Jurisprudence and Political Philosophy in the 21st Century

Central and Eastern European Forum for Legal, Political, and Social Theory Yearbook

Edited by Jürgen Busch / Péter Cserne
Michael Hein / Miodrag Jovanović / Marta Soniewicka

Volume 2

PETER LANG
Frankfurt am Main · Berlin · Bern · Bruxelles · New York · Oxford · Wien

Miodrag A. Jovanović / Bojan Spaić (eds.)

Jurisprudence and Political Philosophy in the 21st Century

Reassessing Legacies

PETER LANG
Internationaler Verlag der Wissenschaften

Bibliographic Information published by the Deutsche Nationalbibliothek
The Deutsche Nationalbibliothek lists this publication in the Deutsche Nationalbibliografie; detailed bibliographic data is available in the internet at http://dnb.d-nb.de.

Cover Design:
© Olaf Gloeckler, Atelier Platen, Friedberg

The publication of this yearbook was possible
due to the financial assistance
of the Ministry of Education and Science
of the Republic of Serbia.

ISSN 2191-8317
ISBN 978-3-631-62207-0

www.peterlang.de

Contents

Contributors vii

Introduction
Miodrag A. Jovanović and Bojan Spaić 1

Part I Reassessing Old Jurisprudential Accounts

Are there any natural rights in Aquinas?
Szilárd Tattay 11

Hobbes and Coke on corporations: Parallels and dissonances
Marko Simendić 23

Part II Methodological Debates in Contemporary Jurisprudence

The Nature and Limits of Conceptual Truths
Tomasz Pietrzykowski 37

The Nature of Jurisprudence
Goran Dajović 48

The Concept of Legal Culture Revisited: An East-Central European Perspective
Balázs Fekete 56

Part III Legacies of 20th Century Legal Positivism

Between the 'Metaphysics of the Stone Age' and the 'Brave New World': H. L. A. Hart on the Law's Assumptions about Human Nature
Péter Cserne 71

Hedgehogs, Foxes and Hart's Rule of Recognition: The Concept of Law in the post-Westphalian International Legal Order
Axelle Reiter 88

Hans Kelsen's Critique of Sovereignty
Petra Gümplová 101

Part IV Justice after Rawls

Why is Rawls's Social Contract Hypothetical?
Bojan Vranić 117

Future Generations: An Almost Rawlsian Perspective
Miklós Könczöl 130

Electoral quotas and John Rawls's idea of justice and equality
Anna Kalisz & Magdalena Półtorak 137

From Defending the Minimal State to Examining the Good Life: Continuity and Change in the Work of Robert Nozick
Antonia Geisler 147

Amartya Sen's Justice: An Idea and a Proposal
Jakov Bojović 155

Contributors

Jakov Bojović undergraduate student, University of Belgrade, Serbia

Péter Cserne assistant professor, Pázmány Péter Catholic University, Budapest, Hungary

Goran Dajović assistant professor, University of Belgrade, Serbia

Balázs Fekete lecturer, Pázmány Péter Catholic University; research fellow, Hungarian Academy of Sciences Institute for Legal Studies, Budapest, Hungary

Antonia Geisler research assistant, University of Greifswald, Germany

Petra Gümplová assistant professor, Justus Liebig University, Giessen, Germany

Anna Kalisz assistant professor, Humanitas University, Sosnowiec, Poland

Miklós Könczöl assistant lecturer, Pázmány Péter Catholic University, Budapest, Hungary; PhD student, Durham University, UK

Tomasz Pietrzykowski assistant professor, University of Silesia, Katowice, Poland

Magdalena Półtorak teaching assistant, Humanitas University, Sosnowiec, Poland

Axelle Reiter lecturer, Verona University, Vicenza, Italy

Marko Simendić teaching assistant, University of Belgrade, Serbia

Szilárd Tattay assistant professor, Pázmány Péter Catholic University, Budapest, Hungary

Bojan Vranić teaching assistant, University of Belgrade, Serbia

Editors

Miodrag Jovanović associate professor, University of Belgrade, Serbia

Bojan Spaić lecturer, University of Belgrade, Serbia

Introduction

Miodrag A. Jovanović and Bojan Spaić

This is the Second Yearbook of the Central and Eastern European Forum of Young Legal, Political and Social Theorists. The Forum was instigated due to the idea and enthusiasm of a group of younger Polish academics, who managed to organise the first meeting in Katowice in 2009. The second conference came as a natural follow-up of a successful event, and was hosted by the Pázmány Péter Catholic University in Budapest. This volume is a result of the third reunion, organised at the Faculty of Law, University of Belgrade, from 25 to 26 March 2011. With three annual conferences in a row, we can already claim that a tradition is being established. And as with any tradition, in order to make it our guide, and not our jailer, as once eloquently put by Somerset Maugham, we have to be open for self-reflection. This introduction might be the adequate occasion for such an endeavour.

Indeed, one may wonder whether there is any justification for a network of theorists that is geographically limited to the blurry area of Central and Eastern Europe. This dilemma boils down to the question of whether there is any common denominator for a number of different nations, countries and academic communities – apart from the apparently arbitrary criterion of a common geographical space – that would justify the existence of one such forum. Let us try to answer it by quoting one of the last passages of a much-celebrated 1959 book, *Rodzinna Europa* (translated as *Native Realm: A Search for Self-Definition*), written by a famous Polish poet and Nobel Prize winner, Czesław Miłosz. He says:

> when I compare us (East Europeans) with the inhabitants of calm and orderly countries, I would be inclined, in spite of all our misfortunes and sufferings, to call us happier in one respect. Neither new models of cars, nor travels, nor love affairs provide the elixir of youth. In grabbing our portion of amusements and pleasures, we expose ourselves to the vengeance of time, which dulls receptivity. We, Easterners, on the other hand, precisely because we had to gaze into the hells of our century, made the discovery that the elixir of youth is not a delusion. No one brought himself willingly to look into those hells. Time that was compressed, speeded up, was not psychological time; it, too, avenged itself with a concentration camp, a bullet, or a heart attack. Nevertheless, it taught

> us the meaning of full commitment and exploded the barriers between the individual and the social, between style and institution, between aesthetics and politics. That miraculous elixir is nothing other than the certainty that there are no boundaries to the knowledge of what is human. (Miłosz 1981, 299–300)

Let us, once again, be aware that these words were uttered in 1959. This means that there was still more 'hell' to come for a majority of people from this part of Europe, more 'distress of the East European small states', as prophetically put by a Hungarian lawyer and political theorist, István Bibó, in his well-known post-World War II essay (Bibó 1991, 18–86). We believe, however, that neither this common misery, nor the earlier mentioned perverted form of happiness makes this Forum intelligible enough. For all of those interested in theorising law and state, it is precisely the fact of being long enough on the other side of the fence of those 'calm and orderly countries' that renders this academic networking sensible. A number of the then shared features of those societies, economies, legal and political institutions affected common theoretical views that could be all subsumed under a single heading: 'communist theory of state and law'. In the preface to his exposition of this theory, Kelsen wrote that 'it will show the shameful decline of a social science that is not able to emancipate itself from politics' (Kelsen 1995, viii). It is this history of 'shameful decline', and even more so the post-1989 belief that theoretical disciplines could finally be emancipated from the daily politics and reconnected to some valuable pre-communist legacies, that represented a decisive impetus for a new generation of theorists from Central and Eastern Europe to gather in this forum.

The 2011 Forum had two specially convened panels, *Heritage of 20th century legal positivism* and *Justice after Rawls*, thus celebrating several important anniversaries: one hundred years of the first important theoretical account of Hans Kelsen, *Hauptprobleme der Staatsrechtslehre* (Kelsen 1911); fifty years of one of the most important contemporary books in legal theory: Herbert Hart's *The Concept of Law* (Hart 1961); and forty years of the most influential 20th century account of justice, John Rawls's *A Theory of Justice* (Rawls 1971). It would be certainly interesting to find out whether, apart from these coincidences, there are some further points in which the lives, interests and theoretical contributions of these three great theoretical minds intersect. What follows is a small contribution to what deserves to be the subject of a more thorough investigation.

One might be inclined to think that the such connections are the most likely to exist in the case of Kelsen and Hart, who were both primarily legal theorists. Still, this assumption proves to be dubious, since the most one can come up with in this respect is their famous 1961 meeting at Berkeley Law School. Hart has made an interesting and vivid note of this meeting in his well-known article 'Kelsen Visited'. One of the funny things, in Hart's words, was 'when Kelsen remarked that the dispute between us was of a wholly novel kind because though he agreed with me I did not agree with him' (Hart 1963, 710). Not only for this reason would it be fair to say that a more fruitful exchange of ideas was the one between Hart and Rawls. After completion of his PhD, Rawls had paid visit to Oxford, where he happened to meet Hart, who made a lasting impression on him. Moreover, according to Rawls's explicit statement in his 1990 Preface to the Serbian edition of *A Theory of Justice*, it was exactly Hart's 1973 article 'Rawls on Liberty and Its Priority', which inclined him to make subsequent changes in his concept of liberty (Hart 1973, 534–555). Can any similar connection be established between Kelsen and Rawls? At first glance, it appears as if their views stood at two completely different poles. While Kelsen argues in his essay 'What is Justice?' that it is 'a possible, but not a necessary, quality of a social order regulating the mutual relations of men' (Kelsen 1971, 1), Rawls opens his *A Theory of Justice* with a famous utterance: 'Justice is the first virtue of social institutions' (Rawls 1971, 3). In spite of this, commentators often find some common grounds in the work of the two authors. David Dyzenhaus, for instance, argues that there is an interesting parallel between Kelsen's Pure Theory of Law and Rawls's account of public reason in his *Political Liberalism*, because both were committed to the idea that their theories could be free of any underlying comprehensive political doctrine (Dyzenhaus 1997, 132–149). One may surely come across other attempts of this sort (cf. Hjorth 2011, 2585–2602).

We finish this cursory outline of plausible points of intersection of the lives and scholarship of these famous authors by noticing that they could have all easily ended up by doing something completely different. At young age, Kelsen was keen on writing poems and short novels, and one of his first successes was a poem published in the *Wiener Hausfrauen-Zeitung*, to which his mother was subscribed. Even when he turned to theorising law and state more seriously, he did not completely abandon this affection for literature, as evidenced in one of his very first publications, *Die Staatslehre des Dante Alighieri*, from 1905 (Kelsen 1905). Hart's well-known service during the war in the British intelligence MI5 could have, perhaps, led him to a career of some new 007. Finally, a recent article of Nagel and Cohen demonstrates that during his last two years of studies at Princeton, Rawls was very much into the idea of becoming a priest of the Episcopal Church. No wonder, thus, that Rawls's recently discovered senior thesis, submitted to the philosophy department in December 1942, was entitled *A Brief Inquiry into the Meaning of Sin and Faith: An Interpretation Based on the Concept of Community* (Cohen and Nagel 2009). No one can tell for sure whether Kelsen, Hart and Rawls would be equally successful were they to opt for some other interests and professions. But one thing is certain: our world of legal, political and social theories would be gravely impoverished without their contributions.

There is, however, one obvious difference between these three authors. Unlike Rawls's theory of justice, which received undivided attention and reception all over the world, the same cannot be said for either Kelsen's or Hart's theoretical accounts. It seems that there exists some indivisible barrier between German-speaking and English-speaking (particularly US) communities of legal philosophers, which can only partly be justified with reference to the specificities of legal systems. In the contribution to a recent collection entitled *Kelsen anderswo* (*Kelsen Abroad*), Telman, for instance, persuasively demonstrates, contra our intuitive belief, that Kelsen's theory was never accepted in the Land of Realists, despite thirty years of teaching and scholarship in the United States (Telman 2010, 353–376). To name just one example, the most widely cited American legal theorist, Justice Richard Posner, admitted that, until recently, he had never read Kelsen. On the other hand, German authors from the same field are generally very well acquainted with the latest developments in Anglo-American jurisprudence, and yet, their common point of reference is the work of German authors. For example, at a recent conference on interdisciplinary research in legal theory organised in Bielefeld, the only author who explicitly dealt with Hart was one who argued that, in certain important respects, his work was largely influenced by Max Weber.

For all these reasons, the Third Forum made a small contribution to fostering a more profound dialogue between the two most influential theoretical traditions, by organising a special session of key-note speakers, which included Kenneth Einar Himma, from Seattle Pacific University, who presented the paper *Hart and Austin Together Again for the First Time: Coercive Enforcement and the Theory of Legal Obligation*, Stephen Kirste, from the University of Heidelberg, who delivered a paper on *Positivism and Normativism* and Veronica Rodriguez-Blanco, from the University of Birmingham, whose paper was entitled *Rethinking the Legal Positivism/Natural law Divide: A Note on the Nature of Human Action*. Even though Belgrade served as a neutral ground for the commencement of this dialogue, any other place in Central and Eastern Europe would have served as an equally adequate location, because one of the important features of the new generation of theorists from this region is that they are open to influences from both traditions. Put differently, their work vindicates the commitment to bridging gaps between different traditions, in a way consistent with words of another winner of the Nobel Prize in Literature, Ivo Andrić, who famously uttered:

> From everything that man erects and builds in his urge for living nothing is in my eyes better and more valuable than bridges. They are more important than houses, more sacred than shrines. Belonging to everyone and being equal to everyone, useful, always built with a sense, on the spot where most human needs are crossing, they are more durable than other buildings and they do not serve for anything secret or bad. (Andrić 1977)

This Yearbook is divided into four broad parts keeping in mind the aforementioned structure of the Forum's 2011 annual conference that aspired to capture the debates in legal and political philosophy in the first decade of the 21th century.

Medieval and early modern jurisprudential accounts were reassessed by Szilárd Tattay and Marko Simendić. In his paper entitled *Are There any Natural Rights in Aquinas?*, Tattay examines whether Aquinas complemented his theory of natural law with a conception of natural rights. The author suggests that Aquinas could have derived a doctrine of natural rights from certain elements of his natural law theory, but he deliberately did not choose to do so. Tattay tries to elucidate why this was the case. In *Hobbes and Coke on Corporations: Parallels and Dissonances*, Simendić offers an overview of Thomas Hobbes's account of corporations laid out in *Elements of Law*, *De Cive* and *Leviathan*, and compares it to the legal theory of Sir Edward Coke. Hobbes strongly opposed at least two related ideas presented by Coke. The first was the general notion that the common law is an English version of natural law and that the sovereign's (corporate) personality is derived from, and thus inferior to, it. The second one was that (a group of) people can be united in a 'headless' corporation, unrepresented and ungoverned. In an effort to rebut the ideas that the enemies of absolute sovereignty associated with Coke's notion of corporation, Hobbes responded by arguing that the unity that makes a corporation depends on the singular will of its representative.

The second part of the Yearbook deals with methodological issues in contemporary jurisprudence. It opens with Tomasz Pietrzykowski's inquiry into *The Nature and Limits of Conceptual Truths*. The paper examines the relationship between conceptual claims and their empirical foundations or presuppositions. It is argued that such relationship is trivial only in cases of trivial conceptual theses. In trying to solve any real problem with conceptual claims (beyond reporting of a uniform and uncontroversial linguistic practice), we cannot escape tacit empirical and evaluative assumptions. In such cases the so-called conceptual claims boil down to rather poorly substantiated empirical generalisations. This undermines the cognitive value of most popular argumentation pursued under the name of conceptual analysis in many domains (including legal theory), which is deemed as being able to illuminate substantive problems and controversies. Goran Dajović considers whether jurisprudence, as the discipline of legal knowledge, is philosophy or a science. He argues that the most general aspect of this problem is actually the persisting dilemma between the empirical (which means inductive, observational), and the conceptual approach to the jurisprudential task. The author deals with certain aspects of this dilemma, concluding that the nature of jurisprudence is in some way twofold. *The Concept of Legal Culture Revisited: An East-Central European Perspective*, by Balázs Fekete, examines certain distinctive features of East-Central European legal cultures. Starting from the presumption that a legal culture consists of two different parts, the norm and the non-norm level, it discusses two components of the latter. The paper concludes with the insight that, although on the norm level of these legal cultures one can hardly find significant differences from general Western patterns, certain features highlight that important regional specialities exist on the non-norm level. Therefore, the everyday functioning of these legal systems differs in certain cases from that of Western legal systems in general.

The third part of the Yearbook starts with Péter Cserne's analysis of H. L. A. Hart's views on the epistemic character of the law's assumptions about human behaviour, as articulated in *Causation in the Law* and *Punishment and Responsibility*. *Between the 'Metaphysics of the Stone Age' and the 'Brave New World': H. L. A. Hart on the Law's Assumptions about Human Nature* follows Hart's suggestion that the assumptions behind legal doctrines typically combine common sense factual beliefs, moral intuitions, and philosophical theories of earlier ages with sound moral principles and empirical knowledge. An important task of legal theory is to provide a 'rational and critical foundation' for these doctrines. This does not only imply conceptual clarification in light of an epistemic ideal of objectivity but also involves legal theorists in 'enlightenment' about empirical facts, 'demystification' of metaphysical obscurities. The confrontation of the implicit assumptions behind legal rules and doctrines with findings of psychology and neuro-sciences raises conceptual and normative questions about law as a regulatory technique and a specific mechanism of social control. Axelle Reiter in *Hedgehogs, Foxes and Hart's Rule of Recognition: The Concept of Law in the post-Westphalian International Legal Order* shows the lasting importance and enduring relevance the vision of law exposed by H. L. A. Hart in *The Concept of Law* has for the understanding of contemporary international law. She argues that the international legal order closely mirrors his adherence to inclusive legal positivism and his conception of the separation of law and morals; his reliance on the social pedigree of rules rather than on the presence of centralised mechanisms of coercion and his approach to state sovereignty; his description of law as the union of primary and secondary norms, integrated under a rule of recognition.

Finally, the fourth part is dedicated to some recent debates and interpretations of the most important account in 20th century liberal political theory, Rawls's theory of justice. In *Why is Rawls's Social Contract Hypothetical?*, Bojan Vranić points to the inadequacy of the conceptions of the contractual strategy that aims at the constitution of institutions or the consensus among representative individuals. The paper offers the following two reasons why Rawls's contract needs to be understood as hypothetical: (a) the contract is a necessary element of the original position and as such it can serve only as a theoretical tool without binding force; (b) the contract is the instrument representative individuals use to achieve their goal, which is the fulfilment of 'the sense of the Self.' Miklós Könczöl discusses the concept of 'rights of future generations' which is often used as an argument in debates about public decisions that are likely to have an impact on the life circumstances of future people. *Future Generations: An Almost Rawlsian Perspective* seeks to offer an alternative to the problematic notion of not-yet-existing persons having rights. It is argued that while Rawls does not attempt to solve the tension between just distribution and the lack of inter-generational reciprocity, the general framework of his contractualist theory of justice may serve as an adequate basis for conceiving of present people having rights with respect to their posterity. Anna Kalisz and Magdalena Półtorak employ Rawls' idea of justice in a contemporary political context, claiming that the present policy of electoral quotas is not a feminist *idée-fixe*, but the very rational requirement of justice and equality. *Electoral quotas and John Rawls' Idea of Justice and Equality* goes on by claiming that quota regulations are a politically neutral tool not only for raising the number of female representatives, but also for expressing the substantive aspect of the equality principle as well as for influencing social practice and 'educating' society. Antonia Geisler in her *From Defending the Minimal State to Examining the Good Life: Continuity and Change in the Work of Robert Nozick* outlines Nozick's minimal state and his theory of justice which he both develops and defends in *Anarchy, State and Utopia*. It is shown that Nozick mitigates some aspects of his libertarian political philosophy in later works, but basically sticks to his central arguments developed in *Anarchy, State and Utopia*. In the last piece of this collection, Jakov Bojović discusses Amartya K. Sen's broad conception of justice, drawing two general conclusions regarding the reach of Sen's ideas. First, Sen's comparative conception of justice, together with the capability approach, can be understood as an unfinished theory of democracy that focuses more on ideas and, regrettably, less on the structure of institutions. Second, the author argues that Sen's bottom-up, reason-based approach is a very significant attempt to bring a metaphysical conception back to the real lives people lead.

⋆

The publication of this Yearbook was possible due to the financial assistance of the Ministry of Education and Science of the the Republic of Serbia.

References

Andrić, Ivo. 1977. *The Bridge on the Drina*, translated by Lovett F. Edwards. Chicago: University of Chicago Press.

Bibó, István. 1991. The Distress of East European Small States. In *Democracy, Revolution, and Self-Determination*, 18–86. New York: Columbia University Press.

Cohen, Joshua, and Nagel, Thomas. 2009. 'John Rawls: On My Religion'. *Times Literary Supplement* 18 March 2009.

Dyzenhaus, David. 1997. *Legality and Legitimacy: Carl Schmitt, Hans Kelsen, and Hermann Heller in Weimar.* Oxford: Clarendon Press.

Hart, Herbert. 1963. Kelsen Visited. *UCLA Law Review* 10: 709–728.

Hart, Herbert. 1973. Rawls on Liberty and Its Priority. *University of Chicago Law Review* 40: 534–555.

Hart, Herbert. 1961. *The Concept of Law.* Oxford: Clarendon Press.

Hjorth, Ronnie. 2011. Equality in the Theory of International Society: Kelsen, Rawls and the English School. *Review of International Studies* 37: 2585–2602.

Kelsen, Hans. 1911. *Hauptprobleme der Staatsrechtslehre.* Tübingen: Mohr.

Kelsen, Hans. 1905. *Staatslehre des Dante Alighieri.* Wien, Leipzig: Deuticke.

Kelsen, Hans. 1955. *The Communist Theory of Law.* London: Stevens and Sons.

Kelsen, Hans. 1971. *What Is Justice? Justice, Law and Politics in the Mirror of Science.* Berkeley, Los Angeles, London: University of California Press.

Miłosz, Czesław. 1981. *Native Realm: A Search for Self-Definition*, translated by Catherine S. Leach. Berkeley, Los Angeles, London: University of California Press.

Rawls, John. 1971. *A Theory of Justice.* Cambridge, MA: The Belknap Press of Harvard University Press.

Telman, Jeremy. 2010. A Path Not Taken: Hans Kelsen's Pure Theory of Law in the Land of the Legal Realists. In *Hans Kelsen anderswo – Hans Kelsen abroad: Der Einfluss der Reinen Rechtslehre auf die Rechtstheorie in verschiedenen Ländern, Teil III*, edited by Robert Walter, Clemens Jabloner and Klaus Zeleny, 353–376. Wien: Hans Kelsen Institut, Manz'sche Verlags- und Universitätsbuchhandlung.

Part I
Reassessing Old Jurisprudential Accounts

Are There any Natural Rights in Aquinas?

Szilárd Tattay

The title alludes, of course, to Herbert Hart's classic study 'Are There any Natural Rights?', but all (or almost all) parallels end here. In my paper, I will examine whether or not Aquinas complemented his theory of natural law with a conception of natural rights. First I shall present a kind of 'conceptual algebra', describing Aquinas's different usages of the term *ius*, and then I will turn to the very question of my investigation.

1

In Aquinas's legal philosophy we can find three different meanings of the term *ius*. *Ius* can mean (1) *iustum*, i.e. right action, (2) by metonymy a rule and measure of human acts (*lex*) and (3) occasionally subjective right.

(1) Like other medieval Aristotelians, the *doctor angelicus* understands *ius* fundamentally and primarily as the *iustum*, as the *obiectum iustitiae*, the object of the virtue of justice. Consequently he discusses the Questions '*De iure*' (On Right) and '*De iustitia*' (On Justice) side by side in the *Secunda Secundae* of the *Summa theologiae* [*ST*] (qq. 57–58).

In his discussion of *ius* Aquinas follows accurately Aristotle's analysis of *dikaion*. In Book V of the *Nicomachean Ethics* [*EN*], Aristotle describes *dikaion* as the just thing in a given situation (*EN* 1129a). Aquinas, likewise, conceives of *ius* as the right action that justice requires of the agent under given circumstances (*ST* II-II q. 57 a. 1). Though both of them make frequent use of the term 'just thing', they seem to associate the object of justice rather with an action than with a thing (Brett 1997, 90–91). For there are no *res iustae* without – at least implicit – reference to human acts.[1] That is why the word '*opus*' appears in Aquinas's famous definition of *ius*:

[1] Michel Villey (1983, 47–48) claims that in contrast to the masculine and feminine adjective '*dikaios*', the neuter noun '*to dikaion*' used by Aristotle always denotes an object, a thing, not an agent or an action, and for him the object of justice is the just distribution ('*juste partage*') of goods and burdens. Yet even if we were to accept these claims, we would arrive at a contradiction, since just division presupposes an act of distributing.

'*ius sive iustum est aliquod opus adaequatum alteri secundum aliquem aequalitatis modum*' (the right or the just is an *opus* that is adjusted to another person according to some kind of equality) (*ST* II-II q. 57 a. 2 co). The term '*opus*' is best translated here – in accordance with the meaning of the verb '*operari*' (to work, to be occupied with something) – as 'action' (Kalinowski 1973a, 64 n. 1).

This definition shows, on the other hand, that justice – in contrast with other virtues – is directed *ad alterum* (towards another person), and that the mean at which it aims is not constituted in relation to the subject of the action, but is objectively determined by the requirement of equality in human transactions (Brett 1997, 90). Aquinas's example of right action is the payment of the wage due for a service rendered.[2]

(2) Secondly, it is by no means exceptional that Aquinas uses *ius* to replace *lex* understood as a *rationis ordinatio*, a rational rule of human actions. His general definition of *lex* is to be found in the treatise on law of the *Prima Secundae* (qq. 90–108), in the Question '*De essentia legis*' (On the Essence of Law). According to this definition, *lex* is (1) an ordinance of reason (2) for the common good, (3) made by him who has care of the community, and (4) promulgated.[3]

The problem of the relation between *ius* and *lex* (right and law) is one of the most debated questions among commentators of Aquinas's legal philosophy. Here I shall mention only the debate between Michel Villey and John Finnis. In Villey's view, it is not by chance that Aquinas treats *lex* and *ius* in two completely distinct parts of the *Summa theologiae*. This reflects that for Aquinas, as for Aristotle and in classical Roman law, there is an '*opposition capitale*' (a fundamental opposition) between *ius* and *lex*. According to Villey, Aquinas, as the last great representative of the pure classical tradition of natural law, avoids the interpretation of *ius* as prescriptive law. He asserts that whenever Aquinas writes *ius* instead of *lex*, he does so only because he respects the authorities (Gratian and Isidore of Seville) he cites (Villey 1972a, 408; Villey 1972b, 427–429).[4]

2 *ST* II-II q. 57 a. 1 co.: 'iustitiae proprium est inter alias virtutes ut ordinet hominem in his quae sunt ad alterum. Importat enim aequalitatem quandam, ut ipsum nomen demonstrat, dicuntur enim vulgariter ea quae adaequantur iustari. Aequalitas autem ad alterum est. [...] Rectum vero quod est in opere iustitiae, etiam praeter comparationem ad agentem, constituitur per comparationem ad alium, illud enim in opere nostro dicitur esse iustum quod respondet secundum aliquam aequalitatem alteri, puta recompensatio mercedis debitae pro servitio impenso.'

3 *ST* I-II q. 90 a. 4 co.: 'Et sic ex quatuor praedictis potest colligi definitio legis, quae nihil est aliud quam quaedam rationis ordinatio ad bonum commune, ab eo qui curam communitatis habet, promulgata.'

4 See also Villey (1975) and Villey (1961). For a much more moderate version of this view, see Gelinas (1970).

Finnis criticises with good reason this 'exaggerated distinction between *ius* and *lex*' (Finnis 1980, 228).[5] To be sure, in his treatment of *ius* Aquinas once explicitly distinguishes *ius* and *lex*, saying that 'law is not the same as right'. But in the same sentence he adds that law is the basis of right ('*ratio iuris*').[6] And in the very next article he seems to equate *ius divinum* with *lex divina*; he speaks of the promulgation of *ius divinum*, which can make sense only in the case of divine law (*ST* II-II q. 57 a. 2 ad 3). Finally, in other parts of the *Summa* – first of all in the treatise on law – as well as in his other works he uses *ius* and *lex* quite often interchangeably (not only *ius divinum* and *lex divina* but also *ius naturale* and *lex naturalis*, *ius positivum* and *lex positiva*, and so on) to mean 'law'.[7] Finnis, on the other hand, makes the not less contestable claim that in Aquinas right is derived from law (Finnis 1972, 424–425).[8]

Perhaps the most adequate and plausible solution to this *crux interpretum* has been provided, in my opinion, by Georges Kalinowski. He argues that in Saint Thomas there is a '*lien organique*' (an intimate link) between *ius* and *lex*, and hence his treatise on right and justice and his treatise on law – like two panels of a diptych – cannot be separated from each other (Kalinowski 1973b, 335–336).[9] According to Kalinowski, Aquinas's metonymical use of the term *ius* is legitimated by the fact that the concepts of *ius* and *lex* are connected to each other in a relation of mutual causation: the *ius naturale* (natural right) forms the basis of the *lex naturalis* (natural law) on the one hand, and the *lex positiva* (positive law), be it divine or human, lays the foundation of the *ius positivum* (positive right) on the other (Kalinowski 1973a, 70–71).[10] Divine law, having a double – partly natural, partly positive – character, can perfectly illustrate this complex cause-effect relationship:

> The divine law is that which is promulgated by God. Such things are partly those that are naturally just, yet their justice is hidden to man, and partly are made just by God's decree. Hence also divine law may be divided in respect of these two things, even as human law is. For the divine law commands certain things because they are good, and forbids others, because they are evil, while

5 Finnis (1972, 424) categorically states that 'chez saint Thomas il n'y a pas d' "oppostition capitale… entre droit et loi"'.

6 *ST* II-II q. 57 a. 1 ad 2: 'lex non est ipsum ius, proprie loquendo, sed aliqualis ratio iuris.'

7 See e.g. q. 94 a. 4, q. 94 a. 5 and q. 95 a. 4 of the treatise on law. In his *Commentary on the Sentences* (*In IV Sententiarum* d. 33 q. 1 a. 1 co.), Aquinas even speaks of '*lex naturalis vel ius naturale*'. See also *In III Sententiarum* d. 37 q. 1 a. 3.

8 A similar point of view is presented by Paul Van Overbeke (1955, 534, 537).

9 For a similar view, see Lottin (1931), Crowe (1974), May (1977).

10 It should be mentioned that in the treatise on right (*ST* II-II q. 57 a. 1 ad 1) Aquinas explicitly calls attention to the metaphorical and metonymic use of language, saying that 'it is usual for words to be distorted from their original signification so as to mean something else'. Elsewhere in the *Summa* (I q. 79 a. 13 co.) we can also read that 'it is customary for causes and effects to be called after one another.'

> others are good because they are prescribed, and others evil because they are forbidden.[11]

(3) Thirdly, Thomas sometimes uses *ius* – besides the above two objective meanings – in the subjective sense as well. For example, while discussing restitution he mentions right to property (*ius dominii*), and in reference to theft he speaks of right of possessing (*ius possidendi*).[12] The Dominican master was well acquainted with law (especially with canon and Roman law), and by the time he wrote his works, the subjective meaning of *ius* had widely spread in medieval legal language (cf. Tierney 1989 and 1997, Tuck 1979). One could even say, remarks Jean-Marie Aubert, that 'il aurait été étonnant que saint Thomas, qui a largement utilisé les sources juridiques, n'ait pas été influencé par le langage courant en ces matières' (Aubert 1955, 91). This usage remains, however, sporadic in Aquinas.

2

Is this enough to prove that Aquinas possessed the concept of natural rights or human rights? The large majority of historians of ideas answer this question emphatically in the negative. Annabel Brett's statement clearly represents the majority opinion: 'the scattered usage of the subjective construction of *ius* with the gerund does not affect the theoretical elucidation of *ius* as objective, which is indeed the sense that *ius* normally bears in Aquinas's text; nor does it necessarily imply a concept of subjective right as liberty' (Brett 1997, 91 n. 12).

A major exception to this majoritarian view is John Finnis's book *Aquinas*, in which Finnis makes a strong case for an affirmative answer. He enumerates many examples of subjective use of *ius* in Aquinas – *ius contradicendi*, *ius dandi baptisma*, *ius petendi debitum* and so on –, while on the other hand he has to admit 'the relative rarity of *iura*, the plural of *ius*, with the meaning "rights"' (Finnis 1998, 133–134). This is, however, of little significance, claims Finnis, since 'though he never uses a term translatable as "human rights", Aquinas clearly has the concept' (ibid., 136). But 'isn't Aquinas primarily interested in the moral uprightness, the just character, of the duty-bearer', rather than in the rights of the right-holder? – objects Finnis himself. His perhaps surprising answer is: 'Not at all [...] In Aquinas's understanding of justice, rights are as fundamental as duties' (ibid., 137, 170).

11 *ST* II-II q. 57 a. 2 ad 3: 'ius divinum dicitur quod divinitus promulgatur. Et hoc quidem partim est de his quae sunt naturaliter iusta, sed tamen eorum iustitia homines latet, partim autem est de his quae fiunt iusta institutione divina. Unde etiam ius divinum per haec duo distingui potest, sicut et ius humanum. Sunt enim in lege divina quaedam praecepta quia bona, et prohibita quia mala, quaedam vero bona quia praecepta, et mala quia prohibita.'

12 *ST* II-II q. 62 a. 1 ad 2 and q. 66 a. 5 ad 2. For further examples, see Finnis (1998, 133 n. 10., 134 n. 12) and Aubert (1955, 91 n. 2).

In order to ground these ambitious claims, Finnis undertakes an essential reinterpretation of Aquinas's treatise on right and justice:

> When Aquinas says that *ius* is the object of justice, he means: what justice is about, and what doing justice secures, is the *right* of some other person or persons – what is due to them, what they are entitled to, what is rightfully theirs. This meaning of *ius* is made clear in the Roman law definition which Aquinas adopts: justice is the steady willingness to give others what is *theirs*. [...] What is theirs, or their right, is: what, as a matter of equality, they are entitled to [...] *Almost always* this 'something due (owed) {debetur}' is to the advantage of the person who has the right {ius} to it. [...] So, if I have a natural – as we would now say, human – right I have it by virtue of natural law {ius naturale}; if I have a legal right I have it by virtue of positive law {ius positivum} [...] Thus law, natural or positive, is the basis for one's right(s) {ratio iuris} (ibid., 133, 135).[13]

Finally, Finnis uses a peculiar logical argument too, asserting that Aquinas's discussions of *iniuriae* (injustices) – for example his analysis of the Decalogue and his treatment of the presumption of innnocence – are implicitly discussions of rights, viz. of violations of rights (ibid., 136–137).

However impressive Finnis's argumentation may appear, taking everything into account, it does not seem convincing to me. On the simplest level, it can hardly be purely accidental that Aquinas never uses the term *ius naturale* (or *iura naturalia*) in the subjective sense, or that when he gives a list of the primary and derivative meanings of *ius* – 'the just thing', the law, 'the art whereby it is known what is just', the court and the judicial sentence –, he omits the subjective sense of the word (Tierney 2002, 393 n. 13, 392; Tierney 1997, 258).[14] The Achilles heel of Finnis's attempt of reinterpretation of Aquinas's discussion of *ius* is that, as a matter of fact, Finnis is merely transcribing objective right into subjective in the passages cited. But, as we saw, it is evident that for Aquinas the object of justice is not another person's right but the right action, and law is the 'basis' (or, depending on the translation, 'expression') not of one's right but of 'the just', and so on (Tierney 2002, 392–393). In the treatise on right and justice the word *ius* never occurs in a subjective sense. The sole exception is the Roman law definition of justice took up by Aquinas, which – containing the possessive pronoun '*suum*' – really seems to suggest that *ius* belongs to

[13] Finnis refers to *ST* II-II q. 57 a. 1 and q. 58 a. 1.

[14] *ST* II-II q. 57 a. 1 arg. 2 and ad 1: 'Praeterea, lex, sicut Isidorus dicit, in libro Etymol., iuris est species. [...] Ad primum ergo dicendum quod consuetum est quod nomina a sui prima impositione detorqueantur ad alia significanda [...] Ita etiam hoc nomen ius primo impositum est ad significandum ipsam rem iustam; postmodum autem derivatum est ad artem qua cognoscitur quid sit iustum; et ulterius ad significandum locum in quo ius redditur, sicut dicitur aliquis comparere in iure; et ulterius dicitur etiam ius quod redditur ab eo ad cuius officium pertinet iustitiam facere, licet etiam id quod decernit sit iniquum.'

the recipient of the action, as his right, '*ius suum*' (or simply '*suum*') (Brett 1997, 92).[15] As a result, stresses Annabel Brett, Aquinas has to proceed with great care to reconcile Ulpian's definition with the text of the *Nicomachean Ethics*, equating *dikaion* with the just thing for a just man to do. Brett argues that 'Aquinas is able to harmonise the two languages of right by exploiting the language of due (*debere*, *debitum*). The right thing is due *from* the just man *to* another citizen.' Nevertheless, this occasional shift of meaning by no means provides a conclusive argument on Finnis's side (ibid.); especially as Aquinas is but borrowing here the terminology of Roman law, which, in addition, is far from being unequivocal. Finnis himself acknowledges (tacitly taking in this question Villey's side) that the *ius* of an ancient Roman could also be a punishment: 'Roman law, and still, vestigially, the language of Aquinas's time, accepted that a liability might also be a *ius*; to be given the appropriate penalty is a malefactor's *ius*' (Finnis 1998, 133–134).

As to Finnis's logical argument of implicit entailment, I believe Brian Tierney warns with good reason against

> the error of discerning a doctrine of human or natural rights each time we encounter some congenial ethical claim in any religious or political system. Moral teachings can be expressed in a variety of ways [...] But, if we are trying to understand the history of natural rights thinking, it merely confuses the issue if we see an assertion of natural or human rights whenever we encounter moral or legal teachings that are not inconsistent with the idea of subjective rights but that actually make no appeal to such rights as the basis of their formulations. (Tierney 2002, 394)

On the whole, Finnis seems to write about – as Arthur S. McGrade suggested in his review – 'what Aquinas should have said' (rather than what he actually said), using a language more accessible to modern readers (McGrade 1999, 126–127).[16] His endeavour to derive a doctrine of subjective rights from Aquinas's discussion of objective right and justice can hence be better described as an elegant and inventive re-reading than as an authentic interpretation of Aquinas's theory. This is, of course, not without precedents. Jacques Maritain already accommodated the notion of 'human rights' into the Neo-Thomist system of natural law in the mid-twentieth century (cf. Maritain 1942); and ultimately, all these efforts can be traced back to the sixteenth-seventeenth-century revival of Thomism.

15 Both Brett (ibid.) and Finnis (1998, 133) notice that '*ius suum*' and '*suum*' are used in this context interchangeably by Aquinas.

16 McGrade maintains that we find in Finnis's book 'what Aquinas should have said if he had been putting out a second, improved edition of, for example, the treatise on law in the *Summa theologiae* [...] Finnis's adoption of recent trends in translation and nomenclature [...] suggest that Finnis is presenting us with what he thinks Aquinas would say if he were doing all of the above today.'

3

What Finnis undeniably proves is that Aquinas's ideas are not incompatible with a subjective concept of right, and that consequently the *doctor angelicus* could have complemented his natural law theory with a doctrine of natural rights (Tierney 2002, 394). A commentator of John Locke's rights theory, A. John Simmons went so far as to say that Aquinas's conception of human equality 'cries out for the development of a theory of natural rights' (Simmons 1992, 96 n. 79). This is a manifest exaggeration, but it remains true that it would have been relatively easy for Aquinas – or at least now it is to us – to translate his conception of natural law and justice partly into the language of natural rights (Zuckert 1997, 714). For instance, he could have deduced a series of rights from the natural inclinations that make up the human essence and determine natural law duties (Lisska 1996, 233, 236). Natural rights would be in this case derivative of natural obligations.[17] Or he could perhaps have reformulated the idea of man's dominion of himself in terms of autonomous choice rights, as a natural right to liberty – like the nominalist Conrad Summenhart and the Thomist theologians of the Second Scholasticism did centuries later. This would not have been impossible, since Aquinas's notion of *dominium sui* was underpinned by a conception of autonomy based on human rationality and a strong doctrine of freedom of choice (Tierney 2006, 179–181).

But this is only speculation about what Aquinas could have said. The fact is that these and other possibilities notwithstanding, Aquinas avoided – arguably deliberately – the language of individual rights (Tierney 1997, 258). Finding the reasons of this requires much less speculation. As Michael Zuckert rightly notes, 'there are important elements of Thomistic theory that resist this translation', hence 'the Thomist doctrine does not well serve as a basis for a general natural-rights position' (Zuckert 1997, 715–716). First of all, one can discern a potential tension between *ius* as a subjective right and *ius* as the right action, inasmuch as the former implies free decision, whereas the latter presupposes an obligation of the agent: 'doing the right thing is not a matter of personal choice' (Brett 1997, 91). And it is not necessary to accept the strict Hobbesian dichotomy of *ius* and *lex* to acknowledge that while natural rights define a sphere of individual autonomy and free choice, the precepts and prohibitions of natural law tend to limit freedom of action (Tierney 2002, 395, 399; cf. Zuckert 1997, 716). Nevertheless, this tension can be significantly mitigated

[17] A further consequence is, according to Zuckert (1997, 716), that in this case 'the natural-law-inspired right to liberty is not a right to do or not to do, as each agent determines. Rather, it is a right only to adhere to the natural-law mandate in a truly human way – that is, through the use of the agent's reason and will. It implies nothing whatsoever about a broader moral freedom – a realm of personal sovereignty or of relatively completely free choice'. Zuckert echoes here Herbert Hart's famous definition of right, rephrased by Richard Tuck as 'the individual's sovereignty within the relevant section of his moral world' (see Hart 1955, 184; Tuck 1979, 6).

or eliminated with the adoption of the idea of 'permissive natural law'. The essence of this idea is that natural law does allow and approve certain courses of action without however commanding (or forbidding) them, and thereby gives freedom of choice to man – within the framework determined by the precepts and prohibitions of natural law.

The conception of permissive natural law has its roots in twelfth-century canon law, and was originally inspired by the problem of private property. Gratian caused great difficulty of interpretation to the Decretists, as at the beginning of the *Decretum* he presented a definition of *ius naturale* – taken from Isidore of Seville – encompassing both common possession and acquisition of things,[18] and then he attributed common property to natural law and private ownership to human positive law and custom, writing a bit later that human laws contrary to natural law are invalid.[19] It was Rufinus whose solution to this difficulty became the most widely accepted. He contrasted natural law commands and prohibitions with *demonstrationes* (indications), 'which nature does not forbid nor command but shows to be good', and classified common property only under the *demonstrationes* of natural law susceptible to change by human law.[20] It was another Italian canonist of the twelfth century, Huguccio, who developed this distinction further and thus introduced the concept of 'permissive natural law'.

> By natural law something is mine and something is yours, but this is by permission, not by precept, since divine law never commanded that all things be common or that some things be private, but it permitted that all things be common and some private, and so by natural law something is common and something private.[21]

18 *Concordia discordantium canonum*, d. 1 c.7: 'Ius naturale est commune omnium nationum, eo quod ubique instinctu naturae, non constitutione aliqua habetur, ut viri et feminae coniunctio, liberorum successio et educatio, *communis omnium possessio* et omnium une libertas, *acquisitio eorum, quae celo, terra marique capiuntur*; item depositae rei vel commendatae pecuniae restitutio, violentiae per vim repulsio' (emphasis added). Isidore offered this definition in *Etymologiae* 5.4.1-2.

19 *Concordia discordantium canonum*, d. 8 ante c.1: 'Nam iure naturae sunt omnia communia omnibus [...] Iure vero consuetudinis vel constitutionis hoc meum est, illud vero alterius.' Ibid., post c.1: 'Dignitate vero ius naturale simpliciter prevalet consuetudini et constitutioni. Quecunque enim vel moribus recepta sunt, vel scriptis comprehensa, si naturali iuri fuerint adversa, vana et irrita sunt habenda.'

20 Rufinus, *Summa decretorum* d. 1: 'Consistit autem ius naturale in tribus, scilic.: mandatis, prohibitionibus, demonstrationibus. [...] Detractum autem ei est non utique in mandatis vel prohibitionibus, que derogationem nullam sentire queunt, sed in demonstrationibus – que scil. natura non vetat non precipit, sed bona esse ostendit – et maxime in omnium una libertate et communi possessione; nunc enim iure civili hic est servus meus, ille est ager tuus.'

21 Huguccio, *Summa decretorum* d. 1 c. 7: 'De iure naturali aliquid est meum et aliquid est tuum, set de permissione, non de precepto, quia ius divinum numquam precipit omnia esse communia vel aliqua esse propria, set permittit omnia esse communia et aliqua esse propria et ita de iure naturali aliquid est commune et aliquid est proprium'. Cited by Weigand (1967, 353).

The idea of permissive natural law soon pervaded not only canon law but also theology and was frequently invoked as a ground of natural rights. However, contrary to many other medieval theologians or canon lawyers (but not unlike Hobbes and Locke), Aquinas did not assimilate this idea into his legal philosophy (Lottin 1931, 89). For Brian Tierney, this is a fundamental reason why Saint Thomas did not develop a doctrine of natural rights (Tierney 2002, 406). There is a strong element of truth in this view, nevertheless, I think Aquinas could have easily decided to accommodate the concept of permissie natural law; especially in view of the fact that in the Question '*De effectibus legis*' (On the Effects of Law) he readily accepts that 'some acts are generically indifferent, and in respect of these the law permits'.[22]

Another serious – though more technical – obstacle is that as Aquinas's natural law doctrine is purposefully sketchy and indeterminate in some crucial respects, it does not allow the formulation of specific, conclusive rights based on it (Zuckert 1997, 717–719). As Anthony J. Lisska rightly stresses, 'the concept of "casuistry" is a necessary condition in determining a list of human rights' (Lisska 1996, 239). But Thomistic natural law differs radically from the *more geometrico* elaborated, deductive systems of natural law of the seventeenth and eighteenth centuries (Frivaldszky 2001, 135). An important consequence of this is that 'the ultimate array of duties actually applicable cannot be captured in a simple table or code' in Aquinas; and 'without a natural table of obligations, there can be no derivation of a table of natural rights' (Zuckert 1997, 717, 718).

Taking everything into account, the decisive reason for the absence of natural rights in Aquinas's legal theory seems to lie in his system of thought as a whole, which is, as it is well known, a harmonious but fragile synthesis of Christian theology and Aristotelian philosophy. This being a complex and far-reaching issue, I can only touch the surface of the question here, relying on Frederick Copleston's eloquent and illuminating analysis:

> For the Aristotelian philosopher it is the universal and the totality which really matters, not the individual as such […] Individuals exist for the good of the species: it is the species which persists through the succession of individuals; […] man is an item in, a part of, the universe […] For the Christian on the other hand the individual human being has a supernatural vocation […] the individual stands in a personal relation to God, and however much one may stress the corporate aspect of Christianity, it remains true that each human person is ultimately of more value than the whole material universe, which exists for the sake of man (Copleston 2003, 428).

It appears to me that while on the one hand the individualist aspects of Christianity precluded a total subordination of the individual to the community in the

[22] *ST* I-II q. 92 a. 2 co.: 'Quidam vero ex genere suo sunt actus indifferentes, et respectu horum, lex habet permittere.'

Thomist system, Aristotelian wholism on the other hand, together with the consistent rationalism of Aquinas's thought, did not leave much space for a doctrine of individual rights either. In the next century, the intellectual climate changed in scholastic philosophy in favour of the idea of natural rights, with the rise of nominalism bringing the individual to the forefront, and voluntarism radicalising the freedom of – human and divine – will. The protagonist of this 'nominalist revolution' was the famous (or ill-famed) English philosopher and theologian William Ockham.

References

Aquinas, Thomas. 1929–47. *Scriptum super libros sententiarum magistri Petri Lombardi*. Edited by Pierre Mandonnet and Maria Fabianus Moos, 4 vols. Paris: Lethielleux.

Aquinas, Thomas. 1952–56. *Summa theologiae*. Edited by Pietro Caramello, 3 vols. Torino: Marietti.

Aristotle. 1969. *Nicomachean Ethics of Aristotle*. Translated by Sir David Ross. London: Oxford University Press.

Aubert, Jean-Marie. 1955. *Le droit romain dans l'oeuvre de saint Thomas*. Paris: Vrin.

Brett, Annabel S. 1997. *Liberty, Right and Nature: Individual Rights in Later Scholastic Thought*. Cambridge: University Press.

Copleston, Frederick. 2003. *A History of Philosophy*, vol. 2: *Medieval Philosophy*. London: Continuum.

Crowe, Michael Bertram. 1974. St. Thomas and Ulpian's Natural Law. In *St. Thomas Aquinas, 1274–1974: Commemorative Studies*, edited by Armand A. Maurer, vol. 1, 261–282. Toronto: Pontifical Institute of Medieval Studies.

Finnis, John. 1972. Un ouvrage récent sur Bentham. *Archives de philosophie du droit* 17: 423–427.

Finnis, John. 1980. *Natural Law and Natural Rights*. Oxford: Clarendon Press.

Finnis, John. 1998. *Aquinas: Moral, Political, and Legal Theory*. Oxford: University Press.

Frivaldszky, János. 2001. *Természetjog: Eszmetörténet* [Natural Law: History of the Idea]. Budapest: Szent István Társulat.

Gelinas, Elmer T. 1970. *Ius* and *Lex* in Thomas Aquinas. *American Journal of Jurisprudence* 15: 154–170.

Gratian. 1959. *Concordia discordantium canonum*. In *Corpus iuris canonici*, edited by Emil Friedberg, vol. 1. Graz: Akademische.

Hart, Herbert. 1955. Are There any Natural Rights? *The Philosophical Review* 64: 175–191.

Kalinowski, Georges. 1973a. Le fondement objectif du droit d'après la 'Somme théologique' de saint Thomas d'Aquin. *Archives de philosophie du droit* 18: 59–75.

Kalinowski, Georges. 1973b. Sur l'emploi métonymique du terme 'ius' par Thomas d'Aquin et sur la mutabilité du droit naturel selon Aristote. *Archives de philosophie du droit* 18: 331–339.

Lisska, Anthony J. 1996. *Aquinas's Theory of Natural Law: An Analaytic Reconstruction*. Oxford: Clarendon Press.

Lottin, Odon. 1931. *Le droit naturel chez saint Thomas d'Aquin et ses prédécesseurs*. Bruges: Beyaert.

Maritain, Jacques. 1942. *Les droits de l'homme et la loi naturelle*. New York: Maison française.

May, William E. 1977. The Meaning and Nature of the Natural Law in Thomas Aquinas. *American Journal of Jurisprudence* 22: 168–189.

McGrade, Arthur S. 1999. What Aquinas Should Have Said? Finnis's Reconstruction of Social and Political Thomism. *American Journal of Jurisprudence* 44: 125–149.

Overbeke, Paul Van. 1955. Saint Thomas et le droit. Commentaire de II^{a}-II, q. 57. *Revue thomiste* 55: 519–564.

Simmons, A. John. 1992. *The Lockean Theory of Rights*. Princeton: Princeton University Press.

Singer, Heinrich (ed.) 1963. *Die Summa decretorum des Magister Rufinus*. Aalen: Scientia, 1963.

Tierney, Brian. 1989. Origins of Natural Rights Language: Texts and Contexts, 1150–1250. *History of Political Thought* 10: 615–646.

Tierney, Brian. 1997. *The Idea of Natural Rights: Studies on Natural Rights, Natural Law and Church Law, 1150–1625*. Atlanta: Scholars Press.

Tierney, Brian. 2001. Permissive Natural Law and Property: Gratian to Kant. *Journal of the History of Ideas* 62: 381–399.

Tierney, Brian. 2002. Natural Law and Natural Rights: Old Problems and Recent Approaches. *The Review of Politics* 64: 389–406.

Tierney, Brian. 2006. Dominion of Self and Natural Rights Before Locke and After. In *Transformations in Medieval and Early-Modern Rights Discourse*, edited by Virpi Mäkinen and Petter Korkman, 173–203. New York: Springer, 2006.

Tuck, Richard. 1979. *Natural Rights Theories: Their Origin and Development*. Cambridge: Cambridge University Press.

Villey, Michel. 1961. Abrégé du droit naturel classique. *Archives de philosophie du droit* 6: 27–72.

Villey, Michel. 1972a. Sur les essais d'application de la logique déontique au droit. *Archives de philosophie du droit* 17: 407–412.

Villey, Michel. 1972b. Si la théorie générale du droit, pour saint Thomas, est une théorie de la loi. *Archives de philosophie du droit* 17: 427–431.

Villey, Michel. 1975. *La formation de la pensée juridique moderne: Cours d'histoire de la philosophie du droit*, 4th ed. Paris: Montchrestien.

Villey, Michel. 1983. *Le droit et les droits de l'homme*. Paris: Presses universitaires de France.

Weigand, Rudolf. 1967. *Die Naturrechtslehre der Legisten und Dekretisten von Irnerius bis Accursius und von Gratian bis Johannes Teutonicus*. München: Hueber.

Zuckert, Michael. 1997. Do Natural Rights Derive from Natural Law? *Harvard Journal of Law and Public Policy* 20: 695–731.

Hobbes and Coke on Corporations: Parallels and Dissonances

Marko Simendić

Introduction

During the first half of the 17th century, England faced severe political turmoil culminating in the Civil War that raged throughout most of the 1640s. These troubled times have seen the Parliamentarians and the Royalists clashing both on the battlefield and the plane of political thought. This is where I situate my argument, within a small but important segment of the intellectual exchange that has marked this period. At the fore of my discussion is Thomas Hobbes's (1588–1679) response to the legal aspect of the notion that the people as a corporation or as a body politic exist independently from their sovereign.

This is a very old conception that reaches back to the Middle Ages,[1] but what makes it specific to the circumstances of seventeenth-century England is the 'rise of common law' that started in the 16th century. At the peak of the expansion of common law, Sir Edward Coke (1552–1634) wrote his immensely influential *Institutes of the Lawes of England*. Coke was the most influential author who considered common law as 'natural law applied to English life, determining the rights of king and subject in ways so ideally just that there could be no possibility of an appeal to other principles' (Cromartie 1999, 81–82). This notion has become commonplace throughout the following decades and the juridical approach was embraced both by radical and conservative authors of the time (ibid., 120). The legal theory of incorporation had an important role within these discussions, not least because the Crown was considered a 'corporation sole' since the time of Henry VIII (Runciman and Ryan 2003, xvii; Maitland 2003b).

Hobbes is famous for making a significant contribution to the fiery political debates that characterised seventeenth-century England. In this paper I will present

1 For example, Bartolus de Saxoferrato, the famous fourteenth-century jurist and an early proponent of the idea of the represented group person, considered the state (*civitas*) to be a kind of a corporation: a *collegium* legitimised by *ius gentium* (see Maiolo 2007, 247).

his account of corporations and show how it developed throughout his scholarship. A brief discussion of Coke's formative views on this issue will serve to illustrate, by way of contrast, just what is so remarkable about Hobbes's account. A comparison of the two accounts is revealing not only because Coke was a leading interpreter and a practitioner of English law, but it is also significant because there is no doubt that Hobbes (1651, 72 and 140) was acquainted with Coke's theory, as he referred to him twice in *Leviathan* and wrote *A dialogue between a philosopher and a student of the common laws of England* in the later 1660s, a work in which he challenged Coke's account of law.

Hobbes's argument from *The Elements of Law* to *Leviathan*

Hobbes's account of corporations evolved over time. In Chapter 19 of *The Elements of Law*, Hobbes (1889, 104) discusses the idea of a 'body politic or civil society' as a 'union' of a number of particular wills. In other words, a body politic is an association of multiple individuals whose wills are united through a covenant 'for their common peace, defence, and benefit' (ibid.). There are, however, two kinds of unions of wills: bodies politic (cities or civil societies) and those unions that are subordinate to them. These latter have a distinctive name and Hobbes (ibid.) notes that they are 'usually called corporations'. Hobbes here emphasises the point he will repeatedly make in his subsequent works: those unions of wills that are not constitutive of states have to be subordinate to them.

Hobbes (1889, 120) also suggests that a body politic cannot be held responsible for breaking natural law, 'as it is a fictitious body, so are the faculties and will thereof fictitious also. But to make a particular man unjust, which consisteth of a body and soul natural, there is required a natural and very will.'[2] Obviously, the state as a body politic cannot break civil laws, either. Since the laws are the expression of a state's sovereignty and a consequence of the original contract between its citizens, the state cannot break a law by promulgating another one. On the other hand, any misdoing of a group of people cannot simply be attributed to the corporation of which they are members. The fact that the responsibility lies with the natural persons absolves both states and subordinate corporate bodies from breaking natural law.

In *The Elements of Law* Hobbes describes the relationship between the sovereign and the people as between the head and the body. Even in the case of a group of rebels, their 'one body of rebellion' is united by its head, that is 'the unity […] by which they are directed to one and the same action' (Hobbes 1889, 175). This image

[2] Here Hobbes echoes the famous findings of pope Innocent IV. In the 13th century Innocent IV laid the foundations of the theory of a fictitious group person (*persona ficta*) by deciding that human associations cannot sin because they are not *real* but only *fictitious* persons who do not have souls (Kantorowitz 1997, 305–306; Maclean 1999, 12–13).

was far from uncommon in Hobbes's time. Thomas Blount (1661, 88) in his *Glossographia* defines a corporation as: 'a permanent thing, that may have succession; it is an Assembly and joyning together of many into one fellowship, brotherhood and minde, whereof one is Head and cheif, the rest are the body.'

The structure of Hobbes's argument remained the same in *De Cive* (1642). Here Hobbes (1978, 170) discusses the idea of a 'civil person' ('*persona civilis*') as an overarching category that includes the state ('*civitas*'; 'city' or 'civil society'), corporation ('*societas*'; subordinate 'civil persons'), as well as family. He argues that 'although every city be a civil person, yet every civil person is not a city; for it may happen that many citizens, by the permission of the city, may join together in one person, for the doing of certain things' (ibid.). Such civil persons are 'companies of merchants, and many other convents' (ibid.). The unity of a multitude of different wills is at the foundation of civil personhood and this is what the two kinds of civil persons have in common, 'for when there is one will of all men, it is to be esteemed for one person, and by the word *one*, it is to be known, and distinguished from all particular men, as having its own rights and properties' (ibid.). Finally, a civil person cannot sin: 'the civil person sins not, but those subjects only by whose votes it was decreed; for sine is a consequence of the natural express will, not of the political, which is artificial' (Hobbes 1978, 199).

In *De Cive* (1642), however, Hobbes (1978, 188) suggested that the sovereign should be regarded as the soul and not as the head of the body politic, '[f]or it is the soul by which a man hath a will, that is, can either will, or nill; so by him who hath the supreme power, and no otherwise, the City hath a will, and can either will or nill.' The soul is not mentioned in this context in *The Elements of Law*, but Hobbes (1651, 1; 144; 171–172; 174) will return to using this metaphor throughout *Leviathan*. It should also be noted that the distinction between the soul and the head in Hobbes's theory is not indicative of any kind of a shift in his views. It is simply a consequence of his mechanicist anthropology in which the brain and nerves are 'the necessary Organs of sense', while the soul produces will, 'immediately adhaering to the action' (ibid., 6; 28), so 'the office of the head is to counsell, as the soules is to command' (Hobbes 1978, 188). The unity of a (political) body is therefore a reflection of an action stemming from the single and individual will. Furthermore, according to Hobbes (1651, 172), the soul is actually located in the head or, more precisely, in the brain.

Hobbes was quite reluctant to use the term 'corporation' in English *Leviathan* (1651). In the few instances when he does use the word he uses it in its strictest sense – to denote the associations of merchants or monopolies (ibid., 119–120), public schools (ibid., 370), and illegal associations such as 'Beggars, Theeves and Gipsies' and those 'that by Authority from any forraign Person, unite themselves in anothers Dominion, for the easier propagation of Doctrines, and for making a party, against the Power of the Common-wealth' (ibid., 121). None of these examples can be linked to any of the defining features of the state. It is obvious that this was done on purpose, especially if we have in mind Hobbes's writing style in respect of his use of synonyms. It is not unusual for Hobbes to employ extensive clusters of synonyms to make his argument as clear as possible.[3]

Hobbes (1651, 115) decided to approach the issue by using 'system' ('*systema*' in the Latin *Leviathan*) as a wider and more neutral term to denote 'any numbers of men joyned in one Interest, or one Businesse'. He offers quite an elaborate classification of such systems. They can be regular or irregular, depending on whether a person or an assembly is representing such a system or not; regular systems are further divided into absolute (independent) and dependent (subordinate). Under Hobbes's classification, commonwealths are the only regular absolute (independent) systems. Consequently, corporations are regular subordinate systems and they can be political (also called political bodies), if they are constituted by the sovereign, or private, if they are created by the citizens. Finally, systems of the latter kind can be divided into lawful and unlawful ones. As it was the case in his previous works, within this classification corporations are viewed exclusively in connection to the commonwealth's legal system, where they are defined by their (subordinated) relationship to the state.

Hobbes's classification from *Leviathan* is centred on the *distinction* between commonwealths and corporations. A corporation is not a *genus proximum* of the state. This is not only true in the logical, but also in the generic sense: the transition from the state of nature signifies the creation of a regular absolute system but it does not introduce a corporation. Although a corporation is not (or should not be) a birthplace of a commonwealth, the opposite can be true in the case of regular subordinate public systems. This shows us that Hobbes goes to great lengths to demonstrate that associations (mainly political bodies) within the state should not be allowed to escape their subordinate status in relation to the commonwealth. Hobbes (ibid., 115) argues that

> to give leave to a Body Politique of Subjects, to have an absolute Representative to all intents and purposes, were to abandon the government of so much of the Commonwealth, and to divide the Dominion, contrary to their Peace and Defence, which the Soveraign cannot be understood to doe.

Finally, Hobbes (ibid., 174) famously argues, the 'infirmit[ies] of a Commonwealth' rest in letting the cities (that are subordinate political bodies or systems)

3 This is perhaps most obvious in his discussion of personhood in chapter 16, where Hobbes (1651, 80–81) writes about 'Rector, Master, or Overseer' personating a bridge and notes that someone bearing someone or something else's *persona* is also known 'as a *Representer*, or *Representative*, a *Lieutenant*, a *Vicar*, an *Attorney*, a *Deputy*, a *Procurator*, an *Actor*'.

develop without control or allowing the number of corporations to grow. This is because the corporations are like 'many lesser Common-wealths in the bowels of a greater, like wormes in the entrayles of a naturall man' (ibid.). This rather picturesque metaphor is not only revealing of Hobbes's suspicion of 'subordinate' forms of human association; it also shows how far he is from defining the state as a derivative of a certain kind of corporation. It is a corporation that is defined as a 'lesser Commonwealth' and not *vice versa*. For him, it is dangerous to think about the state as a 'greater corporation' simply because this may provide a pretext for subordinate systems' demands for (greater) autonomy, which might prove fatal in its turn to the unitary nature of the state's sovereignty.

Finally, there is one recent commentary on the place of the corporate theory in Hobbes's theory that captures Hobbes's lack of trust towards corporations. Monica Brito Vieira (2009, 193) argues that

> Hobbes's account of subordinate group life has a strong parallel with the medieval counterpart of the theory of the *persona ficta*: the concession theory of juridical persons. This treated all manner of organisation within the state as a probable threat, except when deriving its power from an express grant of the state, and kept strictly under the state's control.

However, Brito Viera (ibid., 160) is wrong when she suggests that '[f]rom the early 1640s onwards, [Hobbes] maintained that the state was a type of corporation, civil body or person in law, enjoying an existence distinct from that of its members'. Such a conclusion is based on the interpretation of a passage from Hobbes's (1889, 172) *Elements of Law* where he notes that

> though in the charters of subordinate corporations, a corporation be declared to be one person in law, yet the same hath not been taken notice of in the body of a commonwealth or city, nor have any of those innumerable writers of politics observed any such union.

Brito Vieira (2009, 160) claims that '[t]he astonishment is obviously feigned. Hobbes must have known that he was following in the footsteps of his medieval jurist predecessors when working out the state concept from the legal notion of corporation.' However, Hobbes's astonishment could be quite real, provided that he really believed that the legal notion of corporation was a true example of unity. It seems that Brito Vieira does not take into consideration a sentence directly preceding the one on which she bases her interpretation: 'The error concerning mixed government hath proceeded from want of understanding of what is meant by this word *body politic*, and how it signifieth not the concord, but the union of many men' (Hobbes 1889, 172).

What Hobbes is astonished about is not his predecessors' and contemporaries' inability to properly understand the medieval concept of corporations. Instead, he is *truly* astonished by what he sees as their habit of treating the body politic as a *concord* and not the *union* of many men. This is potentially disastrous to Hobbes's mind since he sees this 'understanding of what is meant by this word *body politic*' as leading to a notion of mixed constitution and, eventually, to the division of sovereignty (ibid.). It is no wonder then that he places this discussion about corporations in the chapter titled 'Of the causes of rebellion'.

Hobbes wants to show that all human associations are united through their representative and not through their membership. We can find traces of this account in *Elements of Law* when Hobbes (1889, 63) argues that: 'involving of many wills in one or more [is] called UNION'. Accordingly, 'a person civil' is defined as 'either one man, or one council, in the will whereof is included and involved the will of every one in particular' (ibid., 124). This idea was, of course, more fully developed in *Leviathan* where it is integrated with Hobbes's accounts of representation and personhood: '[f]or it is the *Unity* of the Representer, not the *Unity* of the Represented, that maketh the Person One' (Hobbes 1651, 82).

Coke, Hobbes and the idea of a corporation

Except by dubbing the subordinate unions of wills 'corporations', Hobbes did not significantly modify the structure of this aspect of his theory before *Leviathan*. Its most substantial remodelling came with Hobbes's best-known work and I will here contrast Hobbes's views with Coke's account of corporations. There are two primary sources that are indicative of Coke's theory of corporations: his ruling in the *Case of Sutton's Hospital* (1612) and his *Institutes*, published in the first half of the 17th century. Coke (*Institutes*, L1. 250.a.) refers to a corporation as 'a body politike, [...] or a body incorporate, because the persons are made into a body, and are of capacity to take and grant, &c.', that is contrasted to 'naturall men'.[4] He also notes that 'this body politike, or corporate, aggregate of many, is by the civilians called *collegium* or *universitas*' (ibid.). Although he does not normally use the term in his writings, Coke usually refers to a corporation as a 'body politike, or [in]corporate'). He starts his *Commentary upon Littleton* (the first part of *Institutes*) by defining corporations as legal persons in a manner similar to Hobbes's:

> Persons capable of purchase are of two sorts, persons natural created by God [...] and persons incorporate or politique created by the policy of man (and therefore they are called bodies politique); and those be of two sorts, *viz.* either sole, or aggregate of many: again, aggregate of many, either of all persons capable, or of one person capable, and the rest incapable or dead in law.[5] (*Institutes*, L1. 2.a)

4 Here I am using the 1832 edition of the *Institutes*.

5 Coke's (*Institutes* L1. 250.a) *classification* of corporations differs from Hobbes's, as he offers three

Such a definition became commonplace in the English legal system. As Frederic Maitland (2003a, 9) argues, invoking Coke's work, this definition comprises a foundation of 'an orthodox beginning for a chapter on the English Law of Persons'. It is obvious that Coke's view matches Hobbes's pre-*Leviathan* account of corporations. When they are predicated by 'corporate' or 'politic', Coke treats the terms 'body' and 'person' as synonymous. Hobbes does the same by putting 'body politic' and 'civil person' in exactly the same context in *The Elements of Law* and *De Cive*. Coke's and Hobbes's accounts have one more important feature in common: Coke also denies that corporations can be held responsible and he also does that on the basis of their artificiality. Coke (2003, 371–327) therefore argues that

> [c]orporation itself is onely *in abstracto*, and resteth onely in intendment and consideration of the Law; for a Corporation aggregate of many is invisible, immortal, & resteth only in intendment and consideration of the Law; [...] They may not commit treason, nor be outlawed, nor excommunicate, for they have no souls, neither can they appear in person, but by Attorney [...]. A Corporation aggregate of many cannot do fealty, for an invisible body cannot be in person, nor can swear, [...] it is not subject to imbecilities, or death of the natural, body, and divers other cases.

For the same reason Coke and Hobbes believe that corporations cannot be held responsible. Hobbes attributes this to their artificiality or fictitiousness while Coke maintains that they cannot be considered responsible due to their abstract existence. So far, then, Hobbes's pre-*Leviathan* account does not differ much from the dominant juristic approach of his time.

Nevertheless, there are some important differences between the two accounts. Unlike Hobbes, Coke lists a rather elaborate set of conditions that a group entity has to fulfil in order to be considered a corporation. In the report regarding the Case of Sutton's Hospital, Coke (ibid., 363–365) argues that the essence of a corporation consists of: (1) 'Lawful authority of Incorporation'; (2) 'persons to be incorporated, and that in two manners, persons natural, or bodies incorporate and political'; (3) 'A name by which they are Incorporated'; (4) 'a place'; (5) incorporation '[b]y words sufficient in Law, but not restrained to any certain, legal and prescript form of words'. The interpretation of Coke's conditions depends on what is regarded as law. Hobbes would probably agree with Coke if these conditions were situated within the context of statutory law. In that case, they would be inapplicable to the state and restricted to those corporations or bodies politic that Hobbes calls 'subordinate'. This is especially true for conditions (1) and (5) which would merely underline the corporations' subordination in relation to the state and the respective legal system.

---

main ways of classifying them: as 'ecclesiasticall and lay', as 'either elective, presentative, collative, or donative' and, finally, as 'sole, or aggregate of many'.

However, Coke's (ibid., 363) 'Lawful authority of Incorporation' was far from limited to statutory law, as it was to be obtained by four means: '*scil.* by the Common Law, as the King himself, &c. by authority of Parliament; by the King's Charter (as in this case) and by prescription'. Clearly for Coke 'the King himself' is a corporation whose authority is derived from the common law. He is a corporation sole, a class of corporations that was almost exclusively made of ecclesiastical persons. Maitland (2003a, 14) notes that 'Coke knew two corporations sole that were not ecclesiastical[. T]hey were a strange pair: the king and the chamberlain of the city of London'. He then goes on to suggest that 'Coke himself was living when men first called the king a corporation sole, though many had called him the head of a corporation' (ibid., 13–14).

Either way, Hobbes could not be satisfied with Coke's account. Although Coke's corporations that derive authority from the state institutions are undoubtedly subordinated to the state, the sovereign still remains a kind of corporation that derives its authority from the common law and not from natural principles, as was the case with the earlier Hobbes. This is highly problematic for Hobbes and the attack on Coke's account of common law as 'the realisation of natural law in English circumstances' was one of the main purposes behind Hobbes's *Dialogue* (Cromartie 2005, xxxi). Coke's views are problematic for Hobbes primarily because they establish the supremacy of common law. Even if one does not argue in favour of the rule of (common) law, it can be quite easily argued from Coke's standpoint that sovereignty is not exclusively vested in one body.

Coke's account is not less unlovable for Hobbes even if we put Coke's classification of corporations aside and regard it as a refined version of a more commonplace theory of that period, namely the theory that regarded the sovereign as the head of the popular body politic. Needless to say, the account by which the people are seen as a corporation that is run by the sovereign would be much more in accordance with Hobbes's project. However, the fact that Coke does not deny the status of a corporation to those groups of people that are 'without a head' destroys even the possibility of reading his theory in a way to which Hobbes could be sympathetic. Coke (2003, 365) argues this in the *Case of Sutton's Hospital* and points to the merchant guilds as the historical examples of headless incorporation:[6]

> where the opinion of *Fineux* in 13 H. 8. 3. b. and of *Prisot* in 39 H. 6. 13. b. was cited at the barre, that a corporation aggregate of many cannot be a body only without a Head; the same was utterly denied: For at first most part of the Corporations were a body without any head by force of these words *Gilda*

6 There is one earlier description of a headless incorporation. In the 15th century Sir John Fortescue in his *De laudibus legum Anglie* 'criticize[d] Augustine's understanding of a people or body politic for being headless (*acephalous*)' (Heyking 1999, 550).

> *Mercatoria*. And that a Corporation aggregate of many may be without a head, see 18 Edw. 2.

On the other hand, as we have seen, Hobbes insists that the unity of a corporation is realised in its head. It is important to note here that Hobbes's objection is not aimed at the possibility of a group of people representing a corporation. What Hobbes argues for is the unity of the wills. Although it is easier to maintain such a unity if the representative is also a single natural person, it is not impossible for a corporation to be guided by a unified will of an assembly, encompassing some of its members, or even all of them.[7] What is impossible, however, is the existence of a corporation that has no representative. Therefore, even those corporations that could appear as headless on the first sight must have some kind of leadership. Even if all the members of a corporation are equals, it does not follow that there is no head, it is just that all of them constitute the representative.

Conclusion

Coke's theory of corporations was far from being acceptable to Hobbes. It was a theoretical reiteration of the late medieval accounts that emphasised the supremacy of natural law (which is in Coke's view embodied in the common law) and the juristic personality of the sovereign that is detached from the body of the people. Coke's view on corporations also grants the status of a body politic to various social groups without requiring 'a head' or a representative, thus putting their joint interest before their unity. Coke's theory is in line with theories that, as Otto von Gierke argues (1958, 45) 'explain the personality of the People as a corporate (and not a collective) unity'. Such accounts have been offered by the proponents of both popular and mixed sovereignty, as well as by the supporters of the idea of rulers' limited sovereignty (ibid.). These are all views that Hobbes strongly disagrees with and tries to discredit. In contrast, he emphasises the union of the members of a body politic who are united through their leader ('by a common power'), as well as the conceptual integrity of the sovereign's person with the person of the commonwealth.

Acknowledgement Research on this paper was funded by the Ministry of Education and Science, Republic of Serbia, project no. 47026.

7 Although Hobbes does not write about a corporation represented by the assembly consisting of all of its members, such a possibility should not be discarded since this is exactly how he defines democracy which is a no less a 'kind of commonwealth' than, for example, an aristocracy. Cf. Hobbes (1651, 94 and 116).

References

Blount, Thomas. 1661. *Glossographia, or, A dictionary interpreting all such hard words of whatsoever language now used in our refined English tongue with etymologies, definitions and historical observations on the same: also the terms of divinity, law, physick, mathematicks and other arts and sciences explicated.* London.

Brito Vieira, Monica. 2009. *The Elements of Representation in Hobbes: Aesthetics, Theatre, Law, and Theology in the Construction of Hobbes's Theory of the State.* Leiden: Brill.

Coke, Edward. 1832. *The First Part of the Institutes of the Laws of England; or a Commentary Upon Littleton, Vol. 2.* London.

Coke, Edward. 2003. The Case of Sutton's Hospital. *In The Selected Writings of Sir Edward Coke, Vol. 1*, 347–377. Indianapolis (Indiana): Liberty Fund.

Cromartie, Alan. 1999. The Constitutionalist Revolution: The Transformation of Political Culture in Early Stuart England. *Past & Present* 163: 76–120.

Cromartie, Alan. 2005. General Introduction. In *Writings on Common Law and Hereditary Right*, edited by Alan Cromartie and Quentin Skinner, xiv–lxvi. Oxford: Oxford University Press.

Gierke, Otto. 1958. *Natural Law and the Theory of Society, 1500 to 1800*, translated by Ernes Barker. Cambridge: Cambridge University Press.

Heyking, John. 1999. A Headless Body Politic?: Augustine's Understanding Of a Populus and Its Representation. *History of Political Thought* 20: 549–574.

Hobbes, Thomas. 1651. *Leviathan, or, The matter, form, and power of a commonwealth ecclesiastical and civil.* London.

Hobbes, Thomas. 1889. *The Elements of Law*, edited by Ferdinand Tönnies. InteLex Corporation [http://pm.nlx.com/, accessed on 10. 08. 2011].

Hobbes, Thomas. 1978. *Man and Citizen.* Indianapolis/Cambridge: Hackett Publishing Company.

Kantorowitz, Ernst. 1997. *The King's Two Bodies.* Princeton: Princeton University Press.

Maclean, Ian. 1999. Legal Fictions and Fictional Entities in Renaissance Jurisprudence. *The Journal of Legal History* 20: 1–24.

Maiolo, Francesco. 2007. *Medieval Sovereignty: Marsilius of Padua and Bartolus of Saxoferrato.* Delft (The Netherlands): Eburon Academic Publishers.

Maitland, Frederic. 2003a. 'The Corporation Sole'. In *State, Trust and Corporation*, edited by David Runciman and Magnus Ryan, 9–41. Cambridge: Cambridge University Press.

Maitland, Frederic. 2003b. 'The Crown as Corporation'. In *State, Trust and Corporation*, edited by David Runciman and Magnus Ryan, 32–51. Cambridge: Cambridge University Press.

Runciman, David and Ryan, Magnus. 2003. Editors' introduction. In Maitland: *State, Trust and Corporation,* edited by David Runciman and Magnus Ryan, ix–xxx. Cambridge: Cambridge University Press.

Part II
Methodological Debates in Contemporary Jurisprudence

The Nature and Limits of Conceptual Truths

Tomasz Pietrzykowski

Claims regarded as conceptual are prevalent in contemporary legal theory.[1] Scholarship is full of inquiries into the concepts of rules, state, constitution, equality, obligation, validity, interpretation, etc. The most famous example is obviously the long-lasting discussion on the concept of law itself, including such ideas as Austin's law as 'commands backed by a threat of sanction', Hart's 'union of primary and secondary rules', Raz's 'exclusionary reasons for action' or Alexy's '*Anspruch auf Richtigkeit*'. All those accounts purport to elucidate conceptual truths about law. Moreover, many substantive legal and moral disputes are influenced by what is believed to be conceptual truths about marriage, person, right, freedom, contract, guilt, discrimination, interest, company, etc.

The very basis of conceptual analysis has been famously challenged by V. W. O. Quine's argument against the analytic/synthetic distinction (Quine 1951). According to Quine, there is no possible explanation of analyticity that avoids circularity and thus the idea of analytic truths should be abandoned.[2] Although Quine's attack turned out very influential in philosophy and remains a subject of intense controversies, it has had relatively little impact on the place of conceptual analysis in legal theory. A notable exception is the idea of 'naturalisation' of legal theory championed mainly by B. Leiter. Apart from that, few eminent legal philosophers have bothered to explicitly discuss the validity and implications of Quine's objections for jurisprudential inquiries. Generally, it may not be unfair to say that Quine's challenge has been hardly noticed in legal theory.

1 The text is an extended follow-up of the several discussions on the value of conceptual claims that took place during the sessions of the 2011 CEE Forum in Belgrade, particularly motivated by the opening presentation delivered by K. E. Himma.

2 Quine argued that except for simple logical truths such as *p* is *p* or *p* v –*p*, the notion of analytic truth involves the notion of synonymy (e.g. when 'an unmarried male is an unmarried male' is substituted by 'a bachelor is an unmarried male'). There is no way, however, to explain synonymy without the notion of analyticity. Thus, there is a hidden circularity in the definition of analytic statements. For a classic critique of Quine's position see H. P. Grice, P. Strawson (1956).

Despite this spirit of 'business as usual', I would like to raise some doubts concerning the nature and value of conceptual claims that might be at least partially independent of Quine's argument (even if deeply influenced by his ideas).[3] My comments are, in turn, directly inspired by a brilliant defence of the validity of conceptual analysis, against i.a. Quine, offered recently by K. E. Himma (2008).[4]

Thus, for the sake of argument, I assume that the distinction between analytic and synthetic truths is sound. Typical 'conceptual truths' such as 'all bachelors are unmarried males' or '2 is a number' may be regarded as true by virtue of the meaning of words used to express them (nevertheless, we have to be aware how debatable it is which propositions are actually analytical – as revealed by many discussions concerning such sentences as 'cats are animals', 'water is H2O', 'sun rises in the east' or, my favorite example, 'students study'). There is an unquestionable difference between statements purporting to express such analytic truths and typical synthetic propositions like 'today the temperature in Katowice is 20 degrees Celsius', 'the Sun was formed 4.5 billion years ago' or 'some bachelors are handsome'.[5] Analytical sentences, as K. E. Himma points out, seem to depend on empirical facts only in a very elementary and trivial way. Namely, they depend on the existence of certain linguistic conventions on the basis of which concept-words mean what they mean. As long as such conventions exist, the truth of a conceptual claim remains independent of any other extra-linguistic reality. In contrast, the truth of synthetic propositions (understood traditionally, as *adaequatio rei et intellectus)* is related to empirical reality in a twofold way. First, it relies (just as analytic propositions do) on the existence and content of linguistic conventions. Second, more importantly, it depends on what is actually the case in respect of the state of affairs a given proposition refers to.

Nevertheless, the status, character and, finally, the epistemological value of 'conceptual' truths seems to remain deeply problematic, particularly if we bear in mind that the real question is whether the distinction between analytic and synthetic propositions is able to provide a cognitively reliable basis for most of what goes under the name of 'conceptual analysis' (in particular within the field of legal theory). In particular, it is dubious whether conceptual claims, at least in most interesting cases, have any distinct character in virtue of which they could produce 'truths' that would not boil down to some combinations of various kinds of disguised (and

3 I feel also deeply indebted to other classic philosophical writings on the subject of 'conceptual' and 'necessary' truths, such as Putnam or Kripke, although I do not accept substantial parts of their arguments.

4 I will limit my repeated references to Himma's argument, even if much more points I make refer to some parts of his essay.

5 For a classic explanation of the analytic sentences as those which 'sagen im Prädikate nichts als das, was im Begriffe des Subjekts schon wirklich, obgleich nicht so klar und mit gleichem Bewußtsein gedacht war' see Kant (1794, 25).

not always well-founded) empirical hypotheses and normative linguistic postulations.

If we take the most typical examples of conceptual truths such as 'no bachelor is married' or 'red is a color', it seems perfectly right to point out (as Himma insists) that their relation to the empirical fact of some existing linguistic conventions is utterly trivial. Everyone knows, after all, that 'bachelor' just *means* a male who is not yet married. To this extent, conceptual truths are simple and unilluminating reports of uncontestable, uniform linguistic conventions governing the use of a concept-term to refer to a class of objects having certain properties.[6] Moreover, conceptual reasoning may also involve some more or less complex chain of inferences from the content of such conventions (e.g. that an unmarried *woman* 'is not' a bachelor or that it is not conceptually 'possible' that there exists a bachelor who is married). They may also purport to explicate relations between such conventions (e.g. presuppositions or commitments implied by the way certain concepts relate to one another, as revealed by the way relevant concept-terms are conventionally used, as in case of Himma's 'you cannot touch 2' example).

Thus, Himma is again perfectly right in arguing that conceptual analysis, unlike lexicography, may actually go 'well beyond the empirical task of identifying shared intuitions or core conventions' and hence become 'something radically different from what lexicographers are doing'. More doubtfully, this 'radically different task' consists in putting forward 'metaphysical claims'.[7] Is 'you cannot touch 2' or 'it is not possible to be a married bachelor' really a metaphysical claim that goes beyond logical or practical consequences of the empirical report of how conventions govern concept-terms' usages? At best, they shed some light on how 'we' conceive the set of properties constituting certain classes of objects. This, in turn, is a purely empirical generalisation based on some (more or less precise and comprehensive) report of how we tend to use respective concept-terms in our linguistic practice. One may doubt whether 'it is not possible to be a married bachelor' needs any more pretentious interpretation that 'as long as linguistic community use the word "bachelor" as it currently does, nobody who is known to be married shall be or should be referred

6 If not just implications of one's own individual understanding of a given concept-term. Such an ambiguity of 'analytical' inferences can be traced back to Kant's original account, where he elaborates on the famous example of 'gold is yellow metal' and claims that 'um dieses zu wissen, brauche ich keiner weitern Erfahrung, außer *meinem* Begriffe vom Golde, der enthielte, daß dieser Körper gelb und Metall sei: denn dieses machte eben *meinen* Begriff aus, und ich durfte nichts tun, als diesen zergliedern, ohne mich außer demselben wornach anders umzusehen.' (Kant 1794, 26, italics added).

7 Himma (2008, 5–6); the very concept of 'metaphysical necessity', quite widespread in some parts of philosophical discourse, seems fundamentally confused and misleading (as long as it is meant to designate something beyond empirical description and causal relations combined with linguistic conventions). It is particularly noticeable in its use to elucidate 'necessary' qualities of legal phenomena. For the general discussion of the concept see e.g. R. Cameron (2009).

to as a "bachelor"'.[8] Is there any metaphysics in such claims beyond the empirical or normative implications of some assumed facts about linguistic practices and the underlying attitudes of language users?[9]

In view of that, we should notice first that conceptual claims undeniably involve empirical hypotheses concerning the convergence of linguistic conventions: the attitudes towards using terms to refer to objects in virtue of some properties of the latter. These conventions do not come from the air. They result from overlapping mental representations of objects and their shared properties that language speakers develop by learning and experience. Such mental representations are usually rather vague and to some extent idiosyncratic even if they largely overlap on some core of 'prototypical' objects belonging to each conceptual category (rather than precise definitions). Such psychological concepts are reflected in linguistic conventions governing the use of relevant concept-terms in linguistic practice. Thus, trivial conceptual claims are true in virtue of an accurate report of those conventions (and their underlying representations), at least as long as relevant conventions remain uniform and unchanged. Thus, they provide, at best, thoroughly contingent truths depending on the actual converging attitudes of language speakers. A bachelor is each and only unmarried male as long as the linguistic community converges in referring such a word to objects that have just that set of properties (male, not yet married) and refrain from referring it to objects having different qualities (say, chairs or numbers). The existence of such uniform and commonly known conventions makes the relation between the claim and its empirical foundation trivial. Such triviality comes with a price, however. It is a triviality either of a conceptual claim itself (as in the case of 'no bachelor is unmarried' or of its various logical transformations).

In other words, the more 'conceptual' a given claim is (namely, its relation to some assumed empirical facts is trivial), the more uninformative it remains. Things radically change, however, when a conceptual analysis purports to answer non-trivial problems. Numerous examples of such conceptual arguments include questions such as whether an unborn child 'is' a person, animals 'may' have rights, legally recognized homosexual relationship 'is' a marriage, international or primi-

8 Which, in my opinion, is roughly equivalent to saying that language speakers (members of a linguistic community) have a certain 'concept' that is the mental representation of a set of properties constituting the typical bachelor, among which is, obviously, the property of being unmarried. This is why they refer this concept-word only to objects (persons) having such properties. On the other hand, such mental representations develop mainly under the influence of a perceived linguistic practice of the community.

9 I will not discuss here a related claim of linguistic philosophy, according to which the way we use words is 'criterial' evidence of attributing some mental states. This idea itself seems to me a very bold and utterly doubtful empirical generalisation rather than a logical, *a priori* truth. Its actual foundations that would not involve *petitio principii* seem rather obscure.

tive law 'is' really law, etc. Roughly, the less trivial an addressed issue becomes, the less trivial becomes also the relation of respective conceptual claims to empirical data.

Let us use an famously and often discussed example: whether a Pope 'is' a bachelor. Its controversiality (non-triviality) seems to reflect the lack of an uniform and uncontestable convention what, in turn, results from the lack of sufficiently precise mental representations of both categories. Thus, on the level of empirical reality there is no obvious convergence of attitudes that would allow to be trivially reported. Therefore, whether or not a Pope 'is' a bachelor ceases to be a purely 'conceptual' truth only trivially dependent on empirical facts. There are some (empirical!) similarities between a 'typical' Pope and a 'typical' example of a bachelor (both are unmarried) and some equally clear dissimilarities (a Pope is not allowed to and probably not willing to marry). Presumably (empirical guess, again!), some competent language users would tend to qualify a Pope as a 'bachelor' (due to similarities between his and 'bachelor's' properties) while others would tend to exclude him from the category (due to coexisting dissimilarities).

Thus, arguably, conceptual claims in such problematic cases may be interpreted in two alternative ways. First, they may be construed as empirical predictions of attitudes that would prevail among language users should they be confronted with the problem of referring a word to a given kind of objects. Notably, conceptual arguments (in particular descriptive ordinary language analysis) typically involve claims of what 'we would say' or 'would not be said' in a given situation (in respect of the applicability of a given concept-term in various potential cases).[10] Second, conceptual claims may be construed (more plausibly) as propositions on what would be a 'proper' decision in respect of the applicability of a given concept-term to this or that kind of objects, in virtue of how the concept-term as well as other related notions have been applied in linguistic practice up to the moment.[11]

10 E.g. H. L. A. Hart (1961, 22): 'what is usually intended by those who speak of laws being 'addressed' to certain persons, is that…', (ibid., 53): 'it could not be intelligibly said to exist' (34), 'we may have good reason for saying', (ibid., 80): 'it is, however, equally certain that we would misdescribe the situation if we said…'. M. Bennett and P. M. S. Hacker (2007, 143): 'that is not the way the concept of being conscious is deployed', 'so in the ordinary sense of knowledge there can be no knowledge recorded, contained in or possessed by the brain', (ibid., 151): 'the stomach can be said to be digesting food but the brain cannot be said to be thinking' (143), 'a being can be said to be following a rule'; M. Pardo and D. Patterson (2010, 7): 'if Smith had no knowledge of the rule prior to his entrance the club it is difficult to say that he was 'following' the rule', (ibid., 15): 'many circumstances in which an ascription of knowledge is inappropriate'; S. Kripke (1981, 119): 'We would say of such a thing that though it has all the appearances…', (ibid., 157): 'in that case we cannot say that…', (ibid., 158): 'one cannot say of any possible person', etc.

11 This kind of normativity based on postulates of coherence or logical consequence has been dubbed 'epistemic' as opposed to 'moral' normativity. Epistemic normativity seems, in turn, to be one of the core elements of rationality of beliefs (Szaniawski 1994). According to Searle, this kind of normativity is implicated in almost every meaningful speech act (Searle 2001).

In both interpretations the truth of conceptual claims is directly and by no means trivially dependent on sets of facts ascertainable and verifiable through empirical inquiry. Whether a conceptual claim is construed as an empirical prediction of language users' attitudes or as a normative stipulation of the 'proper' use of a given concept-term, it has to be based on one's own reconstruction of existing linguistic conventions governing the way a given concept-word and related concept-terms are actually used. Thus, it states what would or ought to happen on the basis of a certain set of assumed objective data. These consist of what 'we would say' or 'we would not say' on the basis of underlying principles and criteria of linguistic conventions governing word usages. Such data may not only be correctly or incorrectly reconstructed (on the basis of better or worse material) but there is no reason to assume that in non-trivial cases it is sufficient to determine any conclusion.

Let us return to the example of a question whether or not a Pope 'is' a bachelor. Now, it seems plausible to distinguish once again two kinds of conceptual claims. In its first type it compares properties decisive for being a bachelor identified as the content of relevant linguistic convention with a set of properties that a given Pope is believed to possess. The fact whether a Pope has such set of properties (e.g. is a male, has never been married, is committed not to marry, does not intend to marry) is a purely empirical question. The direct dependence of the solution of a conceptual question on the accuracy of empirical assumptions is therefore clear. What kind of 'conceptual truth' is expressed by a proposition that the Pope is a bachelor in case, say, the Pope has recently secretly married a woman (let's imagine there is a very long tradition, kept in strict confidence, that Popes marry women soon after being elected to the office)? What kind of 'conceptual truth' would it be in respect of a Pope who actually turns out to be a woman (as in case of the legendary medieval Popess Joanna)? Conceptual claims of this kind, purporting to solve the problem whether an object 'is' (conceptually) a referent of a given concept-term, collapses into a comparison of two sets of empirical qualities (what is the content of a convention, what are the properties of an object). The truth of the claim thus depends on the accuracy of how they have been ascertained.

Two more comments will be in place. First, non-trivial conceptual problems of this kind may result from the fact that there are some similarities as well as some differences between both sets of properties (identified as the content of a linguistic convention and found as actually possessed by an object). Therefore, the conceptual claim in such cases would involve an element of normative stipulation based on the evaluation of relative relevance of similarities and dissimilarities between the properties of 'typical' referents of a concept-term (its 'core') and objects that would be its less typical referents (the 'penumbra').[12] In other words, if a Pope is believed

12 Normativity here is of epistemic rather than moral character, namely it relies on postulates of coherence and logical consistency with the content of the conventional criteria of its applicability as

to be a person who is a male, not married and not willing to marry due to his religious and ecclesiastical commitments, one has to evaluate which of these properties are more critical ('essential') aspects of his empirical description. Those which he shares with more typical bachelors (as the fact that he is a male that has never been married) or those that distinguish him from more typical bachelors (the fact that he is committed not to marry and presumably is not willing to do so). The answer to whether an X is conceptually Y in such circumstances must be 'it depends' (on the choice of identified properties one decides to take into account, and those one decides to ignore). In effect, a conceptual solution to a non-trivial problem could involve a normative claim based at best on a set of deliberately worked out empirical and evaluative judgments, at worst being some kind of an intuitive, definitional *fiat*.

Comparison of criteria governing the applicability of a concept-term and actual properties of some objects or phenomena may support conceptual distinctions of objects of different actual qualities, previously conventionally included into the scope of the same concept-term (as e.g. Austin's 'law in the proper sense' of the word and law 'in the improper sense', or the exclusion of persons whose brain activity irreversibly ceased from the extent of a concept of 'living human being', by the famous Harvard definition of 'death'). On the other hand, it may lead to an extension of the scope of a concept-term to objects found to possess the same critical properties as those to which the use of a term has been conventionally limited (as in case of same-sex relationships to become some kind of 'marriage', fetuses or genetic chimaeras included into the concept of 'human person' etc.).

Second, there is some risk in conceptual analysis aimed at resolving problems as whether X is (conceptually) Y on the basis of a comparison of its actual properties with those associated with typical 'paradigmatic' examples of objects to which a concept-term refers. It is a risk of a tacit reversal of the reasoning from the one in which actual properties decide about conceptual qualification of an object into the one in which its conceptual qualification is purported to decide about empirical qualities of the object. This peril has been noticed e.g. by Hart himself when he cautioned that the idea of a conceptual link between law and morality may turn into a belief that each existing law (everything qualified as law) is actually morally good (because each law, by conceptual necessity, is linked to morality). In trivial cases nobody would probably assume that since the Pope (let us say) 'is not' conceptually a bachelor it is not possible or 'meaningful' that he may actually intend to marry. In many less trivial cases, however, there are serious arguments that seem hardly to avoid this type of fallacy.[13]

---

reflected in the way the concept-term and related concept-terms have been used in the linguistic practice up to the moment.

13 E.g. Bennet and Hacker (2003, 209–210): 'Emotion words do not apply to brain states at all, but to

The second type of a possible conceptual claim identifiable on the basis of 'the Pope is (not) a bachelor' example, compares typical properties involved in linguistic convention (who 'is' a bachelor) not with any actual properties possessed by a real object (real Popes) but some other set of abstract properties fixed by another convention (of either linguistic or extra-linguistic character). What matters, then, is not whether this or that person elected to be a particular Pope has a wife or is a woman rather than a man, but what is the 'concept' of a Pope, that is what it takes 'for us' to be a Pope. The Pope is conceived here not as an actual person having a certain set of properties but rather an abstract figure composed of properties we ascribe to 'someone like a Pope' (the mental representation of a 'typical' Pope). Thus, a conceptual claim becomes a comparison of two conventions determined by two sets of abstract qualities associated with two linguistic labels.

Again, the empirical correctness of their reconstructions is the basic foundation of any conceptual truth here. And again, if such a conceptual problem is not trivial (as it is in the case of this example, let alone serious conceptual analysis of the concepts of law, rights, contracts etc.), then there are some similarities and dissimilarities between the sets of properties involved in the two compared conventions. Thus, the conceptual claim becomes a normative proposition based on the evaluation of their relative importance.

Moreover, it leaves unanswered the problem of which real objects (due to the possession of features required by the content of a convention) qualify as genuine referents of the concept-term. If we claim that the Pope 'is' or 'is not' a bachelor due to the fact that Popes are expected to be males, not expected to have a wife or intend to marry, the question arises whether this or that actual person elected to the position of the Pope is a 'true' Pope (as Joanna or a Pope that turned out to have secretly married a woman or actually intends to marry one). Thus, it is a case discussed by Putnam's example of the sentence 'all cats are animals' in the context of a hypothetical discovery that cats are actually Martian-controlled robots only

creatures who feels emotions and exhibit them in their behavior. [...] Emotions, as we have noted, are not brain states or bodily responses. They are neither objects of perceptions nor sensations that are felt'; (ibid., 128): 'forms of behavior that manifest possession of a given perceptual faculty are [...] logical criteria for a creature's seeing things. [...] the brain is not an organ of perception [...] the neural events in the brain are not forms of perceiving behavior and nothing in the brain can do could count as a criterion of its perceiving something in its vinicinity. The neurons without which we could not see anything are located in our heads, but, of course, it is not those neurons that see or that "do" the seeing'. Pardo, Patterson (2010, 6): 'Rule following is something only human beings do and they do it not alone with their brains but in concert with others', (ibid., 19–20): 'suppose we had an fMRi scan of a defendants brain while committing allegedly criminal acts. Now suppose we have to determine whether he knew the suitcase he walked off was not his [...] or he knew about illegal drugs in his suitcase [...]. Exactly where in his brain would we find this information? Because knowledge is an ability and not a state of the brain, the answer is nowhere. [...] As a conceptual matter neural states of the brain do not fit the criteria for ascriptions of knowledge'.

pretending to be organic creatures similar to other animals. In such a case, we can either conclude that the objects we designated as cats (i.e. robots) turn out not to actually possess empirical properties (including their origin and self-control) implied by our concept of a 'cat' (including those that would lead to their qualification as animals). Hence, despite our common belief, what we took to be a cat proved empirically false. Alternatively, we may conclude that 'cats are animals' is a conceptual ('necessary') truth unable to be falsified by any empirical discovery, since it concerns what we 'take' to be a cat (the set of properties we associate with objects in order to qualify as 'cats'). Then, the discovery proves only that we were in error in referring the concept-term 'cat' to objects that have turned out to be actually Martian-controlled machines instead of 'genuine' cats (even if the latter have never existed in the real world). Then we compare two linguistic conventions and underlying sets of properties required for objects to be included into the relevant category rather than a convention with any real objects.

To summarise, the conceptuality of a claim, arguably, comes in degrees. The more 'conceptual' a claim it is (that is, the more obvious the truth of underlying facts is) the more trivial is the claim itself. The more problematic a question is that a conceptual claim purports to address, the more ambiguous becomes also its relation to empirical reality. There is only a trivial relation between the truth of sentences like 'all bachelors are unmarried' and the actual shape of relevant linguistic conventions. It is much less trivial, however, in case of claims like 'the Pope is a bachelor', 'Nazi law is not law' or 'rights cannot be attributed to animals'. In such cases, where there is no obvious empirical reality that would make the conceptual claim trivially true or false, it may be construed either as a prediction of the behaviour of a linguistic community or as the postulated 'right' use of the concept-term, based on the way in which the existing convention has been governing its operation. In these situations the correctness of the conceptual claim clearly depends on the empirical adequacy of an assumed reconstruction of facts concerning linguistic practice as well as the properties of objects whose character is to be 'conceptually' elucidated. Therefore, conceptual claims often involve some combination of tacit empirical generalisations and normative stipulations based not only on a comparison between reconstructed conventional criteria of linguistic usages and generalised properties of extra-linguistic phenomena but also involve an evaluation of their relative relevance. The plausibility of a normative stipulation may thus depend on both: the adequacy of an empirical description as well as an evaluative judgment concerning the relative weight of particular properties.

I would like to finish by two closing remarks. First, conceptual analysis, let alone the use of concepts themselves, is an unavoidable part of philosophical inquiry. We develop concepts, we think by them and need to analyse their content in view of what they are used to refer to. Thus, to some extent its presence is a matter of clear causal necessity. Beyond doubt, the more we know about the real qualities of a given kind of objects the more we are able to refine the intension and extension of a given concept-term. As long as conceptual analysis is perceived as an attempt to clarify and adjust our conceptual apparatus to what are the actual qualities of relevant phenomena, it has a fundamental value to 'sharpen our awareness' of both words and facts. It has, however, its limitations and brings severe risks. The facts making conceptual claims 'trivially' true of false are a matter of empirical investigation not of speculative inferences or ex cathedra definitional establishments imposed under the name of 'conceptual analysis'. In spite of that, conceptual claims very often seem to be based mainly on an intuitive grasp of underlying sets of facts (of both linguistic and extra-linguistic character) taken as sufficient basis for rather bold and far-reaching generalisations. Such an intuitive, dim image of what is actually the case may always, upon closer empirical scrutiny, turn out to be imprecise or even plainly wrong, thus overturning apparently 'necessary' truths.[14] Moreover, knowledge of reality develops and makes related attitudes and linguistic conventions evolve. Such an evolution itself may often turn today's conceptual truths into tomorrow's empirical or even conceptual fallacies. The history of human thought is full of beliefs once taken to be 'necessarily' or 'conceptually' true (to mention just Anselm's medieval proof of the existence of the perfect God implied by His very concept). Whatever features make empirical and conceptual truths non-superficially distinct, contingency is certainly not one of them.

References

Cameron, R. 2009, What is Metaphysical About Metaphysical Necessity? *Philosophy and Phenomenological Research* 79.1: 1–16

Grice, H. P., and Strawson, P. 1956. In defense of a Dogma. *Philosophical Review* 65: 141–158.

Hacker, P. M. S., Bennett M. 2003. *Philosophical Foundations of Neuroscience.* Malden (MA), Oxford: Blackwell.

Hacker, P. M. S., Bennett, M., Dennett, D., and Searle, J. 2007. *Neuroscience & Philosophy.* New York: Columbia University Press.

Hart, H. L. A. 1961. *The Concept of Law.* Oxford: Clarendon.

Himma, K. E. 2008. Reconsidering a Dogma. Conceptual Analysis, the Naturalistic Turn, and Legal Philosophy. In *Law and Philosophy: Current Legal Is-*

[14] I believe that this is also the case with e.g. R. Alexy's 'claim to correctness' as a necessary quality of genuine law. This argument, however, I will develop elsewhere.

sues, edited by R. Harrison. Oxford: Oxford University Press (available on-line: SSRN Papers, 952910).

Kant, I. 1794. *Prolegomena zu einer jeden künftigen Metaphysik.* Frankfurt, Leipzig.

Kripke, S. 1981. *Naming and Necessity.* Malden (MA), Oxford: Blackwell.

Pardo, M., and Patterson, D. 2009. *Minds, Brains and Norms.* SSRN Papers 1432476.

Pardo, M., and Patterson, D. 2010. Philosophical Foundations of Law and Neuroscience. *University of Illinois Law Review* 4: 1211–1250.

Quine, V. W. 1951. Two Dogmas of Empiricism. *Philosophical Review* 60: 20–43.

Searle, J. 2001. *Rationality in Action.* Cambridge (MA): MIT Press.

Szaniawski, K. 1994. Racjonalność jako wartość [Rationality as Value]. In *O nauce, rozumowaniu i wartościach: Pisma wybrane [On Science, Reasoning and Values: Selected Works],* edited by J. Wolenski, 531–540. Warszawa: PWN.

The Nature of Jurisprudence

Goran Dajović

Introduction

One of the salient features of modern jurisprudence is its preoccupation with methodological and generally with, let us say, *metajurisprudential* issues. Without doubt, one of the basic metajurisprudential questions is: What is the nature of jurisprudence? This kind of question, I admit, sounds fairly frightening, especially if one tries to answer it in a brief report like this one. Actually, this question elicits a long array of others, which are not less perplexing. These *meta* questions, which particularly draw the attention of legal scholars are, for instance: Can jurisprudence be only descriptive or does it need to be a normative discipline as well? Is it universal or parochial, and generally, what is the reach of its theories, theses and concepts: are they concerned with all legal systems in all times or with some legal systems (for instance with *our* legal systems)?[1] Further, if jurisprudence is general, does it deal with those features of law which are shared by all legal systems, or only with essential features of the law, i.e. those without which it would not be the law? Otherwise put, does jurisprudence search for universal elements of different legal systems as a matter of sheer fact (which is a more empirical job), or as a matter of conceptual necessity (which is strictly speaking conceptual work)?[2]

All of these questions (and, surely, not only these) refer to the proper subject-matter and to the method of jurisprudence, and must be solved to get the answer concerning the nature of jurisprudence. But there is an assumption that debates about these questions are debates within jurisprudence. In other words, that the province of jurisprudence is determined, at least roughly. However, if we look more

1 This difference is not the same as the difference between general and particular (or special) jurisprudence, which has been established since Austin as the inner division of labour within jurisprudence itself.

2 This kind of tension between empirical and conceptual can be seen everywhere in jurisprudence. For instance, as Brian Tamanaha pointed out, Hart's theory of law is torn between a conventionalism that serves as a theoretical explanation of any phenomenon treated as law within a social group, and a more essentialist position that assumes that law has some essential and invariant structural features (Tamanaha, 2001, 135).

closely at most metajurisprudential problems, it seems that there is one question which pervades the others: whether jurisprudence, as a discipline of legal knowledge is philosophy or a science? And it is a kind of question which pertains to the province of jurisprudence itself. So, I think it may be useful to solve this question before dealing with other metajurisprudential problems. Although this last question can imply different interpretations and it can raise a few important sub-questions, I will try to shed some light on the most general aspect of this problem, which can be formulated as the persisting dilemma between the empirical (which means inductive, observational), and the conceptual approach to the jurisprudential task.

What is jurisprudence?

If I asked my nine year old daughter what jurisprudence is, I assume she would say that jurisprudence is when jurists become prudent. And this answer is not so superficial as it seems to be at first sight. If prudence in this context means wisdom, a theoretical reflection about law, then before the nineteenth century, jurists had not been prudent. Theorising about law was primarily a privilege of philosophers, political thinkers or theologians. Therefore, the rise of jurisprudence as a legal discipline is closely connected with the lawyers who began to tackle theoretical legal questions. Nevertheless, instead of looking at the law *only* in a larger framework of the world, state or society, as most philosophers did, they focused primarily on the legal system itself.

The first among these was surely John Austin who defined jurisprudence as a 'science concerned with the exposition of the principles, notions and distinctions which are common to system of law' or with 'what is essential to law'. Other than that, Austin made (or, more precisely, took over from Bentham) a distinction between the so-called expository jurisprudence or the knowledge of law as a science and censorial jurisprudence or the science of what ought to be done towards making good laws (Lloyd 1959, 14, 16). This definition of the province of jurisprudence has persisted up to our days, although legal scholars after Austin have also offered others. However, despite different determinations of the province of jurisprudence, there has always been a shared belief among jurisprudential thinkers that they engage themselves with theoretical problems, but not with practical ones. It is an old idea that jurisprudence goes one step back and reflects on the ideas that define our legal practice, or, as Alf Ross said (1958, 26) 'jurisprudence is one store higher than the study of law and looks down upon it'. It amounts to that jurisprudence does not seek to take part in ordinary legal discourse and to help lawyers solve their everyday dilemmas. So, jurisprudents do not reflect about legal practice itself, but on the ideas that underlie it. Today, it is almost a unanimous opinion of legal theorists that the purpose of jurisprudence has always been to better understand the phenomenon of law. It also implies a 'better understanding of the resemblances and differences between law, coercion, and morality as types of social phenomena' (Hart 1994, 17). Therefore, jurisprudence does not only ask questions about the nature of law or *its point* but also in this way it gives us a broader picture of the law and a general understanding of the relation between law and other social normative practices and institutions.

However, from the perspective of this report, the main problem with determining the province of jurisprudence today can be perceived if we analyse one famous remark from the very beginning of Hart's seminal work, *The Concept of Law*. There, Hart says that his book is an essay in analytical jurisprudence because 'it is concerned with the general framework of legal thought, rather than with the criticism of law'. Only one paragraph later, he states that 'notwithstanding concern with analysis, the book may also be regarded as an essay in descriptive sociology' (ibid., vi). Since the very publishing of *The Concept of Law*, the first thesis is accepted as an accurate description of Hart's work, but the second is repeatedly and steadily refuted.[3] It is not our topic now, and I am not going into the analysis of the empirical dimension of Hart's jurisprudence. I have quoted Hart's words about his own book just to hint at his understanding of the nature of the book and, I suppose, his understanding of the task of jurisprudence itself. And, despite how much Hart really attended to such a task in his theory, he drew our attention to the likeness of jurisprudence with the Roman god Janus. These two faces of jurisprudence, broadly speaking, are an empirical and descriptive (and therefore scientific), and a conceptual (philosophical) one.

Jurisprudence: philosophy or science

So, what do we in fact mean when we say that jurisprudence is both a scientific and a philosophical discipline? Most English dictionaries suggest that it is a correct understanding because they define the word 'jurisprudence' as 'the science or philosophy of law'.[4] What is then controversial, if anything, in such a determination of jurisprudence as a legal discipline?

As we know, every discipline is a branch of systematic knowledge about its subject matter, and this knowledge is composed of concepts and propositions as a result of applying its method (experimental, analytical, or observational) to this subject. But a discipline can be a discipline of science, discipline of philosophy, discipline of skill. It should be emphasized that one and the same subject matter (I am talking

[3] Frederick Schauer notes that the 'tricky issue' of the empirical extent of Hart's methodology 'is a subject of continuing jurisprudential debate and one connected to a larger debate in philosophy about conceptual analysis generally' (Schauer 2006, 852, 860).

[4] *The American heritage dictionary of the English language* (2007).

about social phenomena) can be studied from different angles and with different methods and purposes. For instance, it is widely accepted that there is a clear distinction between political science as a general and empirical discipline about political institutions, which deals with the comparison of many different political systems, and political philosophy, which is always concerned with what a state ought to be and what is the justification of the exercise of a state's power over the citizens (Lindsay 1962, 30).

In this respect, if we now take a closer look at jurisprudence, it has been clear since Austin that the so-called censorial jurisprudence actually is a branch of philosophy to the same extent as political philosophy because they are both normatively oriented. On the other hand, with respect to the explicative dimension of jurisprudence, because of the widespread use of the method of conceptual analysis, expository jurisprudence is today often identified as a purely philosophical discipline. Therefore, the philosophical nature of modern jurisprudence seems undeniable.

But there is a rebuke from one prominent empiricist to philosophers who are involved with jurisprudence. It goes as follows: why should we study the concept (of law) if we can study the thing itself, the actual phenomenon instead? Since the law is a set of social practices, its nature is not best discovered through armchair reflections, but by an empirical research of these practices.

Is it possible, due to this objection, to designate jurisprudence as a merely empirical discipline, as a science? In a limited sense, in which political science is a science, the answer is surely yes. It means that jurisprudence is a discipline of knowledge that is concerned with patterns of human behaviour in a political society, and with recognizing regularities of this behaviour. In this aspect, jurisprudence would be an empirical discipline, and, moreover, it would be inevitably led to a certain level of coordination with other social sciences, especially sociology and anthropology.

However, should someone suggest that the investigation of the nature of law is only and purely empirical/sociological, that thesis could be refuted by Jules Coleman's argument offered against Leiter's attempt to 'naturalise' jurisprudence. Coleman asks how one can have a naturalised or sociological theory of law if one does not have at least a rough prior notion of what is or what is not 'law' (Bix 2003, 537–559). In other words, conceptual analysis is a prior inquiry: we cannot study law until we know what we mean by 'law'. Actually, not just the concept of law,[5] but all conceptual apparatus for empirical observations stem from philosophy or are purified by its method of conceptual analysis. As professor Coleman says, 'the naturalized project can proceed only after a good deal of philosophical spadework' (Coleman 2001, 213).

[5] Concerning the concept of law itself, Bix correctly notices that 'there is [...] a sense in which conceptual work must be prior to empirical work[...] For the focus is inevitably on the boundaries of the category – here, what makes something "law" or "not law"?' (Bix 2003, 543).

Yet, this argument notwithstanding, it seems that no matter how great a mistake it would be to ground a theory of the nature of law solely on empirical grounds (without reference to conceptual analysis), it would equally be a mistake to ground such a theory solely on conceptual analysis, without reference to empirical realities.

As an additional illustration of these theses and the useful connections between the empirical and conceptual dimensions of jurisprudence, I want to mention two possible points of intersection where philosophical and empirical elements within the jurisprudence, i.e. the conceptual and the scientific method, must cooperate.

The first one is about a special kind of concepts: novel and theoretical concepts. Namely, jurisprudence can form some concepts that have not yet been used in actual legal practice. They are formed by legal theory as a tool for formulating theories of law and for a better understanding of the practice (Summers 1968, 2). In this stage of theoretical work, i.e. at the level of concept formation, a crude distinction between conceptual and empirical propositions cannot be maintained, because we are always in the intermediate position of examining phenomena and trying to capture their essential properties in definitions of theoretical concepts. Also, checking the adequacy of such kinds of concepts is not possible but through empirical observation (Moore 2002, 99).

Let me point out one example. Hart claims that all modern municipal legal systems possess a rule of recognition. This claim can plausibly be interpreted as introducing a novel and theoretical concept as part of an empirical assertion. Although the Rule of Recognition is not one of the terms which participants in modern legal systems use in their own practice, this concept *can be empirically checked* because it describes and explains the social phenomenon of law. Actually, this work has been undertaken, for instance, by professors Himma (2009), Adler (2006), Carey (2009), and others, in their articles about the Rule of Recognition in the US legal system.[6]

The second point of intersection is, as Nicola Lacey argues, when we enter the realm of special jurisprudence. She contends that it may be easier to get a clear view of the mutual dependence of analytic-conceptual and empirical and social aspects of legal theory through a discussion of 'micro' rather than 'macro' legal theory. For instance, when Hart analyses legal concepts such as causation, intention, or negligence, the connection between the two aspects of legal theory is much stronger than in the case of the concept of law or legal validity.[7] The same is valid for any kind of theorising which demands a richer description of law's social basis: its institutional forms, its various types of rules, and its functions. After all, some legal issues cannot be thought through adequately except in a way which takes seriously empirical work focused on the broader political and institutional context. Law is

6 Some of these articles are collected and published in Adler and Himma (2009).

7 However, as it was argued, it is possible and useful that a higly theorethical concept, like the concept of the Rule of Recognition for instance, be 'compared' with empirical realities.

part of the political system and it works as such, i.e., it is sensitive to other aspects of the political system's functioning.

Finally, paying attention to the problem that has just been sketched can help us, I think, to manage other crucial metajurisprudential problems which I mentioned at the beginning of this report. These problems are, I repeat, about the normative or descriptive dimension, universality or particularity, and the conceptual nature of jurisprudence. Indeed, roughly speaking, if we take jurisprudence as a science, then it becomes a more descriptive, more particular and of course, empirical discipline. On the other hand, jurisprudence as philosophy can be normative and not only descriptive; it is always conceptual, speculative and finally it entails the universality of its theses.[8] But again, owing to the points of overlapping and, most of all, owing to the paramount purpose of all forms of jurisprudence (and, I emphasise, this is a better understanding of the nature of law), neither of these two approaches should be disregarded.

Brief conclusion

It seems convenient to conclude with one interesting remark. Just two years before Hart's *Concept of Law* was published (precisely, 1959), Dennis Lloyd in his *Introduction to Jurisprudence* wrote that 'the whole attitude towards jurisprudence has undergone a sweeping change in the last half century', because on the one side there has been a growing tendency to stress the sociological factors which underlie legal systems and condition their development, and on the other side a tendency 'to neglect if not a total rejection of the conceptual aspects of legal method'.[9] Today, half a century later, we can reverse Lloyd's statement. Namely, the post-Hartian transformation of jurisprudence from theoretical legal discipline into a (partly) philosophical one has had one far-reaching consequence. While this transformation has put on the jurisprudential table an array of philosophical problems which previously had not been considered by legal scholars, this shift has been done at the cost of diminishing the empirical dimension of jurisprudence. Moreover, contrary to the situation described by Dennis Lloyd, the shift was made towards the analysis of the conceptual framework of our legal thought. Even Hart's eternal adversary, Ronald Dworkin has agreed with this general approach, and (speaking about Holmes' theory) he has stigmatised the history of the so-called social-theoretic jurisprudence in the twentieth century as 'depressing'.

8 'The universality of the theses of the general theory of law is a result of the fact that they claim to be necessary truths, and there is nothing less that they can claim' (Raz 1996, 2).

9 Lloyd (1959, 9).

This turnabout of the wheel of fortune shows us that the tension between philosophical method and empirical inquiry is older than all the other problems of metajurisprudence and that it is a source of longstanding debates and differences among legal theorists.

It is an important insight that there is a certain degree of tension between philosophical method and empirical enquiry. However, I hope that it is clear from this brief report that it would be an over-simplification to treat these two approaches in jurisprudence as antitheses and that the nature of jurisprudence actually is in some way twofold.

References

Adler, Matthew and Himma, Kenneth (eds.) 2009. *The Rule of Recognition and the U.S. Constitution*, New York: Oxford University Press.

Adler, Matthew. 2006. Popular Constitutionalism and the Rule of Recognition: whose Practices Ground U.S. Law? *Northwestern University Law Review* 100: 719–805.

Bix, Brian. 2003. Raz on Necessity. *Law and Philosophy* 22: 537–559.

Bix, Brian. 2007. Joseph Raz and Conceptual Analysis. *APA Newsletters* 6: 1–7.

Carey, Stephen. 2009. What is the Rule of Recognition in the United States? *University of Pennsylvania Law Review* 157: 1161–1197.

Coleman, Jules. 2001. *The Practice of Principle.* New York: Oxford University Press.

Dickson, Julie. 2004. Methodology in Jurisprudence: A Critical Survey. *Legal Theory* 10. 117–156.

Farrell, Ian. 2006. H.L.A. Hart and the Methodology of Jurisprudence. *Texas Law Review* 84: 983-1011.

Hart, Herbert. 1994. *The Concept of Law.* Second Edition with Postscript. Oxford: Oxford University Press.

Himma, Kenneth E. 2009. Understanding the Relationship between the U.S. Constitution and the Conventional Rule of Recognition, [http://ssrn.com/abstract=1269748].

Himma, Kenneth Einar. 2007. Reconsidering a Dogma: Conceptual Analysis, the Naturalistic Turn, and Legal Philosophy. In *Law and Philosophy*, edited by Michael Freeman and Ross Harrison, Oxford: Oxford University Press.

Jackson, Frank. 1998. *From Metaphysics to Ethics: A Defence of Conceptual Analysis.* Oxford: Oxford University Press.

Leiter, Brian. 2003. Beyond the Hart/Dworkin Debate: The Methodology Problem in Jurisprudence. *American Journal of Jurisprudence* 48: 17–51.

Lindsay, A. D. 1962. *Modern Democratic State.* Oxford: Oxford University Press.

Lloyd, Dennis. 1959. *Introduction to Jurisprudence.* London: Stevens & Sons.

Moore, Leighton. 2002. Description and analysis in The Concept of Law. *Legal Theory* 8: 91–114.

Moore, Michael S. 1987. Metaphysics, Epistemology and Legal Theory. *Southern California Law Review.* 60: 453–506.

Raz, Joseph. 1996. On the Nature of Law. *Archiv für Rechts und Sozialphilosophie* 82: 1–25.

Raz, Joseph. 2001. Two Views of the Nature of the Theory of Law: A Partial Comparison. In *Hart's Postscript: Essays on the Postscript to The Concept of Law*, edited by Coleman, Jules, 1–38. Oxford: Oxford University Press.

Raz, Joseph. 2004. Can There Be a Theory of Law. In *The Blackwell Guide to Philosophy of Law and Legal Theory*, edited by Edmundson and Golding, 324–342. New York: Blackwell Publishing.

Rodriguez-Blanco, Veronica. 2003. A Defence of Hart's Semantics as nonambitious conceptual analysis. *Legal Theory* 9: 99–124.

Ross, Alf. 1958. *On Law and Justice.* London, Stevens & Sons.

Schauer, Frederick. 2006. (Re)Taking Hart. *Harvard Law Review* 119: 852–883.

Summers, Robert (ed.) 1968. *Essays in Legal Philosophy.* London: Basil Blackwell.

Tamanaha, Brian. 2001. *A General Jurisprudence of Law and Society.* New York: Oxford University Press.

The American Heritage Dictionary of the English Language. 2007. s.v. 'Jurisprudence' [http://www.credoreference.com/entry/hmdictenglang/jurisprudence accessed 17.03.2012].

The Concept of Legal Culture Revisited: An East-Central European Perspective

Balázs Fekete

The concept of legal culture and comparative law

The main, and perhaps the most interesting trend of the last twenty years' comparative law thinking, is a direction change in the research and comparison of legal cultures. Until the end of the Cold War comparative law mostly focused on the functional similarities of legal rules and institutions, and also tried to classify the legal systems into legal families or other units. However, it seems that this traditional orientation coined by such classic authors as René David, Konrad Zweigert and Hein Kötz has undergone considerable transformation in the last twenty years.

From the nineties, some scholars made considerable efforts in order to reformulate the conceptual basis of comparative law. It has been led by many motives, primarily a dissatisfaction with both the conceptual tools and research achievements of traditional comparative law scholarship aligned with secondary, mostly critical, reasons. Common to all of these divergent approaches was that they aimed to renew the methodology by integrating the concept of legal culture into the comparative study. Although these scholars attributed different definitions and components to legal culture, it was obvious that they wanted to integrate elements into the research that were fully or partially neglected by the classic, or leading way of comparative law thinking. But, they referred to too many different components,[1]

[1] To illustrate this diversity it is worthwhile to mention three examples. Pierre Legrand argues that the main points of a cultural research of law are: (i) the nature of legal reasoning, (ii) the role of systematisation, (iii) the character of rules, (iv) the role of facts, (v) the meaning of rights, and (vi) the presence of the past (Legrand 1996, 64–74). In the eyes of van Hoecke and Warrington, the main components of legal culture are: (i) the concept of law, (ii) the theory of legal sources, (iii) the methodology of law, (iv) the theory of argumentation, (v) the theory of legitimation of law, and (vi) a basic ideology (van Hoecke and Warrington 1998, 514–515). For David Nelken, legal culture mostly consist of various attitudes towards law including the attitudes of the professionals as well as those of the citizens (Nelken 1995, 437–440).

and due to this richness of constitutive parts of legal culture it was impossible to reach a comprehensive and commonly shared definition thereof.

It cannot be denied that comparative law dealing with legal cultures implies various difficult challenges. The concept of legal culture is a very problematic one, and its scientific value is doubtful (for different positions see Mezey 2001, Cotterrell 2006). It may also be used in such a broad and vague way that it loses all scientific explanatory potential. In addition, since it is a pattern, or a patchwork, of very different, mostly non-legal elements, it may be too excessive for ordinary lawyers. The claim of interdisciplinarity is strongly implied in it, and, therefore, it may make the whole comparison simply unrealistic (cf. Palmer 2004). However, contrary to all these problematic points, it should also be accepted that a cultural approach of law renders it possible to discuss such important elements as attitudes, ideology, emotions, history and psychology. These 'unofficial' components help to achieve a more suitable understanding of that extremely complex phenomenon which we call law.

Hence, while a cultural approach in comparative law has its own advantages and disadvantages, that does not mean that its application should entirely be rejected. With some caution and methodological discipline, the researcher can avoid the main dangers including dilettantism and an unscientific attitude. In order to do so, this study does not try to formulate a concept of legal culture, nor does it enlist its constitutive components. It simply accepts that legal culture exists and it refers to the elements of legal life including norms and those that are behind or beyond the official norm-level. Thus, legal culture consists of two fundamental parts: the norm and the non-norm level, and both of these are composed of many other interdependent components. In addition, a certain constellation of these constitutive elements in time and space constitutes a specific legal culture.

The hypothesis of this research

The most important starting point of this approach, the complexity of legal cultures, should be stressed at the very beginning. Therefore, this paper selects only two elements of East-Central European legal cultures, from the richness of various features, being worthy of further study. Their common point is that they have not been comprehensively discussed in the general comparative law literature thus far; however, they had a strong influence on the recent shape of these legal systems.

Further, the starting hypothesis of this paper is the existence of Western Law. It implies that there is a legal phenomenon that can be labeled as Western Law due to some common features of certain legal cultures. Obviously, this starting point can be questioned from many aspects. For instance, the national legal cultures composing Western Law differ from each other in many respects. The underlying differences of the two big legal cultures of Western Europe, Civil Law and Common

Law, have already been convincingly proved by Pierre Legrand (1996). Moreover, the uniqueness of European national legal cultures should also be accepted without question; stating that the French and the Swiss legal systems are identical is foolish.

However, one can also imagine such a level of abstraction where it is not impossible to find some common features, even though there are many differing points. René David plausibly argued that the multi-coloured legal systems of the West can be united under the label of *droit occidental*. It is possible, since these legal systems share a common idea and this idea determines them. This is the idea of the rule of law, i.e., the notion that in social life law uniting justice and order should play a prominent role (David 1961). Of course, it also has its special repercussions in the historically conditioned national legal cultures; it is called rule of law in the Common Law countries, *suprematie de droit* in France, or *Rechtsstaat* in German-speaking legal systems. Furthermore, it seems to be the *communis opinio doctorum* that Western legal systems share various common values besides this fundamental idea, such as constitutionalism, predictability, unity, order, secularism, and rationalism; and this value basis distinguishes them from other groups of legal cultures, for example from Middle or Far Eastern legal thinking.[2]

This paper admits as a hypothesis, that contrary to all differences at the level of precise norms and certain historical points, it is possible to find a common denominator in Western laws. This common point, in very broad terms, is related to the idea of rule of law and the autonomy of law. Each Western legal institution implies to a certain degree this fundamental idea and reflects it in its specific field. So, Western legal culture, in this sense, has its own face compared to other big legal cultures of the world. Obviously, this does not exclude the differences in Western legal systems; on lower levels of abstractions, or closer to the norm level of legal cultures, many interesting points can be studied.

In the following sections, the paper will highlight two features of East-Central European legal cultures which are below the surface of the official sphere of norms and may indicate a certain deviation from the general Western model. These components are related to emotions and attitudes, so findings of both law and emotions scholarship and sociology of law are to be applied.

2 The unity of Western legal systems on an abstract level, of course, can be approached from other directions, too. For instance, from Harold J. Berman's point of view the unity of 'Western Legal Tradition' is founded on nine premises. He refers, among others, to the autonomous administration of justice, the training of legal professionals, the view of law as an integrated system and the supremacy of law over politics (Berman 1999, 7–10). Applying a historical approach, Carl Otto Lenz argues that Christianity, Roman law, Enlightenment and the French Revolution provide a basis for the value-community of Western legal systems (Lenz 1996).

The influence of Western Law in the region after 1989 and its limits

It is commonly accepted that the region of East-Central Europe has been strongly influenced by Western legal models following the start of the political transition in 1989. The former Socialist countries incorporated many Western legal institutions into their legal systems. Certain key components, such as constitutional courts providing strong constitutional review of legislative acts (Schwartz 1991–1992), human rights as international and constitutional standards (Sajó 1996b, 143–145), and ombudspersons and equality bodies devoted to anti-discrimination issues (Moon 2007, 872–880) flourished in the region due to European integration aspirations and various legal assistance activities of the nineties. Thus, Western Law comprehensively shaped these legal systems whereby many new institutions and instruments arrived from Western countries to the earlier Socialist systems.

While this import and the wide transformation that followed mostly affected the norm-level of these legal cultures, one of the most exciting questions is whether the other layers of East-Central European legal cultures also changed, and if they did, in which direction? To put the point in sharp focus: did westernisation deeply influence the non-norm layers of legal cultures, i.e., attitudes, emotions, etc.? This is a crucial question, since the everyday functioning and application of law is mostly determined by these factors combined with the precise formulation of legal rules.

Distinctive features I: The role of historical emotions

It sounds a bit unusual, even today, that emotions and sentiments can have an impact on legal cultures, but, contrary to all counter-arguments based on the rationality of law, they cannot obviously be disregarded. Law and emotions scholarship has created an extensive range of literature about this dimension of law in the last twenty years, and it has even emerged as a distinct field of study with its own unique research interests.[3] Hence, scholarship agrees that emotions can be found anywhere in law from criminal trials to family law issues (Bandes 1999, 1–15). In addition, one can identify emotions even in constitutional law since it is beyond doubt that, among others, fear is always an important motive in constitution-making. Modern

[3] The classification of law and emotions studies is possible on various grounds. Abrams and Keren (2009–2010, 2033–2034) suggest three useful dimensions: (a) 'Illumination' presenting how emotions are implicated in legal phenomena, (b) 'Investigation' applying the results of other fields of studies on emotions for legal discussion, and (c) 'Integration' trying to formulate normative suggestions that take into account new findings on emotions in law. In a different vein, Maroney (2006, 125–133) drafts six different approaches in law and emotions researches: (a) emotion-centered, (b) emotional phenomenon, (c) emotion theory, (d) legal doctrine, (e) theory of law, and (f) legal actor. These different, but slightly converging views point out the potential of this way of research.

constitutions, in general, can effectively provide guarantees against political oppression and disorder, so they are able to decrease the fear from unpredictable, future political events (Sajó 2006).

Interestingly, the influence of emotions in the formation of legal cultures has generally been out of the scope of this line of thought thus far. However, law and emotions research cannot be excluded when studying features of legal cultures. For instance, religious sentiments, such as empathy, solidarity, modesty, or even passion for justice, are also able to shape the substance of legal cultures, as the examples of medieval Christian law or Japanese law illustrate.[4] Therefore, legal cultures as such, are worthy of an emotion-oriented analysis. The outcome may offer a more detailed picture by highlighting certain important, but almost invisible cultural aspects. Obviously, the features discovered through it will always remain only an additional dimension, being able to complete the picture gained by more usual ways of research.

Another problem should also be discussed briefly. What are emotions? For an emotional-oriented analysis a certain definition, as a starting point, is indispensable. However, one should also face the complexity of this problem, since it can be approached from the aspect of psychology, biology, moral philosophy or even neurosciences (Kagan 2007, 1–54). An ordinary lawyer is obviously incompetent in these fields. In order to avoid the trap of dilettantism, the focus of the whole question should be changed. Emotions are obviously related to the individual,[5] but one can also speak of collective emotions rooted in the public thinking of an era (Sajó 2006, 2–3). Since we are dealing with legal cultures, the study of this macro level of emotions, i.e. public emotions, will be adequate. Moreover, this macro study does not need such a refined tool as the abovementioned fields offer for the study of the individual, since this problem can be handled with the application of the historical method.[6] The most influential public emotions or sentiments dominating an era can be identified retrospectively by reviewing the expressions of the main trends of

[4] A few examples: Harold J. Berman (1999, 64–66) stresses that Christianity, having love and sanctity in its focus, significantly altered Germanic folk-law to 'more just and more humane', so to say, it humanised it. Lawrence Rosen (2000, 173) argues that the central concept of Islamic legal culture is justice and it is 'the most essential, if indeterminate, of virtues for Arabs'. So, justice in Islam has obvious emotional dimensions, too, since virtues cannot solely operate on the grounds of reason. Chin Kim and Craig M. Lawson (1979, 497–498) point out that one of the main reasons of the distinctiveness of Japanese legal culture is the fundamentally emotional-centered character of the people. The formulation and interpretation of certain penal law articles in Stalinist era was manifestly influenced by fear and hate towards 'the enemies of the system' (Solzhenitsyn 1974, 60–68).

[5] Eric A. Posner offers a wide and comprehensive analysis of the role of emotions in individual decision-making (Posner 2000–2001).

[6] One of the experts, Kagan (2007, 47–49) explicitly accepts that emotions and their interpretations are culturally and historically influenced. So, they can also be studied on a macro level through historical research.

public thinking in various spheres of life. Media, literature, popular and high arts, for instance, and even law, can reveal so many telling points of the dominant public emotions.

In our region one should sharply differentiate between two waves of emotions having impact on post-Socialist legal development at the very beginning. Firstly, a short-run perspective should be analysed. This is related to the fall of the Iron Curtain and the start of political transition, i.e. the early 1990s. It is not too difficult to recognise that the significance of national sentiments drastically increased in the regional public thinking in these years. A large part of the public emotions in the last Socialist decades were centred on the official Socialist internationalism, therefore nationalist themes remained frozen. However, this situation radically changed and some scholars even talk about the presence of a strong ethno-nationalism or aggressive nationalism in the region (Roth 1996, 274–275; Sajó 1996b, 146–147), but this labeling may exaggerate a certainly existing phenomenon. This impressive rise and broad spread of national emotions – just think of the emergence of the Baltic States, the fast dissolution of Czechoslovakia and Yugoslavia, and the birth of entirely new 'nation states' – was one of the consequences of the imperialistic and internationalist policies of the Soviet Union. The nations of this region simply tried to re-establish and revitalise their national-historical identity after more than forty years of pressure from a fundamentally ahistoric and oppressive culture (cf. Wandycz 1992, 244–265).

However, these national sentiments have also been a real engine of post-Socialist legal development. Among others, they have led to the formation of legal solutions that manifestly differ from general Western patterns. Such acts as the language and citizenship laws of the Baltic countries, openly discriminating against former USSR Russian inhabitants;[7] the 'status laws' in Slovakia, Romania, Hungary and Slovenia providing preferential treatment and protection for co-national minorities living outside of these countries (Halász, Majétnyi, and Vizi 2004); or the 'national responsibility clauses'[8] – declaring state obligations concerning those parts of the

7 A good example can be the case of the *Latvian Citizenship Law* (22 July 1994), which excluded all persons from Latvian citizenship who came into the country after 1940 (Art 2 (1)), and this provision mostly effected the former Russian USSR inhabitants having a permanent residence in Latvia. In theory they could apply for naturalisation, however, it was de facto impossible because of the rather demanding linguistic requirements (Art 12 (1), esp. 2, 3, 4). At the end, the status of these Russian persons was settled by the *Law on the Status of Former USSR Citizens who do not have the Citizenship of Latvia or any Other State* (1995). For the assessment of these problems see the report of Klaus Berchtold (1993) on the draft prepared for the Venice Commission.

8 E.g. *Constitution of Romania* Art 7. 'The State shall support the strengthening of links with the Romanians living abroad and shall act accordingly for the preservation, development and expression of their ethnic, cultural, linguistic and religious identity, with the observance of the legislation of the State whose citizens they are.'; *The Constitution of the Slovak Republic* Art 7a 'The Slovak Republic promotes national awareness and cultural identity of Slovaks living abroad, supports their

given nation that lives outside of the national borders – of the regional constitutions, are almost unknown in Western Europe. Thus, rising national feelings significantly contributed to the emergence of certain unique legal measures trying to answer special regional challenges stemming from the recent past.

In addition, the long-term role of emotions should also be assessed. The overwhelming majority of constitutional preambles contain references to the century-long historical fights for national independence.[9] These solemn sentences might be regarded as mere declarations and having no normative value, but they are undeniably important expressions of public sentiment. They can be studied as important litmus papers indicating the reappearance of historical emotions, as for instance the passion for independence. Furthermore, emotions embedded in these texts have strong repercussions for certain constitutional provisions.

The emotional nature of these century-long fights for independence strongly influenced those constitutional measures that made EU accession legally possible, that is, the so-called EU-clauses. The protection of the recently regained sovereignty against the supra-nationalistic claims of the European Union is unambiguous from the relevant provisions of East-Central European constitutions. In general, these articles that made possible the transfer of certain competences to the EU, i.e. open up the closed national legal system towards community law, have restrictive and minimalist wordings and they reflect strong sovereignty concerns (Albi 2005, 415–420; Sajó 2004, 197–198). For instance, the Hungarian constitution declares that 'The Republic of Hungary may exercise competences [...] in conjunction with the other member states [...] to the extent that is necessary [...]' in order to fulfill EU obligations (*The Constitution of the Hungarian Republic* Art. 2/A). The minimalist and sovereignty-focused nature of this provision can hardly be denied. Another good example is the EU-clause of the Czech constitution. It declares, concerning the same issue, that 'certain powers [...] may be transferred by treaty to an international organization or institution' and if a constitutional act requires it, it must be approved by a referendum besides the traditional parliamentary way of ratification (*The Constitution of the Czech Republic* Art. 10/a (1) and (2)). Thus, the decision of the po-

institutions intended to achieve this aim and their relations with the mother country.'; *The Constitution of the Republic of Slovenia* Art 5. 'Slovenians not holding Slovenian citizenship shall enjoy special rights and privileges in Slovenia. The nature and extent of those rights and privileges shall be determined by statute.'; *The Constitution of the Republic of Croatia* Art 10. 'Parts of the Croatian nation in other states shall be guaranteed special concern and the protection by the Republic of Croatia.'

9 E.g. *The Constitution of the Republic of Poland*: 'Beholden to our ancestors for their labours, their struggle for independence achieved at great sacrifice, [...]'; *The Constitution of the Republic of Slovenia*: 'And, acknowledging that we Slovenians created our own national identity and attained our nationhood [...] as a result of our historical and centuries-long struggle for the liberation of our people.'; *Constitution of the Republic of Lithuania*: 'The Lithuanian Nation [...] having for centuries defended its freedom and independence, [...].'

litical sphere is not enough in itself in such a vital question, but the consent of the people is also required. One may conclude that two main public emotions strongly influenced these clauses: the intent to preserve national independence and the fear of losing it in the future.

One can determine from this 'law and emotions approach' that even the norm-level of East-Central European legal cultures could also be influenced by short and long run public sentiments, and, indeed, it properly illustrates to what extent emotions can play a decisive role in the shaping of legal cultures. Here, emotions triggered the emergence of particular regional legal instruments and special constitutional measures.

Distinctive features II: 'Hidden or shadow cultures' in the attitudes towards law

It can be accepted without reservation, that the citizens' attitudes towards law also have a crucial impact on the face of a given legal culture (Nelken 1995). Compare the Japanese way of legal thinking to the general Western attitude. Far-Eastern people do not have too much confidence in the law in general and, therefore, they prefer non-legal ways, such as mediation, in conflict settlement (Kim and Lawson 1979). By comparison, law is the most frequently used way to solve problems and conflicts in the Western world. Obviously, this difference in attitudes decisively shaped the general picture of legal cultures.

In the region of East-Central Europe, one can also find some interesting points, and these may indicate a certain deviation from the general Western model. These differences are coupled to 'the non-official cultures of law', so they are mostly invisible from the point of view of professional legal discourse. They are called 'hidden or shadow cultures' in scholarly literature, since they cannot evidently be recognised on the surface of professional legal culture, but they need a more socially oriented research. Additionally, these 'hidden cultures' are mainly rooted in the Socialist era when citizens had to develop certain special attitudes due to the pressure of official state policies, and, obviously, they were a way of social adjustment, too (Los 1996, 474–475). Therefore, the heritage of the Socialist era still influences current legal cultures in East-Central Europe, because these 'hidden or shadow cultures' can create important normative claims towards the legislator.

As a primary example, one can mention the widely spread 'culture of legal scepticism' in the region. It can be proved empirically, on the basis of the comparison of Western and former Socialist data, that the public opinion of the population is determined by a deep institutional scepticism (Beers 2006, 11; Los 1996, 475). Eurobarometer surveys harshly illustrate this gap between the old and new EU member states in terms of institutional trust. For instance, the overall average of trust in the legal systems in the EU was 43% in 2009. This data was significantly lower in the newly entrant countries. In the Czech Republic 29%, in Hungary 41%, and in Poland 31% of the population answered that they tend to trust in the legal system (Eurobarometer 2009). This gap is more apparent if one compares, for instance, the data of Germany and the Netherlands to those of the above three former-Socialist countries. In Germany 58% and in the Netherlands 51% of the citizens tended to trust in the legal system in the same year. Thus, the general level of institutional trust is significantly higher in these traditional Western countries (ibid.).

This could be a legacy of the Socialist period, during which the governments and the political elites regularly misused the law for their political goals (Varga 1995, 50–57). Basically, they regarded the law as a means to realise their special and ideologically biased group interests over the whole, not necessarily supportive, society. As a consequence, this caution and awareness of people towards the law will not disappear in one or two years following the start of the transition. Alternatively, it could also be a consequence of the general institutional performance in the years of the transition. A fundamental renewal of the whole system of administration of justice was simply impossible at the beginning of the nineties, due to human resources and political reasons (Fleck 2003). Therefore citizens experienced the continuation of former institutional attitudes and practices. This transitory phase and its bad consequences – for instance: disregard of the interest of the ordinary people, the birth of politically motivated judgments, the low effectiveness of criminal investigation, etc. – considerably weakened the trust in legal institutions (ibid., 40–49; Beers 2006, 11). In conclusion, citizens' attitudes towards legal institutions are not the most favourable compared to the general Western setting. People here tend to trust less in the legal system than citizens do in Western Europe. Whether this trust can be increased to a general EU level is a considerable challenge, but one should admit that this low level can seriously affect or even bias, in certain cases, the functioning of the entire legal system.

Another special feature of these 'hidden cultures' is the attitudes related to overemphasised welfare expectations. Because of the weaker performance of post-Socialist economies and the paternalist legacy of the Socialist period, there is a general attitude in the region which regards social security benefits as an expected solution to any kind of problems. People generally tend to establish their life expectations on social security benefits provided by the state rather than on their autonomous acts guaranteed by their fundamental rights. This, however, can also have serious repercussions on these legal systems. First of all, these social justice expectations create a strong pressure on legislation concerning social and economic rights as well as social security law. Secondly, these also lead to a considerable dependency on state policies, and this can impede the formation of a legal culture based on civic autonomy. Therefore, these inherited welfare expectations also shape the content of these legal systems in a certain direction, as for instance an unusually broad interpretation of social rights (Sajó 1996a; 2004, 208–212).

The above feature is strongly related to another regional peculiarity: the unstable and not completely developed 'rights culture'. For various reasons,[10] the ability of the 'rights revolution' to replace the culture of political privileges and state paternalism rooted in the Socialist era has not yet been accomplished. On the norm level, one can see a comprehensive development, since the ratification of international human rights documents and the reformulation of constitutional provisions have already happened since the beginning of the transitory period. The constitutions of the region fully endorsed human rights logic and language, and an institutional framework comprising constitutional courts and ombudspersons also emerged. But, partly due to the Socialist legacy, partly to the ambiguous nature of the transition process, one cannot talk about a perfect 'rights culture' in Western terms. Shortcomings of the economic systems, structural problems of the societies and the overrepresentation of the political sphere are all able to distort the formation of such legal cultures, where rights are not only regarded as instruments in different hands, but autonomous legal claims having a *sui generis* value. The situation of rights, therefore, needs refinement and more development in these legal cultures to be comparable to the general Western standard (Sajó 1996b, 156–157).

Conclusions

What are the main lessons to be learned for legal theory and comparative law? First of all, if we regard East-Central European legal systems as not only a simple set of legal rules but as complex legal cultures, their unique features cannot be denied from a comparative aspect. They seem to formally adhere to 'Western Law', since they imported many important and manifestly Western legal institutions in the last twenty years, and one can even assert that on the norm-level it is not really possible to find highly relevant and serious differences between the Western legal systems and the East-Central European ones. This considerable level of similarity can be very tempting to declare the general similarity of Western and East-Central European legal systems.[11]

10 András Sajó (1996b, 146–151) lists six 'interdependent factors': (i) aggressive nationalism, (ii) antiminoritarian attitudes, (iii) unstable state system, (iv) the state is uninterested in 'destroying' its former economic and cultural monopolies, (v) the distortion of the emerging market economy, (vi) the lack of trust in economic transactions.

11 There is a line of thought in the comparative law of the last sixty years arguing that Central and Eastern European legal systems do not essentially differ from the general Western patterns. This position is represented by such authors as for instance J. H. Merrymann or Tomasz Giaro in the recent times (for a general overview see Osakwe 1986–1987; further see Merryman 1996, 109, 118–119; Giaro 2011).

However, the features analysed here also show that important differences exist regarding the non-norm layers of these legal cultures. These are not only of theoretical or sociological relevance, but they are also able to influence the norm-level and the general functioning of these systems. There are many options. These unique features can distort the ordinary functioning of law, as the so-called 'hidden cultures' do, or they can even be engines for the formation of peculiar regional legal solutions, as pointed out by the example of emotions. Therefore, the similarity of our legal cultures to the Western one should be regarded cautiously. From the aspect of norms it seems to be correct, but the non-norm elements can suggest slightly different conclusions.

Moreover, this may also indicate that comparative law strictly focusing on the functional similarity of legal rules or concentrating on the simple comparison or juxtaposition of norms is inadequate for the comprehensive understanding of these legal systems. Layers of legal cultures, although they are very complex and sometimes controversial, should also play a prominent role in these studies. Therefore, the continued development of the classical theses of comparative law towards the integration of cultural elements should be continued, as the lessons arising from the study of East-Central European legal cultures teaches us.

References

Abrams, Kathryn, and Keren, Hila. 2009-2010. Who's Afraid of Law and Emotions? *Minnesota Law Review* 94: 1998–2074.

Albi, Anneli. 2005. 'Europe' Articles in the Constitutions of Central and Eastern European Countries. *Common Market Law Review* 42: 399–423.

Bandes, Susan A. 1999. Introduction. In *The Passions of Law*, edited by Susan A. Bandes, 1–15. New York, London: New York University Press.

Berman, Harold J. 1999. *Law and Revolution. The Formation of the Western Legal Tradition.* Cambridge, MA, London: Harvard University Press.

Beers, Daniel J. 2006. Mass Attitudes toward the Law in Postcommunist Europe: Normative Support vs. Institutional Trust. Prepared for delivery at the 2006 Annual Meeting of the American Political Science Association [now at http://www.allacademic.com/meta/p151258_index.html].

Berchtold, Klaus. 1993. Report on the draft Law on Citizenship in Latvia. CDL(1993)005 [http://www.venice.coe.int/docs/1993/CDL%281993%29005-e.asp]

Cotterrell, Roger. 2006. The Concept of Legal Culture. In *Law, Culture and Society: Legal Ideas in the Mirror of Social Theory*, 81–96. Burlingon: Ashgate.

David, René. 1961. Existe-t-il un droit occidental? In *XXth Century Comparative and Conflicts Law. Legal Essays in Honor of Hessel E. Yntema*, edited by Kurt H. Nadelmann, Arthur. T. von Meheren, John N. Hazard, 56–64. Leiden: A. W. Sythoff.

Eurobarometer. 2009. *Eurobarometer survey about the trust in the national legal system* 11/2009 [http://ec.europa.eu/public_opinion/cf/showchart].

Fleck Zoltán. 2003. Jogintézmények átépítése (Bevezetés a közép-európai új demokráciák bírói jogalkalmazásának szociológiájába) [Reconstruction of legal institutions (Introduction to the legal sociology of the administration of justice in the new democracies of Central-Europe)]. *Kontroll* 1: 28–55.

Giaro, Tomasz. 2011. Legal Tradition of Eastern Europe. Its Rise and Demise. *Comparative Law Review* 2: 1–23.

Halász, Iván, Majtényi, Balázs, and Vizi, Balázs. 2004. A New Regime of Minority Protection? Preferential Treatment of Kin-Minorities under National and International Law. In *The Hungarian Status Law: Nation Building and/or Minority Protection*, edited by Zoltán Kántor et al., 328–349. Sapporo: Slavic Research Center, Hokkaido University.

Kagan, Jerome. 2007. *What is emotion? History, Measures and Meanings*. New Heaven, Conn: Yale University Press.

Kim, Chin, and Lawson, Craig M. 1979. The Law of the Subtle Mind: the Traditional Japanese Conception of Law. *International and Comparative Law Quaterly* 28: 491–513.

Legrand, Pierre. 1996. European Legal Systems are not Converging. *The International and Comparative Law Quaterly* 45: 52–81.

Lenz, Carl Otto. 1996. Common Bases and Fundamental Values of European Community Law. In *European Legal Cultures*, edited by Volkmar Gessner, Armin Hoeland, Csaba Varga, 78–86. Aldershot, etc.: Dartmouth.

Los, Maria. 1996. Legitimation, State and Law in the Central European Return to Democracy. In *European Legal Cultures*, edited by Volkmar Gessner, Armin Hoeland, Csaba Varga, 473–481. Aldershot, etc.: Dartmouth.

Maroney, Terry A. 2006. Law and Emotion: A Proposed Taxonomy of an Emerging Field. *Law and Human Behavior* 30: 119–142.

Mezey, Naomi. 2001. Law as Culture. *Yale Journal of Law and Humanities* 13: 35–67.

Moon, Gay. 2007. Enforcement Bodies. In *Cases, Materials, and Text on National, Supranational and International Non-Discrimination Law*, edited by Dagmar Schiek, Lisa Waddington, Mark Bell, 871–954. Oxford, Portland, Oregon: Hart Publishing.

Nelken, David. 1995. Disclosing/Invoking Legal Culture: An introduction. *Social and Legal Studies* 4: 435–452.

Osakwe, Christopher. 1986–1987. The Greening of Socialist Law as an Academic Discipline. *Tulane Law Review* 51: 1257–1278.

Palmer, Vernon Valentin. 2004. From Lerotholi to Lando: Some Examples of Comparative Law Methodology. *Global Jurist Frontiers* 4:2. [http://www.bepress.com/gj/frontiers/vol4/iss2/art1]

Posner, Eric A. 2000–2001. Law and Emotions. *Georgetown Law Journal* 89: 1977–2012.

Rosen, Lawrence. 2000. *The Justice of Islam*. Oxford: Oxford University Press.

Roth, Stephen J. 1996. The Effect of Ethno-Nationalism on Citizens' Rights in the Former Communist Countries. In *Western Rights? Post-Communist Application*, edited by András Sajó, 273–290. The Hague, London, Boston: Kluwer Law International.

Sajó András. 1996a. How the Rule of Law Killed Hungarian Welfare Reform. *East European Constitutional Review* 5: 31–41.

Sajó András. 1996b. Rights in Post-Communism. In *Western Rights? Post-Communist Application*, edited by András Sajó, 139–157. The Hague, London, Boston: Kluwer Law International.

Sajó András. 2004. The Impacts of EU Accession on Post-communist Constitutionalism. *Acta Juridica Hungarica* 45: 193–212.

Sajó András. 2006. Constitutional Sentiments. *Acta Juridica Hungarica* 47: 1–13.

Schwartz, Herman. 1991–1992. The New East European Constitutional Courts. *Michigan Journal of International Law* 13: 741–785.

Solzhenitsyn, Aleksandr. 1974. *The Gulag Archipelago 1918–1956: An experiment in Literary Investigation*. New York, Evanston, San Francisco, London: Harper & Row.

Varga Csaba. 1995. What is needed to have Law? In *Transition to Rule of Law. On the Democratic Transformation in Hungary*, 38–61. Budapest: Tempus.

Wandycz, Piotr S. 1992. *The Price of Freedom. A History of East Central Europe from the Middle Ages to the Present*. London, New York: Routledge.

Part III
Legacies of 20th Century Legal Positivism

Between the 'Metaphysics of the Stone Age' and the 'Brave New World': H. L. A. Hart on the Law's Assumptions about Human Nature

Péter Cserne

'How the law thinks': reconstructing the law's assumptions

Briefly and metaphorically, a theoretical reconstruction of legal epistemology is concerned with 'how the law thinks' (Teubner 1989). Most generally, the law's assumptions refer to theoretical and empirical presuppositions behind legal concepts, rules, and doctrines about factual and normative features of the world. It seems obvious that the law is based on such assumptions, especially about human nature. It would be hard to imagine a legal system without taking into account, in some ways, certain features of its subjects whose behaviour it purports to regulate or for whom it claims to provide reasons for action.

Legal scholars often discuss the content, the scope or the origins of the law's assumptions. In terms of *content*, they analyse the implicit 'social models' behind civil codes (Wieacker 1953), or ask what legal rules presuppose in terms of selfishness/altruism or rationality (cf. Dagan 2011). In terms of *scope*, they distinguish different levels of abstraction, i.e. whether the assumptions are shared by entire legal cultures ('modern Western law'), legal families ('Continental law') or legal systems ('French law'), or they attach to specific doctrinal constructs ('strict liability'), juristic 'theories' ('contractual capacity') or differ across legal areas (e.g. 'consent' has a different doctrinal meaning in business transactions, marriage or rape). It is also interesting to look at the historical *origin* of the law's assumptions in custom, precedents, philosophical theories or political debates. Sometimes the law makes its assumptions explicit, but mostly these are implicit in legal rules and doctrines. Such unclarity may be a deliberate decision of the legislator, for reasons similar to the case of 'incompletely theorized agreements' (Sunstein 1995) but in any case, as long as assumptions are implicit, there are different ways to discern or reconstruct them.

In this paper I discuss a fourth aspect of the law's assumptions: their *epistemic character*. While legal constructs and doctrinal theories are often well-articulated and on their surface they have a clear technical meaning, they also half-knowingly reflect philosophical ideas of earlier ages ('the metaphysics of the Stone Age', Hart and Honoré 1985, 2) or express common sense beliefs and evaluations (of 'the man on the Clapham omnibus'). Such archaic, naïve and often implicit theories seem satisfactory for everyday operations of the law but at closer look, especially to the eyes of an analytical philosopher or an empirical scientist, this 'legal worldview' turns out to be strange and deeply problematic. More precisely, the law's models of human nature have an epistemic character and methodological status quite different from models in behavioural and social sciences. The questions discussed in this paper revolve around this difference and its consequences for legal theory and legal design.

How seriously should these so-called doctrinal theories be taken in an epistemic sense? Do they claim to be 'true'? What is their methodological role in the functioning of law? What happens when they get confronted with the insights and models of social and behavioural sciences? More fundamentally, which criteria are to be used in judging the adequacy of the law's assumptions? I will approach this problematic through the lense of Herbert Hart's legal theory. The analysis does not only rely on Hart to elucidate a problem in legal theory but also attempts to shed some new light on relatively neglected aspects of Hart's work itself.

To be sure, legal epistemology and the implicit theories behind legal constructs can be analysed from many theoretical perspectives. Legal anthropologists describe and interpret 'primitive' legal cultures and the *Weltanschauung* reflected in their legal concepts. Combining historical inquiry with a critical stance, French legal scholars use a similar methodology to uncover basic ideological commitments behind (modern) Western law and what they call the 'dogmatic nature' of law (Legendre 1974, Supiot 2005). Donald Kelley's equally erudite but less critical historical inquiry (1990) suggests that for centuries, Western jurisprudence (re)presented itself as the 'true science of society', the centre of scientific inquiry on human nature and social interaction but later this humanistic view was challenged and almost completely washed away by modern social sciences. The rise and fall of law as 'the oldest social science' was reconstructed in a different narrative by Tim Murphy (1997). Different versions of systems theory and social constructivism suggest self-referentiality as both a theoretical reconstruction and a philosophical justification of the autonomy of legal epistemology (see e.g. Luhmann 1974, Teubner 1975, 1989). Some Anglo-American legal philosophers also defend the conceptual schemes of modern law against 'realist' attacks, referring to the 'systematicity' of these schemes and the benefits of this 'systematicity' in plural societies (Waldron 2000).

Ordinary language philosophy, conceptual analysis, and the epistemology of law

Compared to these theoretical efforts, what does Hart's analytical positivist legal theory offer for an understanding of the epistemology of law? When in the 1950s Hart set out to build legal philosophy on 'ordinary language philosophy' (see Hart 1953, 1955, 1957) and later in *The Concept of Law* related his methodology to 'descriptive sociology' (Hart 1994, v), he also committed himself to a certain view of legal epistemology. In the following I discuss what Hart said (or could have said) about legal epistemology as he confronted legal doctrines with ordinary people's views, empirical research, and philosophical arguments. Although I do *not* look at Hart's theory merely as intellectual history, in this paper I merely indicate where the theory seems incomplete or undeveloped but do not engage in critical analysis of his views and arguments.

In analysing Hart's views I mainly rely on his book, *Causation in the Law*, co-authored with Tony Honoré (Hart and Honoré 1985) and his essays in *Punishment and Responsibility* (Hart 1968). In particular, I follow the line of argument in the extensive preface to the second edition of *Causation*, referring from time to time to Hart's other writings and adding my comments throughout. There are two main reasons for using this somewhat unusual method. First, the book is generally considered as the prime example and main result of Hart's theoretical programme of using analytical philosophy in legal analysis (Lacey 2006, 962). The second is that the preface, written in May 1983, is one of Hart's latest writings that presents his views on legal epistemology in a developed, although polemic form. While the book discusses doctrinal problems of causation, it reflects Hart's general approach to legal epistemology and relates to fundamental philosophical issues about human nature as well.[1]

1 Cf. Lacey 2006, 962: 'Even in *Causation*... we see in Hart's emphasis on the centrality of voluntary human conduct to the attributions of causation the seeds of the liberal theory of agency and responsibility that dominates his normative criminal law theory.' Some caution is warranted in using this method. As mentioned in the preface itself, the revision for the second edition was almost entirely done by Honoré. Judging from the text of the preface, this does not seem to apply to that piece itself, at least not in the sense that the arguments in the preface would contradict or even be distinguishable from what Hart wrote elsewhere. As for the main text of the second edition, it would indeed be problematic as single evidence or textual basis for attributing a particular view to Hart. Still, the arguments in the preface about the epistemic character of legal doctrinal constructs and the fundamental assumptions behind the law either follow the first edition of the book or developed it in a direction which is consistent with Hart's other writings.

Causation both interprets and reconstructs but at certain point also criticises legal doctrines on causation. Hart, in fact, did not confine himself to conceptual and descriptive analysis. To borrow a term from one of his essays on Bentham (Hart 1973), he was open towards the 'demystifying' role of legal philosophy. We will see how his 'expository' reconstruction of legal doctrine combines with his critical or 'censorial' jurisprudence. As for the representativeness of the preface for Hart's views, reading *Causation* together with Hart's single-authored writings there is clear continuity: most relevant arguments presented in the preface have their counterparts in his other writings.

To be sure, Hart's most frequently discussed arguments on the law's assumptions are related to what he called the 'core of good sense in the doctrine of Natural Law' (Hart 1994, 199), discussed in *The Concept of Law* (ibid., ch.9 s.2) and elsewhere (Hart 1983, 79–82; 111–114). While these insights are crucial for understanding Hart's general jurisprudence, my main goal in this paper is to throw some light on the epistemic and methodological character of particular legal doctrines. For this question Hart's special jurisprudence seems at least as relevant as his ideas on the human predicament and the minimal content of natural law. In addition, Hart's analysis of doctrinal problems of causation and responsibility provides a good starting point for understanding not only his approach to legal epistemology but also his views on fundamental jurisprudential issues and the nature of law (cf. Lacey 2006, 962).

Legal theory as 'rational and critical foundation' of the law

At least in the first edition of *Causation*, Hart and Honoré 'drew on the philosophical currents of the fifties. At that time the analysis of ordinary language was regarded by many as the key to the clarification of conceptual difficulties.' (1985, xxxiii)[2] They argue 'that the language of ordinary people and of lawyers both revealed and obscured the truth about causal concepts.' (ibid., xxxi). This statement is important in

2 Note here that they mention *conceptual* difficulties, not normative or empirical ones. Although the law's assumptions about human behaviour are not only a conceptual but a substantive matter, their view is that these two cannot be separated. Indeed, their analysis of legal theories of causation is based on the assumption that the concern with the duality of 'words and things' is misguided. As Hart argued elsewhere, 'The question "Is analysis concerned with words or with things?" incorporates a most misleading dichotomy. Perhaps its misleading character comes out in the following analogy. Suppose a man to be occupied in focusing through a telescope on a battleship lying in the harbor some distance away. A friend comes up to him and says, "Are you concerned with the image in your glass or with the ship?" Plainly (if well advised) the other would answer "Both. I am endeavoring to align the image in the glass with the battleship in order to see it better." It seems to me that similarly in pursuing analytical inquiries we seek to sharpen our awareness of what we talk about when we use our language. There is no clarification of concepts which can fail to increase our understanding of the world to which we apply them.' (Hart 1957, 967).

several respects. First, it implies a distinction and a potential difference between ordinary people's views and lawyers' views. Second, they claim that there is such thing as truth about (causal) concepts. In other words, they think that one can meaningfully ask whether what the law says about causation corresponds to what causation 'truly' is. To be sure, '*Causation* is about "causation talk" in particular contexts rather than "causation", understood as a metaphysical concept.' (Lacey 2006, 966). Nevertheless, they claim that language has the dual character to 'both reveal and obscure' how things are. I return to this duality below. They summarise the main substantive finding of the book as follows:

> What is revealed, when studied in conjunction with the decisions of courts and the judgements of ordinary people, confronted with various sets of facts, was that the concept of causation, as we use it in ordinary life, is not a unitary one. There is rather a central concept of physical manipulation or intervention round which cluster a whole group of concepts, which can in a broad sense be termed causal, and which are related in different ways to the central case. (Hart and Honoré 1985, xxxi)

The most important thing to note here is their method of distinguishing central cases from peripheral ones. Philosophical analysis should rely on the usage of concepts in ordinary language, be it among competent language users generally or in a special group of professionals. But it is not a mere catalogue or even statistics of actual or potential usage: analysis has to be selective, and identify what is the 'central', 'standard', 'paradigmatic' or 'focal' use of a concept.[3] They also explain why conceptual analysis involves going beyond description:

> if ordinary language and legal discourse contain clues to the existence of these various notions and to the analogies and dysfunctions between them, they also have a pathological aspect. For though in everyday life we make a distinction between conditions and causes [...], we are often unable to explain the principles on which we do so. Hence lawyers in particular, when called upon to give an account of the causal principles they apply, often resort to obscure metaphors of "causal potency", the "exhaustion" of causes, and the "breaking of causal chains." Here our aim was therapeutic. We tried to translate the bewildering metaphors into factual terms and to dissipate the sense of mystification they engender. (ibid., xxxiii–iv)

3 Hart used and reflected upon this 'central-case method' at different points throughout his work (Hart 1957, 968; 1994, 79; 1983, 11–2, 274–5) but never discussed the method's theoretical background explicitly and generally. Probably he thought that there is no general way to give a criterion of 'centrality'. I briefly discuss Hart's 'central-case method' with respect to the concept of law below. The problem of 'what makes central cases central' has been discussed in the literature (see e.g. Rodriguez-Blanco 2007, Finnis 2007, 316–21) and I shall come back to this problem on another occasion.

Their version of ordinary language philosophy thus also takes up a critical task with regard to doctrinal constructs, although the critique here is not in light of moral values. Juxtaposing the 'factual' with 'metaphorical' is certainly one way for theorists to justify, at least rhetorically, a certain combination of description and critique. This raises the question as to how description and therapy are connected: how much of the ordinary views or the professional jargon and metaphors can be retained; what should be demystified or 'translated into factual terms'? If we look at Hart's other writings, e.g. on the principles of punishment and criminal law doctrines (Hart 1968), the legal enforcement of conventional sexual morality (Hart 1958, 1963) or abortion (Hart 1972), we observe that their 'therapeutic' and critical tenor varies, depending on audience, context, the weight of the doctrinal construct on his critical moral scale and a number of other factors.

Even in *Causation*, the link between legal doctrinal constructs, ordinary people's view and the task of the legal theorist is not only an epistemic matter but related to moral issues. Discussing the role of causation they note: 'That we are responsible for the harm we cause is a principle that makes an immediate appeal to *common moral sensibility*.' (Hart and Honoré 1985, xxxv, my emphasis). To be sure, at least formally, 'common moral sensibility' is mentioned here from a detached perspective, referring to conventional social morality. Later in the preface they argue that

> the law of tort cannot be accounted for solely as an instrument for maximizing future wealth or utility or some other socially desirable end. Backward-looking aims, such as redress of wrongs, play at least some part in it and will continue to do so in any society in which regard continues to be paid to *the moral sensibility of ordinary people*. For one of *our most widely shared intuitions* concerns the redress of wrong we do and that we ought in a proper sense to pay compensation for it. (ibid., lxxv, my emphases.)

Again, in this passage there is no clear indication that 'the moral sensibility of ordinary people' would be necessarily endorsed by the authors' critical morality. Still, the quote conveys the idea that not only conceptual but also moral arguments are relevant in the choice between alternative theories of tort law.

Hart indeed thought that common moral views are relevant for legal design (ibid., lxxviii) and for lawyers in general (ibid., 1). But he clearly did *not* think that law should be a simple 'mouthpiece of the moral sentiments of society' (Hart 1968, 170). At another point he suggests that law should 'control resentment, however natural, in the interests of some deliberate forward-looking policy, much as we control our natural fears in the interest of forward-looking prudential aims.' (ibid., 131). In accord with Bentham, he saw that legal theory has a role in the demystification of legal doctrine (Hart 1973). In this 'therapeutic' task, critical deliberation about ends and scientific knowledge about means (facts) should play a key role (Hart 1968, 171).

Coming back to the possible discrepancy between the law's implicit theories and the ordinary man's views, they argue that in case of causation, there is not much difference between them. The former is based on and refines the latter. Consequently, 'the clarification of the structure of ordinary causal statements was and is an indispensable first step towards *understanding* the use of causal notions in the law.' (Hart and Honoré 1985, xxxiv).[4]

What is then the task of legal theorists who want to understand a certain legal concept or doctrine? The answer seems encapsulated in the methodological credo of *Causation*: 'to put a *rational and critical foundation* under the case law as it stands' (ibid., xxxv). Their method was roughly this: in order to understand what causation in the law is, one first has to look at lawyers' 'causation talk' (Lacey 2006, 966). Legal usage of language itself is based on ordinary people's views and moral intuitions. Therefore, in the first part of the book they took the ordinary man's views on causation as an analytical starting point and distinguished its central case from other uses of causal language. In the second part, they 'tried to show that decisions in many jurisdictions stretching over both civil and criminal law were consistent with the view that the courts, whether consciously or unconsciously, apply the causal criteria analysed in the first part of the book' (ibid., xxxv).

This theoretical strategy is a *par excellence* interpretative or 'hermeneutical' way of relating to legal practice (cf. Hart 1983, 13–4, MacCormick 2007, 46–55).[5] They put a philosophical structure behind 'causation talk' by distinguishing the central or paradigmatic case from subsidiary uses of causal terms. On certain points they suggest corrections to the practice by eliminating what they consider as 'obscuring metaphors'. Legal doctrine, case law, ordinary views and philosophical arguments add up to a theory which should feed back to legal practice itself, by providing 'a rational and critical foundation' of it.

Although Hart and Honoré use the term 'critical', it seems that in case of causation their critical morality can largely support what they analysed and clarified from doctrinal views, case law and ordinary people's views. To put it bluntly, for them this segment of the world more or less makes sense and this segment of the law is more or less doing what it should. Towards the end of the preface, Hart and Honoré discuss three main forms of responsibility in their relation to causation and

4 Cf. Hart and Honoré 1985, 1: 'the assertion often made by the courts, especially in England, that it is the plain man's notions of causation (and not the philosopher's or the scientist's) with which the law is concerned, seems to us to be true'. This is not always the case. Elsewhere, Hart notes that 'the judgment of the reasonable man very often is a mere projected shadow, cast by the judge's own moral views or those of his own social class.' Hart 1968, 171.

5 The similarity between Hart's approach in *Causation* and *Punishment and Responsibility* and what later became Dworkin's own 'interpretive' approach was already noted by Dworkin in his review of *Punishment and Responsibility*. See Lacey 2006, 962.

fault. Again applying their central-case method, they explain what makes the central case of responsibility central:

> But what is it *reasonable* for the law to demand when it makes this primary appeal? Plainly no more than normal individuals can *reasonably* hope to deliver; that is, first and foremost, that they will not do those things which are sufficient to produce harm without the intervention of others or of abnormal contingencies. It would be quite *unreasonable* for the law to demand and for any individual to undertake that his action will not be the condition sine qua non of another's voluntary action and so of the harm it produces. It will on the other hand be *reasonable* enough for the law to demand and the subject to undertake, as subsidiary forms of responsibility in a restricted range of cases, liability for providing reasons for others to act or, in defiance of common precautions, providing opportunities for others to do harm. […] It seems, then, that the limits to responsibility set by common sense causal principles are *appropriate* to the law. (Hart and Honoré 1985, lxxix–lxxx, my emphases)

The references to 'reasonableness' and 'appropriateness' are somewhat troubling. As both terms are left undefined, one can only guess what they refer to. Still, it does not seem far-fetched to relate them to something like the Aristotelian notion of practical reasonableness. At any rate, these arguments clearly go beyond a detached view and represent a committed one. They indicate that the criterion of 'centrality' has normative aspects. What remains to be seen is whether causation is a special 'fortunate case' or this method can be generalised to other legal concepts and doctrinal constructs.

Fortunate and unfortunate cases

Looking at Hart's other writings it is noticeable that the interrelations of epistemic and moral common sense with empirical facts and critical morality belong to the argumentative tools, especially in his essays on criminal law. But as Hart generally sticks to conceptual analysis, his remarks on these interrelations are sporadic, context-bound and undeveloped.[6] Still, for heuristic purposes one could roughly define 'fortunate cases' as reference points and contrast them with a typology of possible 'unfortunate cases'.

In a (relatively) 'fortunate case' the ordinary views are reflected in legal doctrines and, in their main lines both are also philosophically (epistemologically, meta-

6 See e.g. Hart 1968, 2 ['orthodox, or common sense principles (untouched by modern psychological doubts)']; 3 (whether the institution of criminal punishment 'has been eroded by, or needs to be adapted to, new beliefs about the human mind'); 32 ('scientists and plain men differ as to the relevance of some excusing conditions'); 97 (the remnants of metaphysical theories); 170–72 (populist references to common moral sentiments); 179 (the ideology of science); 190 (dispute between doctors and lawyers).

physically, normatively) sound. The most fortunate but most unlikely case is when, in addition to these, there is general agreement among theorists and competent participants of the practice that this congruence holds. This last condition is most unlikely to be fulfilled in modern societies characterised by moral pluralism (cf. Hart 1968, 171).

In contrast to this, there are unfortunate cases of various kinds. The first is when the ordinary views are 'unenlightened' (ibid., 136) and the law caters these views. For instance, they are restrictive of individual freedom to an unnecessary extent. Hart discusses a few instances when his moral standpoint differs from the majority view as reflected in conventional morality and sanctioned by criminal law.[7] This kind of unfortunate cases requires 'enlightenment'.

A second type of unfortunate case occurs when the ordinary people's views are diffuse, uninformed or based on false or unproven factual (empirical) assumptions.[8] This lack of clarity is generally reflected in legal doctrine. In this case, the therapy provided (or supported) by the legal theorist should be 'expertise' about facts (Hart 1968, 88; 1957, 973).

In a third type of 'unfortunate cases' Hart criticised accepted legal doctrines or constructs for being expressed in metaphorical terms or based on obsolete or obscure philosophical arguments, in brief representing 'the metaphysics of the Stone Age' (Hart and Honoré 1985, 2) An example in point is his analysis of the legal conceptions of 'intent' and 'voluntary conduct' in English criminal law (Hart 1968, 97–104, 142–5). What is needed here is 'demystification'.

To be sure, 'fortunateness' is a matter of degree and unfortunate cases can be mixed. Two further types of unfortunateness will be discussed in the next sections. The point of this typology is to suggest that when legal theorists provide 'rational and critical foundations' for legal doctrinal constructs, the hermeneutic method of a non-committed understanding is combined with enlightenment, expertise, and demystification. In the specific case of Hart, they reflect how he was able to combine the 'progressive idealist' with 'a hard-headed empiricist' (Gardner 2005, 330). It should also be noted that Hart was generally sceptical about how much useful knowledge social sciences, especially sociology can provide (Sugarman 1995, 289–93).

7 The criminal protection of sexual morality and the use of criminal law for pure retribution are the best known examples; see Hart 1958, 1963, 1968. His goal as a legal theorist was to support legal reform by generating and participating in public moral debate.

8 An example is Hart's denial of the alleged role of criminal law in upholding social cohesion, the 'disintegration thesis' (1983, 259), another is his reference to the 'stock of knowledge' of medical science that would be needed, instead of relying on 'a judge or jury's speculation' about the effect of 'lesser mental abnormalities' on *mens rea* (1968, 262).

Law as a distinctive form of social control

Criticisms of *Causation* clearly showed that others did not see causation as much of a 'fortunate case' as Hart and Honoré. Their theoretical enterprise itself has a polemic aspect. The main target of their criticism is 'causal minimalism' which they see as a legal theory aiming at the wrong kind of 'demystification' or rather over-simplification. Causal minimalists hold that most problems that courts discuss in terms of causes, 'are rather issues of legal policy in disguise, better answered by asking whether, all things considered, the defendant should be held liable for the harm which ensued' (Hart and Honoré 1985, xxxiv–v). They argue that to reduce causality to a matter of legal policy is a theoretical mistake that leads to less, rather than more conceptual clarity: 'in the interests of clarity... causal issues should be kept separate from issues of legal policy' and the different policy goals themselves 'should be carefully distinguished from one another' (ibid., xxxv–vi).

Hart and Honoré do not deny that to determine the basis of legal responsibility and the role of causation within this is a matter of legal policy (ibid, xlii). The reason why they reject causal minimalism is resistance to sceptical temptations to reduce causal issues to policy issues *tout court*. Legal theorists should not blur distinctions and categories in ordinary use of language that can also be interpreted in a philosophically sound manner. This methodological principle could be called Hart's 'Aristotelian perspective' in legal philosophy.

As John Gardner notes, the reference in *Causation* to common sense 'signals rejection of the reductivist thesis that there is a secret "real" nature of things lurking behind our understanding of their nature.' The book is 'located firmly in the Aristotelian tradition of "respect for appearances", which are rightly held up by Hart as partly constitutive of realities' (Gardner 2005, 331). This 'Aristotelian perspective' is reflected in Hart's other work as well, when he discusses examples of this wrong kind of reductionism, concerning the different *kinds* of rules (Hart 1994, ch.3 s.1), the difference between a tax and a fine (Hart 1983, 111), and most importantly, the notion of an obligation (Hart 1994, ch.5 s.2). Oversimplification could be called a fourth type of 'unfortunate case' when legal theorists do not take ordinary people's views and legal doctrine seriously. It seems that within the confines of Hart's theory there is no general answer as to which distinctions are relevant. This is yet another aspect of his unreflective use of the central-case method.

After responding to causal minimalists who are sceptical about the legal vocabulary of causation they turn to 'causal maximalists' who want to eliminate the requirement of fault from responsibility; then to sceptics who question the justifiability of the entire institution of legal responsibility; finally to those real or imaginary discussants who doubt that the law is preferable to psychological manipulation. This polemic takes Hart and Honoré into discussing complex philosophical matters and exposing their deeper reasons for the rejection of scepticism towards causation and legal responsibility.

One sceptical question they face is this: 'Why should a legal system bent on minimizing the harm arising from human conduct by its regulation of that conduct pay attention to our ordinary concepts of action? Why should it attend to the way in which we identify separate actions, and so the limits of action?' (Hart and Honoré 1985, lxxix) This question touches upon the very problem this paper is concerned with: the epistemic and methodological character of doctrinal constructs, in this case, legal responsibility. Should it reflect ordinary people's views and common sense psychology? Do we need the construct at all?

Hart and Honoré give an answer that might be surprising at first: 'the answer to the sceptic must be thought mainly in the *virtues of the distinctive form which the legal control of conduct takes*.' (ibid., my emphasis) This argument, as it were, refers to the *nature of things*. The legal way of controlling human conduct seems to have, if not an essence, at least a distinctive form. Hart and Honoré's response to 'responsibility-scepticism' shows close parallels with both Fuller's ideas on 'the view of man implicit in legal morality' (1969, 162–167)[9] and Hart's own 'minimal content of natural law' argument (Hart 1994, 199; 1983, 113). The 'necessary' content of the law is required by empirical facts about the human predicament. Hart stresses that these features are not conceptually necessary: they are only necessary 'in our world'. In our world, as we know it, people individuate actions and think of each other as responsible for their doings, at least in central cases. This is not logically necessary: we could imagine a different world without the institution of legal responsibility but it would be fundamentally different from ours.[10] Hart refers to features of human behaviour which are so basic that they could even be called 'natural' necessity. The logical possibility of their change is not a real prospect for any predictable future: it rather belongs to 'science fiction' (Hart 1983, 80). Of course, many scientific and technological achievements that in Hart's lifetime seemed to belong to science fiction turned out to be real and part of human practice.

9 In *The Morality of Law* (1969) Fuller argued that the inner morality of law is an expression of the *nature* of the institutions of legislation and adjudication, in the Aristotelian teleological sense of the term. The eight requirements of law's inner morality follow from the nature of the law in the sense of its distinctive form. Fuller also stated that '[t]o embark on the enterprise of subjecting human conduct to the governance of rules involves of necessity a commitment to the view of man that is, or can become, a responsible agent, capable of understanding and following rules, and answerable for his defaults.' (ibid., 162) and that 'the whole body of the law is permeated by two recurring standards of decision: fault and intent' (ibid., 167).

10 We could imagine that instead of being moderately selfish, people were angels; or that instead of moderate scarcity, they would enjoy abundance in all resources necessary for human needs (or at least for peaceful survival); or that instead of being vulnerable to physical violence, humans 'were clad perhaps like giant crabs with an impenetrable carapace' (Hart 1983, 80) that made one person's injuring another more difficult.

Law and the Brave New World

In Hart's 'workmanlike prose' (Gardner 2005, 331) there are scarce references to fictive literary worlds, such as Huxley's *Brave New World* (e.g. Hart 1968, 23, 209) or Butler's *Erewhon* (ibid., 52–3, 181).[11] Towards the end of the preface, there is such a reference:

> It is thinkable that legal control of conduct might take the form of Brave New World conditioning, so that people were never tempted to disobey the law, or of preventive or incapacitating measures, so that people were unable to disobey. In contrast with such forms of control the law of crime and tort, quite apart from sanctions, makes its primary appeal to individuals as intelligent beings who are assumed to have the capacity to control their conduct, and invites them to do so. It defers coercion and punitive measures until it is shown that this primary appeal has broken down, viz. until a crime has been committed or some harm has been done. The latter is the price to be paid for a form of control that invites the subject's obedience and so, by preserving the possibility of disobeying, maximizes freedom within the framework of coercive sanctions. (Hart and Honoré 1985, lxxix)

This quote confirms Hart's commitment to the normative ideal of the law as a 'method of social control which maximises individual freedom within the coercive framework of law' (Hart 1968, 23). Coercion is seen as the necessary evil in a system of primarily voluntary cooperation; it is necessary for protecting the cooperative members against free riders. At the end of the preface, Hart and Honoré add a further argument against the sceptic:

> [T]he idea that individuals are primarily responsible for the harm which their actions are sufficient to produce without the intervention of others or of extraordinary natural events is important, not merely to law and morality, but to the preservation of something else of great moment in human life. This is the individual's sense of himself as a separate person whose character is manifested in such actions. [...] This sense of *respect for ourselves and others as distinct persons* would be much weakened, if not dissolved, if we could not think of ourselves as separate authors of the changes we make in the world. (Hart and Honoré 1985, lxxx–lxxxi)

11 *Erewhon: or, Over the Range* is a novel by Samuel Butler, published anonymously in 1872. *Erewhon* satirises various aspects of Victorian society, including criminal punishment. According to Erewhonian law, offenders are treated as if they were ill whilst ill people are looked upon as criminals. The reference to the *Brave New World* also shows a parallel with Fuller who hints at an alternative fictional world where people are made 'happy without rules', i.e. by a non-legal governance mechanism run by 'psychiatrists and experts in public relations' (Fuller 1969, 38).

A variant of this argument was raised by Hart in an earlier essay:

> Human society is a society of persons; and persons do not view themselves or each other merely as so many bodies moving in ways which are sometimes harmful and have to be prevented or altered. Instead persons interpret each other's movements as manifestations of intentions and choices, and these subjective factors are often more important to their social relations than the movements by which they are manifested or their effects. […] This is how human nature in human society actually is and as yet we have no power to alter it. The bearing of this fundamental fact on the law is this. If [...] it is important for the law to reflect common judgments of morality, it is surely even more important that it should in general reflect in its judgments on human conduct distinctions which not only underlie morality, but pervade the whole of our social life. (Hart 1968, 182–3).

Common sense moral intuitions assume that persons consider themselves and each other as authors of their doings and, as Fuller (1969, 167) also mentioned, care about intentions and faults of each other. These are 'fundamental facts' about human nature and human society that the law should take into account.

But what kind of 'should' exactly is this? Where does the law end? How much cure, manipulation, conditioning and propaganda are allowed? The question is ambiguous. In one sense, it concerns a conceptual problem and the criteria that could disqualify these techniques of 'governance' from the semantic field of law (as a means of social control). But the question can also be understood as asking for a point where too much use of these practices in a legal system would turn the system into non-law in a substantive sense, even if the rules that authorise these governance techniques are formally valid.

Hart's contrast between law as a goad (the Brave New World) and law as a guide (governance by rules that maximize individual freedom within a coercive framework) makes clear which one he would like to prevail (Hart 1968, 44). On this point he does not only formulate a hypothetical imperative for a rational rulemaker but takes a substantive 'moral position' (ibid., 181). Still, it would impute him too much jusnaturalism to say that he would define the concept of law through this substantive idea, thus calling brave-new-world-like rules non-law, less legal or the perversion of law.[12]

[12] This is Hart's argument against Finnis's analysis of the concept of law (1983, 11–12). Praising Finnis for 'foster[ing] awareness of the way in which unspoken assumptions, common sense, and moral aims influence the law', Hart claims that 'these valuable lessons can be taught in other ways.' (ibid., 11) While he does not explain what those 'other ways' are, he stresses the conceptual clarity we can gain and the confusions and obfuscation that we can avoid if we maintain the separation between conceptual analysis and moral evaluation. Hart claims that the focal meaning of the concept of law cannot or even if it could, should not be identified in light of the moral values served by the law.

Naturalism, constructivism, and instrumentalism in legal epistemology

The quotes in the previous section elaborated on the idea that the law is (or should be) closely linked to 'our world', i.e. the phenomenological world, including moral intuitions and deep-rooted factual beliefs. Now, here seems to lurk a fifth type of unfortunate case, probably the most difficult one. If epistemic and moral common sense, legal doctrine and powerful moral arguments are on one side, empirical science and naturalised epistemology on the other, is it obvious that legal theory should side with the former?

This unfortunate case is different from the second one where factual mistakes and false beliefs about issues of 'local importance' can be corrected by expertise. This case is about a potential conflict between generally held fundamental ideas about human nature on the one hand and a 'naturalistic' worldview on the other. From a 'naturalistic' perspective, the phenomenological worldview according to which people are responsible agents, capable of following rules, and conceive of themselves as authors of their doings, is an illusion. This allows for the possibility that what science says about how things 'really are' on the one hand, and what the law says or assumes about our phenomenological world on the other, become fundamentally distinct, at least on certain points (Greene and Cohen 2004).

Hart does not seem to have an elaborate solution to this problem. Still, *Causation* and *Punishment and Responsibility* indicate what his take on naturalism would be. Although legal doctrines and practice can be rightly criticised in light of empirical facts about the external world or human nature, Hart considers it 'reasonable' to uphold certain fundamental legal notions, such as responsibility, even if, to borrow Kelsen's phrase, they cannot stand firm 'before the tribunal of science' (Kelsen 1949).

This, however, is not the end of the story. On the one hand, it might turn out that Hart's ideas about personhood or the nature of responsibility are philosophically naïve (Gardner 2005, 332), his neglect of empirical sciences not only impoverishes but discredits his legal theory (Lacey 2006), or his fears from a Brave New World were groundless. On the other hand, the fifth unfortunate case, although unfortunate, may provide an opportunity for thinking about an epistemic position where legal theory does not 'take sides' between 'naturalistic' and 'phenomenological' perspectives but simply 'observes' the discontinuity between them and draws

---

They 'cannot', if we think that we cannot attribute any meaningful general goal or purpose to the law. They should not, if we care about the epistemic value of 'clear thought', and we want to adopt a 'balanced perspective' and avoid 'distortion' (ibid., 12). These arguments do not seem conclusive. In fact, this issue has been the subject to extensive methodological discussion in jurisprudence, see e.g. MacCormick 2007, 202–206; Gardner 2010.

conclusions from this discontinuity for legal design and legal practice. This position could be called a 'constructivist' epistemology of law (Teubner 1989).

Finally, Hart's views on legal epistemology could also be developed in an instrumental direction. This interpretation is supported by Hart's view of law as an artefact; a social phenomenon formed by the group whose law it is (MacCormick 2007, 49–50). Whether we should look at the law from a technological perspective (Albert 1986) is controversial but from Hart's writings it can be clearly reconstructed that he looked at the law as a means of social control (Hart 1957, 953). It also seems difficult to conceive of law as something else than a means, i.e. something without any instrumental value (Green 2010). From this instrumental perspective, law's assumptions about human nature can, and in some sense should be counter-factual.

Conclusion

Taking H.L.A. Hart's legal theory as a starting point, I suggested that the assumptions about human behaviour behind legal doctrines typically combine common sense factual beliefs, moral intuitions, philosophical theories of earlier ages and scientific knowledge. According to Hart, the main task of legal theory with respect to legal doctrines is to provide a 'rational and critical foundation' for them. This task includes conceptual clarification, 'enlightenment' about empirical facts and 'demystification' in the form of normative, including moral, argumentation. Finally, Hart argues convincingly that embedded in legal doctrines are assumptions about human agency and personhood that are potentially in conflict with naturalistic theories about human behaviour.

References

Albert, Hans. 1986. Law as an Instrument of Rational Practice. In *Contract and Organization: Legal Analysis in the Light of Economic and Social Theory*, edited by Terence Daintith and Gunther Teubner, 25–51. Berlin: Walter de Gruyter.

Dagan, Hanoch. 2011. Between Rationality and Benevolence: The Happy Ambivalence of Law and Legal Theory. *Alabama Law Review* 62: 191–206.

Finnis, John. 2007. Grounds of Law and Legal Theory: A Response. *Legal Theory* 13: 315–344.

Fuller, Lon L. 1969. *The Morality of Law*, 2d ed. New Haven: Yale Univesity Press.

Gardner, John. 2005. [Book review of] A Life of H. L. A. Hart: The Nightmare and the Noble Dream. *Law Quarterly Review* 121: 329–334.

Gardner, John. 2010. Hart on Legality, Justice, and Morality. *Jurisprudence* 1: 253–265.

Green, Leslie. 2010. Law as a Means. In *The Hart–Fuller Debate in the Twenty-First Century*, edited by Peter Cane, 169–188. Oxford: Hart.

Greene, Joshua, and Cohen, Jonathan. 2004. 'For the law, neuroscience changes nothing and everything' *Philosophical Transactions of the Royal Society B* 359: 1775–1785.

Hart, H. L. A. 1953. *Definition and Theory in Jurisprudence. An Inaugural Lecture delivered before the University of Oxford on 30 May 1953*. Oxford: Clarendon Press.

Hart, H. L. A. 1955. Theory and Definition in Jurisprudence. *Proceedings of the Aristotelian Society, Supplementary Volumes* 29: 239–264.

Hart, H. L. A. 1957. Analytical Jurisprudence in Mid-Twentieth Century: Reply to Professor Bodenheimer. *University of Pennsylvania Law Review* 105: 953–975.

Hart, H. L. A. 1958. Immorality and Treason. *Listener* 59: 162.

Hart, H. L. A. 1963. *Law, Legislation, and Liberty*. Oxford: Oxford University Press.

Hart, H. L. A. 1968. *Punishment and Responsibility. Essays in the Philosophy of Law.* Oxford: Oxford University Press.

Hart, H. L. A. 1972. Abortion Law Reform: The English Experience. *Melbourne University Law Review* 8: 388–411.

Hart, H. L. A. 1973. Bentham and the Demystification of the Law. *Modern Law Review* 36: 2–17.

Hart, H. L. A. 1983. *Essays in Jurisprudence and Philosophy*. Oxford: Clarendon Press.

Hart, H. L. A. 1994. *The Concept of Law*, 2d ed. Oxford: Oxford University Press.

Hart, H. L. A., and Honoré, Tony. 1985. *Causation in the Law*, 2d ed. Oxford: Clarendon Press.

Kelley, Donald R. 1990. *The Human Measure* Social Thought in the Western Legal Tradition. Cambridge, MA: Harvard University Press.

Kelsen, Hans. 1949. The Natural-Law Doctrine before the Tribunal of Science. *Western Political Quarterly* 2: 481–513.

Lacey, Nicola. 2006. Analytical Jurisprudence Versus Descriptive Sociology Revisited. *Texas Law Review* 84: 945–982.

Legendre, Pierre. 1974. *L'amour du censeur: Essai sur l'ordre dogmatique*. Paris: Editions du Seuil.

Luhmann, Niklas. 1974. *Rechtsdogmatik und Rechtssystem*. Stuttgart: Kohlhammer.

MacCormick, Neil 2007. *H. L. A. Hart*, 2d ed. Stanford: Stanford University Press.

Murphy, W. T. 1997. *The Oldest Social Science? Configurations of Law and Modernity.* Oxford: Oxford University Press.

Rodriguez-Blanco, Veronica. 2007. Is Finnis Wrong? Understanding Normative Jurisprudence. *Legal Theory* 13: 257–283.

Sugarman, David. 1995. Hart Interviewed: H. L. A. Hart in Conversation with David Sugarman. *Journal of Law and Society* 32: 267–293.

Sunstein, Cass R. 1995. Incompletely Theorized Agreements. *Harvard Law Review* 108: 1733–1772.

Supiot, Alain. 2005. *Homo juridicus: Essai sur la fonction anthropologique du droit.* Paris: Editions du Seuil.

Teubner, Gunther. 1975. Folgenkontrolle und responsive Dogmatik. *Rechtstheorie* 6: 179–204.

Teubner, Gunther. 1989. How the Law Thinks: Toward a Constructivist Epistemology of Law. *Law and Society Review* 23: 727–757.

Waldron, Jeremy. 2000. Transcendental Nonsense and System in the Law. *Columbia Law Review* 100: 16–55.

Wieacker, Franz. 1953. *Das Sozialmodell der klassischen Privatrechtsgesetzbücher und die Entwicklung in der modernen Gesellschaft*. Karlsruhe: Müller.

Hedgehogs, Foxes and Hart's Rule of Recognition: The Concept of Law in the post-Westphalian International Legal Order

Axelle Reiter

Introduction

At the outset of the 21st century, the main challenge facing international legal scholars remains the understanding of the fluctuating nature of contemporary international law and the actual configuration of the underlying international society. This includes an investigation into the legal character of the international system, as well as into its specificities compared to domestic legal orders. The writings of H. L. A. Hart and, in particular, the vision of law exposed in *The Concept of Law* are truly illuminating in this regard. Unlike most competing theories, his conception of positivism accounts for both the legal character of the international system and its peculiarities. This proves the lasting importance and justness of his analysis, since a notion of law that ignores existing legal systems and phenomena is necessarily reductive and, hence, to some extent inadequate.

The enduring relevance of *The Concept of Law* can be observed at three levels of analysis or in answering three fundamental questions: (1) whether a satisfactory analytical elucidation of the concept of law necessarily includes some reference to morality; (2) whether the absence of a centralised regulatory authority and of centrally organised sanction mechanisms at the international level questions the legal character of the international order; and (3) the existence of a unifying rule that determines the legal validity of international norms and constitutes the ultimate criterion for the identification of other norms as such. In all three respects, the international legal order closely mirrors the Hartian idea of law: his adherence to inclusive legal positivism; his reliance on the social pedigree of rules rather than on the presence of centralised mechanisms of coercion and his approach to state sovereignty; and his description of the union of a set of primary and secondary norms, integrated under a rule of recognition.

Hart's inclusive legal positivism and the separation of law and morals

Hart (1963, 2–4) identifies two important questions to be considered when thinking about the law, which both provide some evidence for the enduring relevance and accurateness of his own conception of law. The first one is definitional. Hart investigates whether a satisfactory analytical description and elucidation of the concept of law necessarily includes some reference to morality. In this sense, he touches upon the distinction between legal positivism and natural law theories. As a result, this question is of keen importance when examining the specificities of contemporary international law, which is often criticised for allegedly flouting positivism. The second question deals with the relation between the validity and legitimacy of laws and the related issue of the criticism of the law from an extralegal normative position, a project sometimes referred to as 'Archimedean'.[1]

In relation to the interaction between law and morals, Hart's inclusive legal positivism explains the methods of interpretation and sources of international law. The interpretation of the law given by most international actors and many scholars in the field is often 'evolutive', keeping in mind the object and purpose of international agreements, and expansive (Dupuy 2003, 416; Guellali 2008, 4–5, 346–348). For instance, the European Court of Human Rights considers that the European Convention on Human Rights is 'a living instrument which must be interpreted in the light of present-day conditions' (*Tyrer v. UK*, 25 Apr. 1978, § 31; *Loizidou v. Turkey*, 23 Mar. 1995, § 71) and that failure to progressively expand upon the actual text of the treaty would entail a regrettable 'bar to reform or improvement' (*Stafford v. UK*, 28 May 2002, § 68). Besides, the positivistic character of the sources of international law has been challenged, because they are not formed through the same type of processes traditionally identified at the domestic level. This applies to international customary law, general principles of international law and, especially, *ius cogens*. The relevant case law and doctrine is often accused of relying on natural law rather than on strictly positivistic legal considerations. In particular, it has

[1] The label comes from a sentence attributed to Archimedes, when explaining the principle of levers; 'give me something to stand on and I can move the world'. Dworkin, whose writings have for main unifying thread the rejection of any form of Archimedeanism, has popularised the term in legal theory to refer to the evaluation of complex philosophical questions from a totally external and neutral perspective. His denial of the possibility to adopt a non-evaluative standpoint is at the core of his condemnation of the positions of Hart and Berlin (Dworkin 1996; Dworkin 2001; Dworkin 2004; Ripstein 2007).

been defended that peremptory norms of international law cannot be reconciled with legal positivism and that only natural law explanations can account for their authority (Dubois 2009). Along similar lines, Dworkin (1977, 14–45) criticises positivism for apparently not taking into account the existence of binding legal norms which do not result from preceding social guidance but are nevertheless applied by judges because of their appropriateness or moral content. However, because of the methodology adopted and his stance on the relation between law and morals, Hart's inclusive legal positivism explains both phenomena in the frame of positive law.

Hart (1963, 2–3) contrasts two possible methodological approaches to an adequate definition of the concept of law: one which is purely linguistic and based on the common perception of the average citizen, whereas the alternative method tries 'to provide, by marking off certain social phenomena from others, a classification useful or illuminating for theoretical purposes'. He attempts to unveil the nature or essence of the concept of law and to elucidate the foundations of legal thinking (Hart 1961, 79 and 151; Hart 1994, 81 and 155; Perry 2001, 323–329). This logic implies focusing on core provisions, primary principles, general direction and patterns of transformation in any given field. Hart (1954, 37) tells apart semantic definitional issues from those that are connected with the distinctiveness, 'the cause or the purpose or the justification or the origin of a legal or political institution'. He dismisses the first method, because reducing questions like 'what is law?' or 'what is a right?' to that of 'what is the meaning of the word "right"?' is actually trivialising the original question, and endorses the second approach. The type of analysis thus adopted needs to be preferred, if one wants to elucidate phenomena that are sitting at the margin of the concept as semantically defined, to give an explanation for the constant evolution of international norms and practices or to form a coherent vision of what international law is about. Moreover, it has the distinctive advantage of being closer to the jurisprudential conception of legal interpretation at the supranational level, which is precisely based on a deeply 'evolutive' vision of the law. Hence, even from a purely descriptive viewpoint, it is more in line with today's global regime.

In addition, Hart's conceptualisation of the link between law and morality partakes to the same vision of that relation as that espoused by international courts and monitoring organs. In this respect, his position diverges from the views of hard positivists on three main points. First, inclusive positivism accepts that moral values permeate all legal orders, a fact usually rejected by exclusive positivists. Second, it conditions the validity of legal systems to the inclusion of some minimal elements of natural law, mostly tied to the formal conditions for the rule of law. Third, the validity of a norm inside a given legal order does not presuppose its legitimacy. Following Hart's Archimedean view, the latter is connected with the foundations and structure of the entire legal edifice and is apprehended from an external normative position.

Hart's (1961, 189–195; 1994, 193–200) conception that legal systems necessarily embody a 'minimum content of natural law' means that legal rules and attachment to the rule of law are not only a matter of actual enforcement but also of respect for core ethical principles. The determination of the contents and the interpretation of positive rules and principles are not only informed by purely social facts but also include a reflection on the concepts and ideas entrenched in legally valid norms. Besides, whereas the rule of recognition of a legal system must exhibit a social pedigree, others do not necessarily flow from a social source. The criteria to assess their validity might well be purely moral or political, as long as a social rule of recognition foresees it (Hart 1994, 258–259; Shapiro 2007, 33–35). Subsequently, the methods of interpretation and sources of international law can be accounted for as the positive law of the international society, since they are internally recognised by the system and conform to its secondary rules. The detractors of this line of argumentation fail to appreciate the complexity of the current international system and its progressive move away from the traditional Westphalian model. In particular, even though *ius cogens* is sometimes relied on for purely instrumental or strategic purposes, one should not forget that – far from constituting 'a "legal word" devoid of any coherent meaning' – it remains an important concept of positive law (Dupuy 2003, 28–33, 207–213, 269–313 and 414–427; Dupuy 2005, 136). The mere fact that it incorporates values of a mostly ethical nature into the fabric of the law does not give reason to refute its crucial position and function in the development of the supranational system.

In relation to the validity and legitimacy of norms, strict positivists like natural lawyers mistakenly conflate both notions, losing analytical clarity in the process. While for natural lawyers the legitimacy of a law determines its validity, strict positivists tend to instil some normative value into their adhesion to positivism and reduce legitimacy to legal validity. Contrastingly, Hart's inclusive positivism permits to evade this oversight, by dissociating the answers offered at each level of analysis. Notwithstanding contrary allegations of its main proponents, the philosophical neutrality of the strict positivist approach is a fallacy. For instance, Kelsen (1960, 63–69) pretends to ground in relativism the inherent value and morality of legal norms. He claims that 'the law constitutes a value precisely by the fact that it is a norm: it constitutes the *legal value* which, at the same time, is a (relative) moral value; which merely means that the law is norm'. Accordingly, he conflates what is good with 'what is lawful'. Yet, this move reintroduces absolute *a priori* values into the analysis, albeit through the backdoor. In fact, strict positivism is, at the same time, a method of interpretation of the law, a theory and an ideology. It is based on an unshakable attachment to the absolute power of sovereign states and entrusts them with a monopoly over both coercion and the formation of legal norms. This Hegelian fixation on the state is founded on an implicit belief in its legitimacy and intrinsic worth; a position that is surely not value-free (Bobbio 1962; Carty 2007; Chwaszcza 2007, 123–128; Dupuy 2003, 27–28 and 208; Guellali 2008, 31–32; Teson 1998). Besides, it prevents strict positivists from acknowledging the peremptoriness of international law and the subjection of states to the dictates of the international community.

Hart's defence of the binding character of international obligations

The tenth chapter of *The Concept of Law* is devoted to the elucidation of the nature of international law. In this last part of his theoretical masterpiece, Hart (1961, 209–211; 1994, 214–216) tackles the misgivings and doubts raised by other theorists in relation to the identification of the international legal order as a fully developed legal system, bearing in mind 'the absence of an international legislature, courts with compulsory jurisdiction, and centrally organised sanctions'. In this view, he dispels the challenges stemming from the misconception of law as 'a matter of orders backed by threats' and 'the obscure belief that states are fundamentally incapable of being the subjects of legal obligations'.

First, the legal status of international norms presupposes that the notion of obligation does not unavoidably mandate a sanction. To be sure, the presence of centralised mechanisms of coercion is a contestable requisite for the identification of a normative structure as legal (Barry 1981, 16 and 40; Hart 1961, 194–195 and 208–215; Hart 1994, 198–199 and 213–220). It cannot account for current developments in international law (Dupuy 2003, 208–209 and 212; Teson 1998, 73; Verdross 1937, 576) and its exclusive focus on national legal orders means that it gives an explanation for neither supranational nor intrastate phenomena. Besides, it imposes domestic legal systems as empirical facts, divorced from the adequate theoretical justification that a reliance on legitimacy presupposes. This poses a serious issue for strict legal positivists. Ironically, by its purely ideological attachment to the statist fiction, this brand of positivism develops the very shortcomings on account of which it opposes natural law theories and 'jumps' from merely descriptive premises to normative conclusions, without attempting to provide an adequate line of reasoning to back up such a contestable move. In spite of the recurrent claim of the so-called 'plain fact' positivists that their theory is the direct and necessary upshot of a relativist position, it is epistemologically untenable. Their criticism of universalism is supposedly grounded in the refutation of the possibility to determine cognitively the set of values that should be legally imposed. Yet, their absolute and uncritical consecration of the rules and practices that govern any given society presupposes that a unified system of norms can be objectively determined, with the sole difference that the values deemed worth to protect are not integrated at the global but at the national level. As such, it is replacing a humanist by a nationalist form of objectivism and eventually serves to justify state absolutism.

Devoid of justification, the state is reduced to the status of an efficient criminal organisation, which is operating on a particularly large scale. Hart (1958, 603) fittingly remarks that the classical positivist account of legal rules as 'the command of the uncommanded commanders of society' -a command grounded in the notion of absolute sovereignty, backed up by sanction, and radically disconnected from morality- boils down to the orders of a gunman to his victims 'writ large'; 'the only difference is that in the case of a legal system the gunman says it to a large number of people who are accustomed to the racket and habitually surrender to it'. Unfortunately, this casts the government in the part of a successful racketeer. Instead of the command theory's identification of law with mere compulsion,[2] Hart (1961, 229; 1994, 234) relies on the internal acceptance of rules and considers that, 'if rules are in fact accepted as standards of conduct, and supported with appropriate forms of social pressure distinctive of obligatory rules, nothing more is required to show that they are binding rules'. This comes very close to the process of formation of norms at the international level.

Even in the absence of some traditional elements usually associated to the notion of law at the municipal level, international law remains binding and generates for his subjects rights and obligations of a strictly legal character. In the post-Westphalian international legal order, the traditional focus on a centralised regulatory authority is replaced by the idea of a spontaneous order; which progressively emerges from the uncoordinated actions of the many agents that make up the international community, following a type of invisible hand process. All subjects of international law participate in the elaboration of the supranational norms that will bind them (Dupuy 2010, 18–19). The mechanisms of creation of the norms are diffuse, basically customary in nature, and the sanction and adjudication procedures are heavily decentralised. The unity of the contemporary international system is less organic than substantive, based on the development of a notion of international public order and the entrenchment of core values at the top of the normative hierarchy through the concept of *ius cogens*. In this frame, the binding character

2 Austin (1954, 10, 13–15 and 24), the leading proponent of the command theory, defines a law as 'a rule laid down for the guidance of an intelligent being by an intelligent being having power over him', as 'a command which obliges a person or persons to a *course* of conduct' and is assorted of a sanction in case of disobedience or non-compliance with the duty it imposes. This theory cannot account for a great many number of forms of law and kinds of legal dispositions (Hart 1961, 27–35; Hart 1994, 27–35). It distorts the typical features of most legal orders, like their temporal continuity, and excludes from the realm of the law many familiar types of legal systems or provisions; including international law, constitutional law, customs, the common law, federal and primitive or tribal legal systems, as well as the enabling or 'power-conferring' rules that constitute the bulk of private law regulations (Barry 1981, 23 and 27–34).

and legality of international norms is uncovered by an analysis of the norms that the international community considers to be binding law.

The presumption that states' sovereignty cannot be reconciled with their subjection to the law is the source of the second challenge that Hart addresses. As a result of their statist ideological bias, strict positivists accept with difficulty the binding character of international law. They simply assume the legitimacy of unconstrained state sovereignty, independently of international law, and then fail to make room for international obligations in the overall picture. Hart (1961, 218; 1994, 224) resists the ensuing confusion by refuting their uncritical use of the idea of sovereignty and examines instead the actual rules of the game. As he rightly underlines, 'there is no way of knowing what sovereignty states have, till we know what the forms of international law are and whether or not they are mere empty forms'. This leads to an inversion of the criticised approach and to a reconstruction of the notion of sovereignty which conforms to states obligations under international law. Far from being absolute, state sovereignty 'includes respect for its legal limitations' (Türk 2003, 765). In fact, 'sovereignty is only a name given to so much of the international field as is left by law to the individual action of states' (Hart 1961, 215–216 and 256; Hart 1994, 220–221 and 305). International norms and states' practice at the international level assume this conception of sovereignty.

In the first place, states' pretensions to sovereignty rest on its recognition in Article 2 §§ 1 and 7 of the Charter of the United Nations. National sovereignty is only appropriate as long as states act inside the limits established by the Charter and respect the norms it protects. The foundational role of the Charter could not be overemphasised. It establishes a set of new institutions and its implementation has initiated a transforming process for the control mechanisms and power dynamics at the global level. Following its adoption, the international legal order has become independent from states' sovereign powers. Even though it was originally established by the expression of states' assent, it progressively developed an existence of its own. In effect, the Charter is analogous to an *actual* social contract (Dupuy 2003, 204, 220–221 and 412). It is a remarkably concrete achievement. The international system is grounded in a real constitutive legal document, which irreversibly binds the parties to this agreement. The Charter operates a radical shift in international relations, going from a state centric to a truly cosmopolitan world order. The development of human rights norms and the creation of transnational institutions further consecrate the evolution 'away from the classic regime of state sovereignty […] toward the firm entrenchment of the liberal regime of international sovereignty' (Held 2002, 94). By moving the focal point from 'sovereignty as control to sovereignty as responsibility', this leads to a purely teleological and gradual conception of sovereignty, closely tied to issues of internal legitimacy (International Commission on Intervention and State Sovereignty 2001, 13; Keohane

2003, 276–277). Sovereignty so conceived becomes 'the outward face of legitimacy' (Teson 1998, 18, 40 and 57).

Hart's rule of recognition and the unity of the international legal order

With respect to the unifying rule that identifies international rules as legal norms and determines their validity inside the system, recent developments in international law demonstrate once again the relevance of Hart's analysis. In the tenth chapter of *The Concept of Law*, Hart (1961, 226; 1994, 232) concedes that international law resembles, at least formalistically, to a simple type of social structure solely composed of primary rules of obligations. In the absence of a unifying rule of recognition posing the criteria for the legal validity of international norms, international law bears more resemblance to 'a set of rules' than a fully fledged legal system. However, Hart (1961, 230–231; 1994, 236) suggests that, if multilateral treaties were generally recognised to bind states that are not parties to these agreements, 'such treaties would in fact be legislative enactments and international law would have distinct criteria of validity for its rules'. Hence, 'a basic rule of recognition could then be formulated' in turn for the international order. Hart concludes that, at the time of writing, international law might be 'in a stage of transition' in exactly that direction. Recent trends in international law have proved him to be right. Half a century after the publication of *The Concept of Law*, international law has reached this stage of development. Article 38 of the 1969 Vienna Convention on the Law of Treaties consecrates the avenue of legislation by treaties mentioned by Hart, through the incorporation of international customs. Yet, the expansion of customary rules and general principles of international law and, chiefly, the notions of *erga omnes* obligations and *ius cogens* constitute the main driving force behind this evolution.

In the absence of the mere possibility to govern the fragmented global polity by majority decision or consensus, reference is made instead as the main legitimising factor and keystone of the supranational legal system to *ius cogens*; peremptory norms of international law from which states cannot either contract out by treaty or derogate under any circumstances. These rules, which boil down to the prohibition of aggression and the respect of human rights in peacetime and armed conflicts, have been regarded as the core principles of international law since their recognition in the United Nations Charter. Their identification by the International Court of Justice (*Barcelona Traction Light and Power Company Limited*, 5 Feb. 1970, § 33) as *erga omnes* obligations means that they consecrate a set of objective standards that are owed by each and every state to the international community as a whole and that, subsequently, all states have the same legal interest in their protection; an interest that is closely tied to the principle of legality and the respect of the rule of law at the international level (Dupuy 2003, 359; Dupuy 2010, 282–283). The International Law Commission has endorsed a similar approach in its 2001 codification of the responsibility of states for the violation of peremptory norms of international law (UN Doc., A/CN.4/L.620/Rev.1).

Peremptory norms encompass the idea of an international public order that binds all states independent of their explicit consent. Following Articles 53 and 64 of the Vienna Convention, treaties which conflict with *ius cogens* at the time of their conclusion are void, while the emergence of new peremptory norms invalidates and terminates all conflicting treaties previously adopted. In consequence, *ius cogens* introduces a hierarchy among international norms and serves as a criterion for the validity of other legal rules and the legality of states' acts (Dupuy 2003, 273, 281, 299–302, 306, 393–394 and 400; Dupuy 2010, 322). For instance, the European Court of Human Rights defends that the European Convention on Human Rights is 'a constitutional instrument of European public order' (*Loizidou v. Turkey*, 23 Mar. 1995, § 93; *Banković et al. v. Belgium et al.*, 12 Dec. 2001, § 80) and that domestic rules and policies which violate basic human rights cannot qualify as the law, at least for the purposes of the Convention (*Streletz, Kessler and Krenz v. Germany*, 22 Mar. 2001, § 87). This is equally valid at the universal level (Schwelb 1976, 275), where the Universal Declaration partakes to 'the constitutional structure of the world community', together with the United Nations Charter (Sohn 1982, 16–17). Namely, peremptory norms serve as criteria for the validity at the supranational level of each and every legal provision otherwise adopted.

In addition to engaging the international liability of the responsible state, violations of peremptory norms raise the issue of the use of force by the international community. The prohibition of aggression constitutes one of the main purposes of the United Nations. The Charter foresees three exceptions to the general ban on the use of armed force entrenched in Article 2 §§ 4 and 7: individual or collective self-defence (Article 51), military actions organised by the Security Council (Article 42) and enforcement actions by regional defence mechanisms under the Security Council's authority and supervision (Articles 52 and 53 § 1). By opposition, it expressly forbids regional enforcement actions that have not been explicitly authorised by the Security Council (ibid.). Article 56, concerning the promotion of human rights, does not derogate to the prohibition of aggression and cannot be considered as a supplementary counter-norm enabling states to use force either collectively or individually. Part of the doctrine calls for 'humanitarian intervention' in states internal affairs, outside of the frame of the Charter, in presence of gross violations of human rights (Cassese 1999; Glennon 1999; Wedgewood 1999). However, this doctrinal theory is contentious at best and deprived of customary status, as it is supported neither by the practice of the majority of states nor by the required *opinio iuris* (Francioni 2000, 117–118). As such, it cannot be relied upon to legitimise military interventions in the absence of self-defence and authorisation by the Security Council. For instance, NATO's 1999 bombing campaign without a mandate of the Security Council is clearly illegal, because it fails to meet the necessary conditions for any of the enumerated exceptions. It constitutes an act of aggression and engages the international responsibility of NATO member states. Finally, the prohibition of aggression benefits from the same peremptory status as the protection of individual rights. It is similarly situated on top of the normative hierarchy and cannot be overruled.

State sovereignty is legally restricted by the respect of *ius cogens*; a duty derived directly from their membership and participation in the international society. Peremptory norms of international law grow to be the law of the land through a transfer of state powers to the international community by adhesion to the United Nations Charter and the Vienna Convention. The creation and progressive extension of international mechanisms of supervision reinforces the ban on their domestic abuse. In a nutshell, the prohibition of aggression and the protection of individual rights effectively function as a Hartian rule of recognition for the international legal system.

Hart (1961, 92–108, 113 and 245–246; 1965, 1292–1294; 1994, 94–112, 116, 250 and 292–294) defines a rule of recognition as 'a very simple form of secondary rule: a rule for conclusive identification of the primary rules of obligation'. It is normally concerned with conferring powers but it can include substantive and even moral conditions. It unifies all other norms into a coherent legal system and operates as a benchmark for their validity. Therefore, it constitutes the defining element and the ultimate foundation of the entire legal order. Hart adds that 'for the most part the rule of recognition is not stated, but its existence is *shown* in the way in which particular rules are identified', in practice, by various actors, chiefly including judicial bodies. This entails a clearly customary aspect. Besides, the validity of that particular rule does not need to be demonstrated. Whereas it serves as a touchstone for the validity of all other rules within a given legal order, it cannot (logically) ground either its own legitimacy or that of the system as a whole. These two issues are clearly interdependent but they require some further justification, as well as an extralegal point of reference from which to assess their truthfulness. Yet, as long as one remains inside the legal paradigm, the rule of recognition functions as a factor of self-validation and rationalisation of that regime. Hence, Hart's rule of recognition is, at the same time, a norm and a blunt (social) fact. It also has both a legal and a meta-legal character. In a way, it is axiomatic precisely because it is the keystone of the system, the main hypothesis on which it is constructed and from which it derives its internal consistency.

This is precisely the role played by the prohibition of aggression and the protection of human rights on the international plane. Their *ius cogens* status does not merely give them a peremptory character but implies also that neither international agreements nor national norms can restrict or oppose them. This means that they work in practice as a standard for the legality of other norms, which is the nature and function Hart ascribes to his rule of recognition. Moreover, they have a customary character and the progressive strengthening of their effective recognition and protection has been tightly linked to the development of international customs. Besides, although not always explicitly articulated, their impact on the pronouncements of international courts, supervisory organs and other institutions is undoubtedly decisive. In consequence, they ground the contemporary evolution and integration of general public international law.

Conclusion

To sum up, *The Concept of Law* provides the most illuminating theorisation of law for the understanding of the nature and structure of international law. Its radical transformation after the creation of the United Nations leads to enquire whether, in the metaphorical words of Isaiah Berlin (1953), the international legal order mirrors a world prearranged by hedgehogs or rather perpetually reinvented by foxes. The universe in which hedgehogs thrive is perfectly ordered and fully integrated, whereas foxes belong to the chaotic and somewhat 'exploded' world of the unprompted. In this sense, general international law reflects the anticipations of foxes much more than the aspirations of hedgehogs. Hart provides a model of law for foxes, which perfectly fits the fox-like characteristics of the global reality. This shows the importance and enduring relevance of his theory for contemporary lawyers.

References

Austin, J. 1954. *The Province of Jurisprudence Determined and the Uses of the Study of Jurisprudence*. London: Weidenfeld and Nicolson.

Barry, N. P. 1981. *An Introduction to Modern Political Theory*. London: Macmillan.

Berlin, I. 1953. *The Hedgehog and the Fox*. London: Weidenfeld and Nicolson.

Bobbio, N. 1962. Giusnaturalismo e positivismo giuridico. *Rivista di diritto civile* 6: 503–515.

Carty, A. 2007. *Philosophy of International Law*. Edinburgh: Edinburgh University Press.

Cassese, A. 1999. Ex iniuria ius oritur. *European Journal of International Law* 10: 23–30.

Chwaszcza, C. 2007. *Moral Responsibility and Global Justice*. Baden-Baden: Nomos.

Dubois, D. 2009. The Authority of Peremptory Norms in International Law. *Nordic Journal of International Law* 78.2: 133–175.

Dupuy, P.-M. 2003. *L'unité de l'ordre juridique international*. Leiden: Nijhoff.

Dupuy, P.-M. 2005. Some Reflections on Contemporary International Law and the Appeal to Universal Values. *European Journal of International Law* 16.1: 131–137.

Dupuy, P.-M. 2010. *Droit international public*, 10th ed. Paris: Dalloz.

Dworkin, R. 1977. *Taking Rights Seriously*. London: Duckworth.

Dworkin, R. 1996. Objectivity and Truth. *Philosophy and Public Affairs* 25: 87–139.

Dworkin, R. 2001. Do Values Conflict? *Arizona Law Review* 43.2: 251–260.

Dworkin, R. 2004. Hart's Postscript and the Character of Political Philosophy. *Oxford Journal of Legal Studies* 24.1: 1–37.

Francioni, F. 2000. Of War, Humanity and Justice. *Max Planck Yearbook of United Nations Law* 4: 107–126.

Glennon, M. 1999. The New Interventionism. *Foreign Affairs* 3: 2–7.

Guellali, A. 2008. *Droit international pénal, droit humanitaire et droits de l'homme*. PhD Thesis, European University Institute.

Hart, H. L. A. 1954. Definition and Theory in Jurisprudence. *Law Quarterly Review* 70: 37–60.

Hart, H. L. A. 1958. Positivism and the Separation of Law and Morals. *Harvard Law Review* 71.4: 593–629.

Hart, H. L. A. 1961. *The Concept of Law*. Oxford: Clarendon.

Hart, H. L. A. 1963. *Law, Liberty and Morality*. Oxford: Oxford University Press.

Hart, H. L. A. 1965. Lon L. Fuller's *The Morality of Law*. *Harvard Law Review* 78.6: 1281–1296.

Hart, H. L. A. 1994. *The Concept of Law*, 2nd ed. Oxford: Clarendon.

Held, D. 2002. Violence, Law, and Justice in a Global Age. In *Understanding September 11*, edited by C. Calhoun, P. Price and A. Timmer, 92–105. New York: New Press.

International Commission on Intervention and State Sovereignty. 2001. *The Responsibility to Protect*. Ottawa: International Development Research Centre.

Kelsen, H. 1960. *Pure Theory of Law*, revised ed. translated by M. Knight. 1989. Gloucester, MA: Peter Smoth.

Keohane, R. O. 2003. Political Authority after Intervention. In *Humanitarian Intervention*, edited by J. L. Holzgrefe and R. O. Keohane, 275–298. Cambridge: Cambridge University Press.

Perry, S. R. 2001. Hart's Methodological Positivism. In *Hart's Postscript*, edited by J. Coleman, 311–354. Oxford: Oxford University Press.

Ripstein, A. 2007. Anti-Archimedeanism. In *Ronald Dworkin*, edited by A. Ripstein, 1–21. Cambridge: Cambridge University Press.

Schwelb, E. 1976. The Law of Treaties and Human Rights. In *Toward World Order and Human Dignity*, edited by W. M. Reisman and B. H. Weston, 262–290. New York: Free Press.

Shapiro, S. J. 2007. The 'Hart–Dworkin' Debate. In *Ronald Dworkin*, edited by A. Ripstein, 22–55. Cambridge: Cambridge University Press.

Sohn, L. B. 1982. The New International Law. *American University Law Review* 32: 1–64.

Teson, F. R. 1998. *A Philosophy of International Law*. Boulder: Westview.

Türk, D. 2003. Reflections on Human Rights, Sovereignty of States and the Principle of Non-Intervention. In *Human Rights and Criminal Justice for the Downtrodden*, edited by M. Bergsmo, 753–766. Leiden: Nijhoff.

Verdross, A. 1937. Forbidden Treaties in International Law. *American Journal of International Law* 31.4: 571–577.

Wedgwood, R. 1999. NATO's Campaign in Yugoslavia. *American Journal of International Law* 93.4: 828–834.

Hans Kelsen's Critique of Sovereignty

Petra Gümplová

Hans Kelsen's critique of sovereignty represents one of the most radical and elaborate attempts of a legal philosopher to eliminate sovereignty both from the internal political realm of the state and the external sphere of international relations. It has become a commonplace to argue that Kelsen's fundamental attack on sovereignty came about as a result of his neo-Kantian epistemological project of pushing for a strictly scientific legal theory purified of all non-juristic elements. Yet, as I would like to suggest, Kelsen's legal theory can also be seen as something driven by a normative goal to 'depersonalise' law, that is, to explain law's validity without reference to the action of any sovereign political authority of a person. In the first place, Kelsen was committed to providing not just an exact and objective description of law, but an account of the normative idea of the rule of law as opposed to the rule of men. He was convinced that what would best prevent arbitrary abuses of state power, bring about freedom in modern society, and help to sustain peace in world politics was the adherence to the ideal of the rule of law.

Critique of the dualism of law and power

Sovereignty, according to Kelsen, represents first and foremost a fundamental obstacle standing in the way of any full realisation of the rule of law. For this reason, what Kelsen attempted to do was to systematically exclude sovereignty from the theory of legal normativity, although not so much because it contaminated legal reasoning with non-jurisprudential phenomena, but rather because he viewed sovereignty as a residue of the absolutist state, disguising within it an autocratic claim to power that lent itself to justifying disregard for existing positive law.

Kelsen proceeded from a common, substantive understanding of sovereignty as the purely political concept referring to the absolute and legally unlimited state power understood as the ultimate source of the validity and compulsoriness of legal norms (Kelsen 1920, 3). This understanding of sovereignty is derived from Hobbes's work in which sovereignty was defined as the supreme authority embodied in one person who has the absolute and unlimited power to make law by his command. Ever since Hobbes most thinkers assumed that sovereign authority is of a substantive kind and amounts to power in the sense of pure facticity inconceivable in legal terms (Arendt 1965; Foucault 2003). Kelsen is no exception in presupposing that the logic of the concept of sovereignty implies that sovereign power must be characterised by non-derivability, originality, indivisibility, and unity of its source and unlimitedness of its exercise. Kelsen's intention was to show that no such concept as sovereignty is necessary to account for the sources and the nature of law. The main reason for his wholesale rejection of sovereignty was normative in nature: Kelsen believed that claim to sovereignty leaves room for uncontrollable, arbitrary, and hence autocratic exercise of political authority.

The concept of sovereignty for the first time made its appearance in Kelsen's work with the publication of *Das Problem der Souveränität und die Theorie des Völkerrechts* in 1920. The most fundamental problem inherent in the concept of sovereignty, Kelsen argued in this book, was that it postulated a purely political notion of political power, hence granting an absolute primacy to state authority based on the irreconcilable duality between law and power. This duality is, in his view, theoretically incoherent since the political authority of the state is conceived prior to the law and potentially dangerous since the capacity to act without legal authorisation is considered the essential element of statehood. Kelsen sets for himself the task to overcome the duality of law and power by proving that the concept of sovereignty is jurisprudentially inconceivable in the first place.

To demonstrate the redundance of the concept of sovereignty in legal theory, Kelsen constructed a purely 'normativist' account of the normativity of law, based on the simple definition of law as a system of valid norms (Kelsen 1992). Unlike most legal positivists, Kelsen did not understand legal rules as commands of the sovereign political will. For Kelsen, legal norms are essentially statements about what ought to be. The 'ought' does not have a deontological meaning. A legal norm is not a categorical imperative telling what people should do, but a morally neutral statement denoting the specific relationship between a certain fact and a certain consequence – in other words, what people ought to do according to a positive legal norm (Kelsen 2006, 35–39). The antithesis of ought is an 'is', that is, the sphere of empirical facts. Inspired by the neo-Kantian methodological distinction between *Sollen* and *Sein*, Kelsen distinguishes ought primarily from is in order to separate the world of legal normativity from that of empirical facticity. Positive law is a system of postulates existing independently of reality and therefore legal science is to deal only with pure legal rules.

The specific normativity of positive law thus must be understood, according to Kelsen, in a neutral, formally prescriptive, and hypothetical sense, and not in the sense of moral imperatives or empirical facts. Legal norms are valid not because they have a content whose binding force is self-evident, because they are compatible with moral values, or because they are compelling as threats of violence based on actual superiority in power. A norm is a valid legal norm, Kelsen claimed, by virtue of the fact that it has been derived from another legal norm. The validity of a legal norm is thus established by the procedural appeal to a higher-level norm, whose validity is established by appeal to its own higher-level norm, and so on, until the highest level of norms is reached – the so-called basic norm. The basic norm is the ultimate norm in a legal system which cannot be derived from any other superior norm. According to Kelsen, it is the postulated ultimate rule according to which the norms of this order are established and annulled and which explains the validity of all norms in a legal system (ibid., 113, 393).

Presuming the basic norm as the source of the validity of legal norms, the widely accepted view that sovereignty is the ultimate source of law placed somewhere above it now appears misconceived. Law cannot be derived from some highest power existing outside of law. For Kelsen, to assume so represented a naive theory derived from the absolutist thought that personified law and the state. No such thing as sovereign power exists prior to the law as an empirical or natural phenomenon. Neither in nature, nor in society, can one find any source of power or motivating cause such that could be considered original and entirely self-sustaining, with no causal connection with another source (Kelsen 1920, 7–9). The only tangible power in the social and political context is the impersonal coercion particular to legal norms. That power exists only as the efficacy of the order regulating the conduct of individuals, and it therefore always refers to a power authorised by valid legal norms. Power is thus nothing more than a right or a competence derived from a legal norm.

In the mainstream legal theory, Kelsen rightly observed, sovereignty was nonetheless considered as an unambiguous fact of real power or violence, one that not only supplied the ultimate source of law but also referred to the facticity of law, that is, to the actual realisation of the legal ought in reality. This was, for him, another misconception, arising from a confusion between the efficacy of law and the power of the state as the expression of its sovereignty (ibid., 16–17). Kelsen argued that the element of coercion, which is essential to law, consists not in physical compulsion, but in the fact that specific sanctions are provided for in specific cases by the rules that form the legal order. Law, for him, was indeed a coercive order which compels to social conduct through a threat of sanctions, but the ultimate normative aim of law was the sustenance of peace, or the condition in which there is no use of force in the relations among individuals. To establish peace, Kelsen argued, law for this reason monopolises the employment of force in the hands of the state, rendering all uses of coercive force in society that are not authorised by the law legally impermissible delicts. The basic norm ensures that coercive force is applied in accordance with the norms authorised by it (ibid., 21–22). This force has nothing to do with the sovereign power, which for Kelsen remained nonsensical as a notion, both jurisprudentially and empirically.

Identity thesis and the problem of legal legitimacy

The conceptual solution to the problem of the duality of law and sovereign power offered by Kelsen is the so called *identity thesis* according to which the state cannot be understood as anything else but the legal order itself. Only by conceiving the state as identical with its legal order it is possible to avoid the error of viewing it alternately from two antithetical perspectives – from the perspective of the legal order and from the perspective of the political power irreducible to legal order. Such a double perspective, for Kelsen, implied that the state had an option to ignore its own commands and exercise political authority in ways that differ from the mechanisms of legality.[1]

I agree with Lars Vinx that the main purpose of Kelsen's identity thesis was to show that understanding political decision-making as distinct from legal decision-making amounted to suggesting that the legitimacy of political decisions could be sought from outside of their legality. Conceiving the matter in this dual manner, according to Kelsen, seriously undermined the resources of legitimacy internal to the legal order. If the state, based on the appeal to its sovereign authority, has the power to override its own constitutional norms, then, Kelsen claimed, these constitutional norms lack legal force. Taking constitutional norms seriously thus means accepting the view that extralegal exercises of sovereign power cannot qualify as expressions of public power; in other words, that they are not lawful acts of the state (Vinx 2008, 21, 81).

Kelsen's identity thesis thus consists in showing that the authority of the state to determine its own legal order is always derived from the rules of this order that are traceable back to the basic norm. There is no ultimate sovereign power, only the ultimate possibility to change the legal order as derived from the basic norm. The state, Kelsen maintained, is neither a person behind the legal order, nor a natural reality of ethical life: it is merely a set of legal rights and duties attributed to real persons. These persons represent organs of the state, but they can do that only if they are authorised to do so by that very order (Kelsen 1920, 8–20). For Kelsen, the state is simply an order of positive norms that are valid, binding, and efficacious. Once the basic norm is presupposed, legal science can reject the dualist view because the

1 Georg Jellinek, one of the most prominent legal positivists in Germany, for instance, had maintained that the state was simultaneously both a fact of violence (*Herrschergewalt*) and a normative order bound to the rule of law. As a legal order, the state was dependent on the state as a fact of violence for its creation and protection, and so the state could not assume an unconditional commitment to act in accordance with the rule of law (Jellinek 1960, 367–375).

state capable of legally unauthorised action is jurisprudentially inconceivable (see also Kelsen 1922, 86–91; Vinx 2008, 20).

Kelsen's identity thesis does represent a landmark achievement in the fields of constitutionalism and the rule of law in continental legal philosophy. All the same, it remains questionable whether it in itself provided sufficient tools to eradicate arbitrariness and domination from politics. Several commentators have correctly pointed out that the identity thesis based on the model of pure legality fails to provide normative constraints on the state's actions and cannot as such sustain the ideal of the rule of law (MacCormick 1999; Raz 1979). Given the failure of legality to provide protection from abuses of power, as witnessed in the course of the past century (and indeed the role that legality itself has played in making such abuses possible), the skepticism towards the conception of pure legality as the sole basis of legitimacy of political power has been justified.

The problem lies, in especial, in Kelsen's insistence that the identity thesis is a neutral methodological principle not intended to side with any particular conception of the state.[2] It follows from the identity thesis that no matter how just or unjust, all states defined by law should be respected merely because they represent instances of legal order. The problem is then that Kelsen's insistence on a strictly normativist identity thesis becomes almost a tautology: law is defined by law. If law is only what the legally constituted government enacts, then anything this government enacts is law merely because it is authorised by law. If the decisions taken in these cases comply with formal rules of competence, the outcomes have to be considered as legitimate acts of the state. It seems unclear, however, whether the rule of law in such a neutral and procedural sense can actually constrain the rule of persons and protect citizens from domination and injustice. To be able to judge the state's actions as legitimate, we may therefore well need a normative conception of legality stronger than that provided by Kelsen's minimal normativist notion of legal validity. Correspondingly, to prevent illegitimate actions by the state, we are likely to need more substantive restrictions on the state's actions to protect citizens from arbitrary exercise of state power (Vinx 2008, 15–29, 59–67, 101; Bellamy 2007, 54–66).

In any case, the notion of legal legitimacy implied by the conception of pure legality is insufficient in itself to fully motivate reasonable acceptance of laws by

2 Kelsen argued that the choice between democratic and autocratic state is impossible to make from the point of view of jurisprudence. According to him, there was no reason for limiting the concept of law to a social order that corresponds to the political ideal of democracy and liberalism. The reason for his seemingly neutral stance towards democracy was his belief that democracy is a political system that can accommodate substantive values of different ideologies—that is, of both socialism and capitalism, the conflict between which can be solved in peaceful form (Kelsen 1942, 4–5; 1929, 1–2; 1955, 68–86).

those laws' addressees. If citizens are to accept laws for reasons other than fear of sanctions, they need laws that are good, just, and reasonable. They must be able to see that the law reflects their reasoned debate about the public good, and that it stems from and makes possible mutually beneficial, reciprocal cooperation among free and equal individuals. Turning the rule by law into the rule of law is thus more of a matter of the method of legislation than of the form of law per se. As Jürgen Habermas has shown in his discourse theory of law and democracy, this can only be achieved when the people understand themselves as the authors of those laws that they are supposed to obey. The source of the legitimacy of law is linked to the democratic participation of citizens in the law-making process (Habermas 1998, 121). The rule of law is thus the form of government rather than legality as such; and only as a democratic self-rule it provides the bulwark against arbitrary rule and domination.

It seems, therefore, that Kelsen's identity thesis can work only when building on a *normative* rather than *normativist* conception of legality that includes ethical-political principles capable of providing more substantive restrictions on the state's actions. The legality-based claim to legitimacy involves the protection against abuses of power by legal means only when combined with participatory creation of general legal norms, the protection of the individual and minority interests by constitutional guarantees, and the impartial administration of law – in other words, when legality is complemented by principles and institutions of constitutional democracy. There are, in fact, ample resources in Kelsen's own work to make this substantive, democratic reading of the identity thesis possible (see Vinx 2008, 25, 66–67, 83). There is a theory of democracy formulated by Kelsen, and it is precisely this much-neglected conception of democracy which supplies the missing ethical-political dimension necessary for understanding his pure legality as a normative political ideal. Before turning to Kelsen's theory of democracy in the last section, I will nonetheless first need to discuss the direct implications that the identity thesis and the concept of the basic norm have for the concept of sovereignty.

Sovereignty of law and the monistic conception of a legal system

Paradoxically, even when reducing the state to its legal order, Kelsen did not entirely abandon the category of sovereignty. Insofar as the state is identical with its legal order, there was no reason, in Kelsen's view, why sovereignty could not be understood as a property of the legal system (Kelsen 1920, 12–14, 74–75). This somewhat surprising argument appears a little less surprising if we take a closer look at the affinity between Kelsen's description of the legal system through his concept of the basic norm and the way he interpreted the concept of sovereignty itself. Ultimately, it is this very affinity that also comes to undermine the plausibility of Kelsen's identity thesis.

Kelsen defines legal order as a self-contained, unified, closed and gapless hierarchy of norms, derived from the basic norm which is the highest norm in a legal system. Legal order is independent and self-referential, singular, discrete, excluding the simultaneous existence of other normative systems within a territory. These distinct features of a legal order, namely unity, exclusivity, and independence, are not, however, outcomes of the political condition. According to Kelsen, they are expressions of the unique juridical condition related to the existence of the singular and ultimate basic norm (ibid., 27, 38–39, 74–75). The basic norm is at the very top of the hierarchical ordering of norms in a legal system and provides the legal system with its unity and exclusivity. All norms in a legal system then have to be deduced from the same basic norm in an unbroken chain of validity, otherwise the unity and the identity of the legal order would be compromised. Resembling Hobbes's sovereign, the basic norm is the ultimate, singular, and indivisible source of validity of legal norms.

Transforming the idea of sovereignty into the notion of the basic norm enables Kelsen to present a purely legalistic theory of the unity and autonomy of a legal system. This theory, however, is based on the preservation of all important tenets of the early modern paradigm of sovereignty which are, then, made essential attributes of the basic norm – singularity, exclusivity, indivisibility, and absoluteness. In a remarkably unproblematic manner, Kelsen translated this absolutist conception of sovereignty into a monistic vision of a legal system with its single ultimate source in the basic norm, thus shifting from one 'monocular' conception to another. Paradoxically, his critique of sovereignty represented by the identity thesis thus relies on precisely those features of sovereignty that made Kelsen reject the concept in the first place.

Kelsen's monistic approach can be challenged on several grounds which I have discussed extensively elsewhere. One of the most controversial issues pertains to the fact that Kelsen's monistic conception of the legal system compels him to adopt a controversial theory of legal cosmopolitanism claiming the primacy of international law over domestic law (Gümplová 2011, 69–83).[3] From the perspective of this paper, let me briefly highlight flaws of the monistic approach from a theoretical and empirical point of view.

As many legal theorists have pointed out, Kelsen's vision of a gapless hierarchical unity of norms and singularity of their source is misconceived. Raz, for example, has shown that it is possible for two laws to belong to the same legal system even if there

3 One of the consequences of Kelsen's cosmopolitan monism is obscuring momentous revolutionary changes such as democratic revolution and their marking the beginning of a new, discontinuous legal order (Kalyvas 2007).

is no common basic norm authorising the creation of both (Raz 1979, 127–128; 1983, 95–108). It is not an unbroken chain of validity leading to one basic norm which determines the membership of a norm in a legal system. The membership of a norm in a legal system can only be determined through the practice of identification that characterises the process of applying law. To answer the question of the identity of a legal order, we must look at facts through which an order is created and applied, especially at courts as its primary law-applying institutions. Any legal norms applied by the domestic courts form part of the same legal system without being necessarily derived from the same basic norm.[4]

Numerous examples telling of today's legal reality prove this criticism, thus contradicting Kelsen's claims concerning the unity, exclusivity, and singularity of normative systems. Domestic law is today more and more overlain by transnational global legal regimes or supranational law making institutions (Fischer-Lescano et al. 2004). The norms created by these legal instances become valid norms in national legal orders without being derived from the same basic norm. In European Union, for example, there is now an independent and autonomous European legal order with its own source of validity in place. It is recognised as valid, directly applicable, and binding in distinct legal systems of the individual member states. As a result, the national legal systems now also include norms whose validity may be derived from sources external to them (MacCormick 1995). The reality of today's Europe-wide legal order and the manner in which it functions is clearly not something that Kelsen's monistic argument can account for. What we need, obviously, is a perspective that enables us to observe different legal systems interacting and mutually recognising one another, partly independent and partly overlapping. A proper analysis must thus take this pluralistic and interactive nature of legal systems into account.

Sovereignty between law and politics

As a way of conclusion of this paper let me summarise Kelsen's misconceived interpretation of sovereignty and discuss the question whether the success of Kelsen's defense of the rule of law does not depend on an alternative conception of sovereignty.

The core of Kelsen's misleading monistic approach is, as already suggested, an essentialist interpretation of the early modern, absolutist conception of sovereignty which assumes that sovereignty necessarily implies that in order to be supreme, the political power has to be located in a singular, unitary source above the legal order. This essentialist understanding is derived mainly from Hobbes's theory which is taken to suggest that sovereignty amounts to the arbitrary exercise of power by the

4 For a similar critique see also Hart's discussion of Kelsen's doctrine of the unity of law (Hart 1983, 309–342).

'sovereign person' (Hobbes 1985, 227) who is not subject to law, although Hobbes (as well as Jean Bodin before him) meant to describe a new, essentially modern idea of the unity of political supremacy and legal authority, not that sovereignty primarily entails arbitrary and unlimited exercise of somebody's will (see Bodin 1955). Hobbes envisioned an absolute and unlimited sovereign power in order to put an end to devastating wars that plagued England in the seventeenth century. The purported unlimited sovereign power can also be interpreted as a 'common power' (Hobbes 1985, 185, 188, 227) imposed above the plurality of different associations, thus making their peaceful coexistence possible by neutralising their claims to power. The absolutist state is not the answer to a corrupt human nature but a historical answer to emerging social plurality and potential conflict that comes with it, which at Hobbes's time was the conflict of the claims of religious factions to orthodoxy. These claims could only be challenged, as Koselleck argued, by creating a new political sphere with a supreme and absolute authority which replaced moral and religious ethics with political claims by rational action of the sovereign (Koselleck 1988, 16, 31).

Sovereignty does not necessarily imply an absolute, original, indivisible power unlimitable by law. This model of sovereignty represents a conceptual variant influenced by the social and political struggles of the era of absolutism; and is inapplicable to the modern constitutional state where sovereignty is a divided and limited condition, dispersed in various government offices and limited by separation of powers, checks and balances and basic rights. The complex structure of the modern state itself renders the indivisible, unitary and unlimited conception of the form and location of sovereign authority implausible. Yet, sovereignty has been and remains, as Martin Loughlin has aptly pronounced, a 'quintessentially political concept' (Loughlin 2003, 56) referring to the highest power. This power is, however, a product of the political relationship between the groups of people and their government. As Kelsen himself rightly stressed, this power is limited if only because it can only be official, conferred by a normative order and invested and exercised through an institutional framework of the modern state.

Being inextricably linked to the modern state, sovereignty has always been expressed through the medium of law and is inseparable from it. Yet, sovereignty cannot be made the feature of law or a solely legal concept as Kelsen believed. Sovereignty remains a political concept even though the method by which the claim to sovereignty is expressed is the medium of law. Law is law by virtue of being a political phenomenon, that is, a means of political rule. The supreme political authority embodied in the apparatus of the modern state is defined legally as the capacity to make decisions in accordance with higher constitutional rules. Law is an expression of sovereignty, but sovereignty is itself constituted and limited by law. For many thinkers this is what indicates the conceptual paradox and incoherence of sovereignty, namely that sovereignty expresses both the power that enacts law and law that restrains power. As Walker rightly pointed out, the claim to sovereignty is only seemingly caught in the antinomy between sovereignty that is legally derivative and hence never politically independent and sovereignty that is politically unconstrained and not so truly legal (Walker 2003, 20–21).

The alleged paradox built into the conceptual structure of sovereignty disappears, as Walker suggests, once we understand it as the key to sovereignty and define sovereignty as a dynamic process of the mutual containment and interdependence of binding positive law and political power (ibid., 21). Kelsen insisted on a strict separation of legal and political theory because he believed that only the scientifically grounded legality is capable of becoming the sole basis of the legitimacy of the political rule, such that represents a normative antidote to the sovereign decision which claims legitimacy for its action derived from some extralegal grounds. This step seems justified by the concept of sovereignty he takes as his starting point. When it is replaced by a 'de-absolutised' concept of sovereignty, the move from political to legal concept of sovereignty appears unnecessary. All the more so, when we take into consideration the normative aims of Kelsen's theory and link Kelsen's theory of pure legality with his theory of constitutional democracy. To conclude I will briefly consider how the redefined concept of sovereignty would fit into Kelsen's theory of constitutional democracy.

The concept of democracy does play an indispensable role in Kelsen's theory. It is inspired by Rousseau's vision of a political order in which an individual submits to a unifying general will and yet remains as free as in the state of nature. Unlike Rousseau, however, Kelsen does not believe in the absolute reconciliation of the individual will and the general will. There is an inherent possibility of conflict between coercive social order and individual freedom, yielding what Kelsen calls 'uneasiness of heteronomy' (Kelsen 1955, 18). Kelsen's defense of democracy is based on the claim that democracy preserves individual freedom to the largest extent possible. Democracy, Kelsen argues, is a transformation of natural freedom from an instinct that leads men to the negation of any social order to a state in which a man, 'while being subject, is subject only to his own but not subject to an alien will' (Kelsen 1929, 4). For Kelsen, it means in practice to be subject to a normative order in the establishment of which one participates.

Kelsen's conception of democracy operates with the ideal of the autonomous social order based on the normative distinction between autonomy and heteronomy. Autonomy is a state of collective life that makes it possible for the people to consider themselves the authors of the norms that coercively regulate their behavior. Only government by the people themselves can create an autonomous political order and thus lessen the torment of heteronomy. It can be argued that Kelsen's conception of democracy qua autonomy relies on a two-fold conception of sovereignty according to which sovereignty is divided between the state's supreme decision making power as conferred by the legal order and popular sovereignty understood essentially as the participation in the process of lawmaking by virtue of which the people can consider themselves the authors of the norms that coercively regulate their behavior.

Democracy can bear the name of constitutional order distinct from autocracy only insofar as it enables participatory lawmaking based on the principle of majority. At the same time, it must conform to the normative ideal of the rule of law. Legislative power must be subject to such conditions of legality that constrain its exercise in a way which ensures that the content of laws is more than the proverbial tyranny of the majority. In other words, the exercise of legislative power must be in accordance with basic political rights, civil liberties and democratic rights of political participation. These secure a successful transformation of natural freedom as the idea of absence of government into the idea of political freedom as the idea of participation in government (Kelsen 1955, 27–28). There is no contradiction between popular sovereignty (understood by Kelsen as democratic majoritarianism) and constitutionalism and its practice of entrenching rights.

Sovereignty in constitutional democracy thus cannot be seen neither as the purely political notion of the absolutely highest power (whoever holds it) standing above the law, nor as a purely legal category embodied in a hypothetical highest norm, but as the concept of autonomy determined by political institutions and arrangements, such as division and organisation of power, method of lawmaking, procedures for resolving disagreement etc. As such, it is a concept that is perfectly suitable for capturing the interaction of law and politics, the co-originality and interdependence of binding positive law and legitimate political power. Getting rid of the political dimension of sovereignty and making sovereignty the feature of law is not necessary for developing the theory of legality adequate to constitutional democracy.

References

Arendt, Hannah. 1965. *On Revolution*. New York: The Viking Press.

Bellamy, Richard. 2007. *Political Constitutionalism*. Cambridge: Cambridge University Press.

Bodin, Jean. 1955. *Six Books of the Commonwealth*. Oxford: Basic Blackwell.

Foucault, Michel. 2003. *Society Must Be Defended*. New York: Picador.

Fischer-Lescano, Andreas, Teubner, Gunther. 2004. Regime Collisions: The Vain Search for Legal Unity in the Fragmentation of Global Law. *Michigan Journal of International Law* 25: 999–1046.

Gümplová, Petra. 2011. *Sovereignty and Constitutional Democracy*. Baden-Baden: Nomos Verlagsgesellschaft.

Habermas, Jürgen. 1998. *Between Facts and Norms*. Cambridge (MA): MIT Press.

Hart, H. L. A. 1983. *Essays in Jurisprudence and Philosophy*. Oxford: Oxford University Press.

Hobbes, Thomas. 1985. *Leviathan*. London: Penguin Books.

Jellinek, Georg. 1960. *Allgemeine Staatslehre*. Darmstadt: Wissenschaftliche Buchgesellschaft.

Kalyvas, Andreas. 2007. The Basic Norm and Democracy in Hans Kelsen's Legal and Political Theory. *Philosophy and Social Criticism* 32: 573–599.

Kelsen, Hans. 1920. *Das Problem der Souveränität und die Theorie des Völkerrechts*. Tübingen: Mohr.

Kelsen, Hans. 1922. *Der soziologische und der juristische Staatsbegriff*. Tübingen: Mohr.

Kelsen, Hans. 1929. *Vom Wesen und Wert der Demokratie*. Tübingen: Mohr.

Kelsen, Hans. 1955. Foundations of Democracy. *Ethics* LXVI, no. 1, Part II: 1–101.

Kelsen, Hans. 1942. *Law and Peace in International Relations*. Cambridge (MA): Harvard University Press.

Kelsen, Hans. 1992. *Introduction to the Problems of Legal Theory. A Translation of the First Edition of the Reine Rechtslehre or Pure Theory of Law*. Oxford: Oxford University Press.

Kelsen, Hans. 2006. *General Theory of Law & State*. New Brunswick, NJ: Transaction Publishers.

Koselleck, Reinhardt. 1988. *Critique and Crisis. Enlightenment and the Pathogenesis of Modern Society*. Cambridge (MA): MIT Press.

Loughlin, Martin. 2003. Ten Tenets of Sovereignty. In *Sovereignty in Transition*, edited by Neil Walker, 55–87. Oxford: Hart Publishing.

MacCormick, Neil. 1995. The Maastricht-Urteil: Sovereignty Now. *European Law Journal* 1: 259–266.

MacCormick, Neil. 1999. *Questioning Sovereignty: Law, State and Nation in the European Commonwealth*. Oxford: Oxford University Press.

Raz, Joseph. 1979. *The Authority of Law. Essays on Law and Morality*. Oxford: Oxford University Press.

Raz, Joseph. 1983. *The Concept of Legal System. An Introduction to the Theory of Legal System*. Oxford: Oxford University Press, 1983.

Vinx, Lars. 2008. *Hans Kelsen's Pure Theory of Law. Legality and Legitimacy.* Oxford: Oxford University Press.

Walker, Neil. 2003. Late Sovereignty in the European Union. In *Sovereignty in Transition*, edited by Neil Walker, 3–32. Oxford: Hart Publishing.

Part IV
Justice after Rawls

Why is Rawls's Social Contract Hypothetical?

Bojan Vranić

It is commonly said that after the publication of *A Theory of Justice*, most contemporary political theorists agreed that this book defined the criteria for the distinction between political philosophy and modern political theory. The significance of Rawls's work is visible not only in the revitalisation of conceptual topics such as justice, freedom and equality, 'but he also gave new life to the discipline of political philosophy, which was largely moribund in the Anglo-American world in the first half of the twentieth century' (Hampton 1996, 132). The epochality of Rawls's work is reflected in the reconstruction of the very basis of liberal political thought. One of the most significant projects of this reconstruction is the reconfiguration of the contract's nature.

The aim of this paper is to explain why Rawls's social contract is hypothetical in its nature.[1] In order to explain this, I first have to give an overview of the interpretations that claim that Rawls's contract exists as a constituting ('the constitutional conception') or consensual act ('the consensual conception'), both of them binding in their nature. After I pinpoint the inadequacies of both of these conceptions, I will analyse and explain the conceptions that claim that Rawls's contract is hypothetical. In these conceptions, the contract is seen as a theoretical means of achieving a goal, i.e. determining the criteria for conceiving justice as fairness. As Jean Hampton points out in her paper about Rawls's contractual strategy, 'contractual agreement on two principles not only *does not* but *ought to* occur in the original position,' which makes the contract hypothetical (1980, 315). I will offer a twofold answer to the question why Rawls's contract is hypothetical. Firstly, it is directed towards finding an adequate model for the distribution of goods, and secondly, it is hypothetical because of the concept of the noumenality of the self, which Rawls refers to when he explains the basic characteristics of representative individuals.

1 I would like to stress that this paper is based only on *A Theory of Justice* and its interpretations. Earlier and later works of Rawls and the corrections of *A Theory of Justice* will not be in the focus the paper.

Is there a contract?

In the first part of *A Theory of Justice*, Rawls states that his contractual theory is based upon the tradition that can be recognised in the works of Locke, Rousseau and Kant, quoted by many later on (Rawls 1971, 11). This can be a rather attractive argument in defence of the declining classical political philosophy in the first half of the 20th century. Therefore, Rawls's contractual strategy can be interpreted as 'a constitutional conception,' or a part of Lockean liberal political theory. The contract can be seen as a constituting act, based on the principles of justice reached by a consensus. Its product is the body politic as the basic structure of society which is the most stable if the principles of justice converge with the principles of liberal democracy. As I said, this idea is appealing, but at the same time misleading. It is simply an inadequate interpretation of Rawls's contractual strategy. Rawls never discusses the constitution of anything beyond the original position. And what is within the original position is assumed to be 'a purely hypothetical situation' (ibid., 120). As I will demonstrate later on, the constitution cannot take place in the original position due to the presence of the veil of ignorance. Since these two theoretical principles are mutually exclusive, the constitutional conception proves to be inadequate. At this point, it is important to emphasise that the contract is neither an act, nor does it possess a constituting function.

When this function is removed, what remains is the fact that Rawls's contractual strategy leads to a consensus on the principles of justice. I believe that the consensus represents the cornerstone of the debate over whether the contract belongs to the consensual or to the hypothetical type. The first type brings Rawls closer to Rousseau's understanding of the general will as a constituting force of political order, while the latter brings Rawls's contract closer to Kant's constructivism. Those authors who believe that the 'consensual' conception lies at the heart of Rawls's contractual strategy support it by the argument that the original position results in a Rousseauian *volonté générale*. In a nutshell, this conception suggests that the contract should be seen as part of the original position, with the aim of giving arguments for the direction in which the overlapping consensus should be formed. The conception furthermore suggests that there is a contract that guarantees that the consensus has a morally binding force for the legislator.

This insistence on consensual strategy can be interpreted as a way of overcoming the essential contestability of justice (Plant 1991, 104–106). Rawls's argument of social contract is directed towards overcoming pluralism and the conflict that exists between various conceptions of justice by providing good reasons for the legitimacy of the consensus concerning the distribution of basic goods. Rawls's strategy directly opposes the then dominant liberal idea, according to which there was no 'neutral' distribution due to the teleological nature of goods (Plant 1991; Pavlović

2005). All goods, in a Kantian sense, serve a specific purpose, and as such they cannot be universal and general. Neither the goods nor their distribution according to a determined pattern can be just, and in that way, binding (Plant 1991). By introducing the rational choice of an individual into the original position, Rawls wanted to demonstrate that we can create formal conditions for neutral distribution, which is the basis for achieving consensus in terms of the principles of justice. The reference to the possibility of consensus over basic goods means an incomplete but significant progress along the path towards justifying the concept of justice as fairness (ibid., 105). What is left to be done is to formulate the contract in accordance with consensus.

But what is, then, the status of the consensus and in what way is it related to the contract? At this point, it is useful to bear in mind the distinction between 'bargain' and consensus made by János Kis (1998, 12–13). The 'bargain' hinders morally neutral agreement because it leaves room for the agreement of a small number of individuals, to the detriment of others. Consensus unconditionally requires the agreement of all sides that participate in deliberation. As an answer to the previous question, one can argue that the consensus serves as the basis for the constitution of a political body resulting from the general will. The difference from Rousseau's concept in this case is in the limitation guaranteed by the right of veto. Indeed, it would be wrong to believe that this political body is a specific institution, some sort of assembly. It should rather be understood in an abstract way, in the same way as Rawls's concept of the basic structure of society. The characteristic of this political body is the replacement of unjust institutions, which means that it has a corrective function. Therefore, according to these interpretations, the aim of Rawls's contractual strategy, as Newey (2001) pointed out, is the creation of a post-political order. The purpose of the basic structure of society is to ensure maximal participation and justice when it comes to the distribution of goods.

The consensual conception generates several problems. Firstly, if we accept that the original position is characterised by a consensus, and not a bargain, then we necessarily exclude the contract. As Hampton (1980, 325) states, 'contracts involve an *exchange*; they are *bargains*'. Even if we keep the contract in the weak sense, as a means of reaching a consensus, this conception proves to be contradictory in the light of Rawls's understanding of the original position. The basic characteristic of the original position is the presence of the veil of ignorance which disables the identification of one's own and other parties' preferences. If they don't know what the dispute is about, or at least what their common goals are, how are representative individuals able to reach consensus? The only thing they can do, due to their distrust of the moves of others, is to stick to their own interest (whatever their interest may be), which does not lead to any consensus on the principles of justice (ibid., 326).

Secondly, although this conception operates on a more abstract level than the constitutional one, it still leads to the conclusion that Rawls's strategy has a constitutive function. Reaching a consensus on the constitution of a political body would collide with the principle of justice as the first virtue of that body. The dominant role of the consensus is necessarily in clash with the lexicographic order of the two principles of justice. Rawls (1971, 19) insists that the principle of equal rights for all individuals needs to be established before any social distribution of goods takes place. The aim should not be to constitute the political body, but to define the procedure for its evaluation. This can be achieved only through the creation of a series of hypothetical agreements on the distribution of primary goods between representative individuals. Such a distribution should prevent the situation in which some individuals are in the position of a hopeless minority, either politically or economically. However, the problem of the consensual conception is that it neglects the fact that there is always a minority to which the previous institution was not unjust. Those minorities also have to participate in reaching the consensus (otherwise we would not be able to call it a consensus), and it is difficult to believe that they would comply with the principles of justice that would deprive them of some of the *primary goods*, such as freedom, health or self-respect. In other words, a consensual strategy according to which the two principles of justice are the key values for which everybody is ready to leave aside their disputes over the distribution of basic goods proves to be unrealistic (Podunavac 2001).

Finally, this conception generates a problem within Rawls's view. If we claimed that there is a clear strategy concerning how to reach the consensus on a rational basis, that would mean that representative individuals possess formed identities. Rawls denies this by eliminating the contextual elements of identity, reducing them to the principles of basic psychology. The consensus that can be reached is the one concerning the basic virtue of society. For Rawls, that virtue should be justice as fairness. That is precisely the level of abstraction which Rawls aims at, and which marks the difference between his work and the classical discourse of liberal political theory. Consequently, the consensual conception lacks general and universal properties, because it insists on the post-political dimension of contractual strategy, and thus neglects the very essence of Rawls's theory.

Why is there no contract?

If what I have so far suggested is convincing, I can draw the conclusion that the aim of Rawls's contract is not the constitution, but the procedural verification of basic structures, which results in adhering to the principle of justice as fairness. The contract's function should be reduced to something similar to the Kantian view. By doing this, we elevate contractual strategy to the highest level of abstraction. In the process of generalisation two effects are achieved: firstly, a consensus is reached concerning the basic criteria for the just distribution of *primary goods* among representative individuals and secondly, based on the criterion of justice thus created, the quality of the basic structure of society is evaluated. This conception is based on the foundation of moral principles from which we derive justice as fairness, which is nothing but a procedure for the evaluation of the basic structure of society. The conception implies that in both cases the contract is a hypothetical assumption. Similarly to Kant's view, the contract is just an "idea of the mind" which in its form and its content determines which laws are just. The contract is a general test (Hampton 1996, 135). It is an instrument that allows individuals in the original position to test the fairness of their needs for primary goods, and to apply the procedure formulated this way to the evaluation of social institutions (Hampton 1996).

The drawback of this conception is the fact that it does not offer an explanation why the contract should remain hypothetical. How can we claim that for a society that strives to be just it is better to leave the basic principles on the hypothetical level than to make them binding through the act of contract? The conception of hypothetical contract is therefore on thin ice, because it 'seems either historically absurd, if it is intended to identify actual promises, or morally insignificant, if it is intended to point out purely hypothetical promises' (Kymlicka 1993, 187–188). Bearing all these aspects in mind, the criticism of the hypothetical contract can serve as a solid argument in favour of Dworkin's claim that such a contract is not binding because it is not a real contract in the first place (Kymlicka 2002). What the conception of the hypothetical contract lacks is a firm basis, which is clearly, but wrongly, expressed in the consensual conception. The conception of the hypothetical contract should be further explored with the view to find which arguments in Rawls's theory can be taken as a firm basis for drawing conclusions. One should also consider the possibility that the basis of the contractual strategy are in fact representative individuals and their willingness to comply with the notion of righteousness, in order to achieve personal autonomy. The purpose of the contract should be searched for in the ends of representative individuals, i.e. the fulfilment of the Self through deliberation in the original position. 'In this sense, the contract is a means for reaching moral autonomy of an individual [...] through adjusting social and political context to moral self-understanding' (Pavićević 2006, 160). Having the freedom of choice (developing autonomous action) and respecting the consensus on the distribution of primary goods (the principle of identicality) are the necessary conditions for achieving this goal.

The original position is a hypothetical condition in which some representative individuals take part with the aim of defining the principle for determining the basic structure of society. 'Rawls's *original position* is *a space of ignorance*, which is [...] nothing else than Rawls's ambition to create an atmosphere for social actors [...] that provide no advantage for anybody in terms of influence of social or political institutions' (Podunavac 1998, 119). Representative individuals are not members of any kind of general assembly or any other representative institution (Rawls 1971, 139). A representative individual can be anybody. I have to stress that 'anybody' does not at the same time mean 'everybody.' The first term in this context stands for the pluralistic structure of society and the particularity of interests, whereas the latter word implies the holism of the social community and a general consensus over social, political and moral principles. I prefer to interpret Rawls's theory from the first of these two perspectives. 'Rawls accepts a version of pluralism [...], holding that reasonable people have various, and sometimes competing, notions about what is good – what is worth pursuing in life' (Gaus, 2000, 200). I believe that the idea that all disputes over general principles among particular parties can be resolved within one hypothetical framework is the basic assumption in the original position. It would be wrong to assume that the entire community participates in this idea. Such a claim would open up the possibility of reducing Rawls's theory to Rousseau's idea of general will functioning as a sovereign legislator.

> The beauty of a contract argument is that it involves each individual in the selection of the best conception of justice, such that any conception that would allow the society to use (or sacrifice) some people for the benefit of others in substantial ways could not be agreed upon. (Hampton, 1996, 134–135)

At this point, it is useful to make a few analytical distinctions concerning the status of representative individuals in the original position. For those who are representative individuals (RI), there are three dimensions that define their situation: (a) what they know, (b) what they are ignorant of, and (c) what they strive to achieve – as presented in the following table.

What do RIs know?	What are RIs ignorant of?	What do RIs strive to achieve?
Concept of the Self (general psychology)	Interests of other representative individuals (mutual disinterest)	Ability to deliberate autonomously and publicly (justice as an idea of the mind)
Intuitive ability for deliberative rationality (the concept of right, the need to acquire goods, self-respect)	Specific psychology (calculating with the conceptions of goods)	Procedural justice and the principle of lexicographic order

Sense of future (genetic principle)	Physical and intellectual abilities	Conceptions of justice
Sense of subjective and objective conditions of justice (political culture, laws, etc.)	Contextual and historical conditions (contingency)	Justice as fairness (general and universal principle)

The primary condition that representative individuals can rely on is 'their concept of the Self', or what Rawls terms basic psychology. '[T]he individual is assumed [...] to be a self-interested rational chooser, with definite conceptions of a plan of life, who will try to minimize losses and maximize benefits in any choice situation' (Vincent 2004, 125). Put into the context of the original position, he/she can only rely on what, hypothetically speaking, is part of his/her identity. At first glance, this seems like a very narrow theory of identity, defined solely as a 'moral personality' (Hampton 1980, 319). This would imply that the main end that individuals strive for is the need for self-fulfilment. In other words, for Rawls, the representative individual is the 'I' which can become anybody in the society (Hampton 1980). In order to fulfil the 'I', representative individuals rely on the intuitive sense for deliberative rationality. What might seem confusing is Rawls's need to point out the purpose of deliberative rationality before he shows what it consists of. The purpose is in fact the sense of justice. As Rawls further develops this argument, he suggests that the sense of justice is reached by means of the intuitive sense of the right. Such a righteous reasoning determines the cluster of characteristics of the Self, which in the original position also includes the need for the acquisition of goods and, most importantly, self-respect (Rawls 1971, 440). Two key characteristics of representative individuals, the basic psychology and the sense of rightness, point to the noumenality of the Self. 'Even these are not given (nor determined), but need to be reconstructed on the basis of moral judgments, or taken from [...] reliable social science practices' (Pavićević 2006, 160). Representative individuals evaluate things in relation to themselves, i.e. according to what they believe to be right. This would imply that in the original position, under the veil of ignorance, the participation of only one individual is enough (Hampton, 1980). Such a position is purely Kantian. It suggests that each individual is free if he/she makes autonomous decisions concerning in what kind of society and with what concept of justice he/she wishes to live. Such decisions are universal and general in the strong moral sense. Rawls expressed this through his view of the Kantian interpretation of justice as fairness:

> My suggestion is that we think of the original position as *the point of view* from which noumenal selves see the world. The parties qua noumenal selves have complete freedom to *choose* whatever principles they wish; but they also have

> a *desire to express* their nature as rational and equal members of the intelligible realm with precisely this liberty to choose, that is, as beings who can look at the world in this way and express this perspective in their life as members of society. They must decide, then, which principles when consciously followed and acted upon in everyday life will best manifest this freedom in their community, most fully reveal their independence from natural contingencies and social accident. (Rawls 1971, 255; my emphasis)

The orientation towards the development of the Self should not be confused with egoism (Rawls 1971). Rather, it should be understood as a disinterest in others since the veil of ignorance conceals from us what others want to gain for themselves. Representative individuals do not want to do harm to each other because they are not envious. However, they are aware of two things: firstly, there are not enough primary goods for everybody to get as much as they wish to get (which are the conditions of moderate scarcity), and secondly, beyond the original position people live in a society in which they have to cooperate (the corporative nature of society). This generates the need for compromise, which takes the form of a consensus. But regarding what? Only regarding the procedure that has to enable the just distribution of goods in congruence with the principles of justice. 'Rawls identifies the principles that would be chosen by instrumentally rational beings to whom he ascribes certain sparsely specified ends not the principles that *could* consistently be chosen regardless of particular ends' (O'Neill 1993, 184). Those principles do not necessarily have to be the ones implied by the conception of justice as fairness. For Rawls, justice as fairness is the best conception. However, which of the conceptions will be selected depends only on the sense of justice shared by representative individuals, and this brings me back to the idea of the noumenal self.

The rightness of reasoning of representative individuals results in Kantian moral maxims. This means that the ultimate goal of self-fulfilment is the creation of an autonomous individual who has a sense of justice. In the original position, the freedom of choice as the basis for autonomy is practiced among a number of competitive conceptions of primary goods. Which conception gets selected depends on the rationality and the interest of the parties to maximise their benefit. Indeed, it is plausible to object to the possibility of a connection between primary goods and individual autonomy (Pavlović 2005). Let us suppose that the moral maxims of an individual are categorical in the Kantian sense. However, if primary goods are partly selected by his/her wants or passions, then his/her Self is not autonomous, but it is under the pressure of heteronomy. 'Kant demanded that our motivation to act be guided by what is just. That is autonomous action, in contrast to the heteronomous one' (ibid., 73). I believe that this objection is partly inadequate because it is based on a wrong understanding of the status of primary goods. Firstly, Hampton states that due to the existence of the veil of ignorance it is irrelevant who and with what interest wants to participate in the process of distribution of goods. In such a position, an individual is acting rationally only if he/she respects 'the desires and goals of every actual member of his society' (Hampton 1980, 335). In this situation, the veil of ignorance does not provide the feeling of certainty that it would be this particular individual that would maximise their needs for goods (Hampton 1980). Goods have intrinsic values, but that should not influence the choice a moral individual makes. At this point it could be argued that Rawls's theory is teleological in the sense that the feeling for deliberative rationality is practiced by means of goods. This does not imply that primary goods are independent from the representative individual's sense of justice. Their value is estimated only in relation to the representative individual's concept of what is right. Any theory of primary goods needs to be subjected to the status of the concept of rightness, which is a way to rule out the possibility of bargain of goods. This should result in choosing only those goods whose intrinsic values could also be universal. Primary goods should be defined by means of descriptive theory (Rawls 1971). This opts for the definite definitions of goods. Two things are implicitly present in this requirement: (a) the definite description of goods is the conception of the concept of goods; and (b) we should treat goods as a function of right.

Once we define the status of primary goods and determine the procedures of their distribution, we also define the maxims for the justness of any social structure. Goods are wanted neither for their practical applicability nor for the maximisation of happiness, but for the values they have for the development of the autonomous Self, which leads to just institutions. The fulfilment of the Self cannot be heteronomous, but only an autonomous act. The limit is set by rationality – according to Rawls (1971, 427–430), rational persons will not allow their abilities for self-development to be restricted or imposed, and they will not wish to treat others in the same way either. When it comes to goods, individuals will not wish the goods as they are per se, but they will wish the goods to be universally acceptable. Such a strategy is rational because it provides a definite descriptive meaning of goods, and also certainty that the selected conception is respected. In that way, a consensual equilibrium is achieved between the sense for righteousness that individuals possess and the need for goods based on which this sense manifests itself (Plant 1991).

Primary goods have to be the ones that, at least *prima facie*, everybody wants. It is contrary to common sense to eliminate the wish for such goods. However, they become value for representative individuals only after their conceptions, which are congruent with rightness, are accepted. As such they become universal values that are positioned on the same category level as moral maxims. Consequently, this also answers the question about the status of goods. It shows that goods have to be formal, because 'bias would be eliminated from the selection among the principles of justice by the fact that goods represent uniform and universal means and conditions for the realization of any individual or collective goal' (Glintić 1998, 141).

The consensus between representative individuals is connected to the formation of the conception of justice which guarantees a just distribution of goods in the society. If the evaluation of the basic structure of the society is the aim of the establishment of procedural justice, then the aim of the original position needs to be the establishment of the model. Such a model, with certain limitations, is formed through the processes of the distribution of primary goods among individuals. The moderate scarcity of primary goods leads to the need for a consensus on their distribution. When reaching the consensus, individuals are led by their sense of Self. If goods are evaluated on the basis of the sense of the concept of right, which characterises each individual, then every individual strives to preserve his/her personal understanding of this concept. We should not neglect the fact that individuals in the original position do collect elements for their rational life plan, which is sufficient motivation for them to want other individuals to regard some goods as more valuable than others. 'A rational plan-constrained as always by the principles of right [...]. Moreover, his fellow associates are likely to support these activities as promoting the common interest and also to take pleasure in them as displays of human excellence' (Rawls 1971, 429). Therefore, they are willing to reach a consensus based on the reflective equilibrium. This way of reaching a consensus has a circular form. Arguments move back and forth until an agreement acceptable for all sides is reached (Kis 1998).

The contract can only be hypothetical, and it is hypothetical in two senses. Firstly, in a Kantian sense, which means that it is directed towards the goods on which the consensus is reached. As I have already shown, goods are the object of wish and as such they can be the subject only of the hypothetical contract. Being hypothetical, the contract does not possess the strength of the highest rank like the categorical imperative. The contract is a loose relation which brings circularity to an end and enables individuals to move on to other goods on which a consensus should be reached. The need for the contract is psychological in its nature, because it creates the feeling that the negotiation progresses along a rational path. The moment when the universality of goods is achieved, i.e. when it is congruent with righteousness the contract as an instrument can be left aside. Hampton (1980) goes so far as to claim that the contract is unnecessary and contradictory to Rawls's conception of the original position. Her argument is that due to the existence of the veil of ignorance there is no need for the existence of the contract, since individuals, in the Kantian sense, can wish their deeds can serve as a universal law. But what is then the factor that stops the deliberation process? Although Hampton (1980, 329) refers to Robert Paul Wolff's objection that in the original position there is a problem of 'arbitration' over the timeframe within which deliberation should take place, she seems to miss that the purpose of the contract is precisely that – achieving the balance among parties when that is rational. Even if only one person takes part in the original position, the need still remains to overcome the inner gap by means of a contract, which can be created when a choice is made between two conceptions of the contested concept.

The second reason why the contract has to be hypothetical is the primacy of the Self. If the contract is a constituting act, that means that the injustice that may be done after the veil of ignorance is eliminated cannot be corrected. From the point of view of an individual, injustice is done when what the individual gained in the original position is abused, mocked or discredited in any other way. 'Therefore the parties in the original position would wish to avoid at almost any cost the social conditions that undermine self-respect' (Rawls 1971, 440). It seems that self-respect is the crucial element of the sense of right, which is, again, the basis of the Self. Even more than that, self-respect is at the same time the self-confirmation of freedom: the choices that 'I' makes belong to it only and are, therefore, rational. When the veil of ignorance is lifted, the Self that is fulfilled in the original position has to stay identical to itself and retain the freedom guaranteed by personal autonomy, or otherwise the entire form of procedural justice collapses. One of the places where Rawls creates room for such a claim is through the formulation of the first formal condition for the principles of justice. The principles of justice need to be general in the sense in which they are acceptable both for current individuals and future generations, also after the veil of ignorance is lifted. Rawls's argument relies on Locke's justification of general moral authority (God): 'if one person is created by another (in the theological sense), then that person has a duty to comply with the precepts set to him by his creator' (Rawls 1971, 132). Due to the absence of God's will as the moral basis of Rawls's theory, the idea is that the 'creator' of personality is in fact a 'moral personality' from the original position. Hampton believes that if we perceive the moral personality as the basis of all future personalities, then according to the rule of 'the identity of indiscernibles', 'there is no reason to claim that more than one person exists in these [the original position – BV] circumstances' (Hampton 1980, 334). The fulfilment of the Self, however, does not require the identification of moral principles, because 'moral personalities' already possess an intuitive ability for deliberative rationality. To claim that 'moral personality' needs to fulfil itself with moral principles would be trivial. The fulfilment of the Self happens through determining the procedure for the just distribution of goods, which represents the property of the intuitive sense for rightness. In that sense the rule of the identity of indiscernibles should be replaced with its converse, i.e. the rule of indiscernibility of indenticals. I will observe this principle through the following definition: 'Necessarily, for any objects, *a* and *b*, if *a* is identical with *b*, then for any property, *P*, a exemplifies *P* if and only if *b* exemplifies *P*' (Loux 2006, 169). Personal autonomy is evaluated on the basis of freedom to use the selected goods to their full extent. Only in that way can we be certain that the Self would be identical to itself. If the contract were not hypothetical, if it had the force of a binding or a constituting act, the injustice that could be generated after the veil of ignorance is removed would turn into a permanent social state. Such an outcome is a complete opposite of Rawls's basic intention and aims.

⋆

Even though there is a valid argument that for a social contract theory it is better to claim that the contract has a constituting force, I have shown why such a claim would be contradictory to Rawls's basic idea. The reasons for accepting the hypotheticity of the contract can be briefly summarised as follows. Firstly, the hypothetical contract is a necessary means which guarantees that in the original position a consensus over goods that are being evaluated is reached. The binding force of this guarantee is not the same as the one of the categorical imperative. Rather, it is loose and instrumental. Although I believe that the interpretation I have offered preserves Rawls's basic idea, that does not leave it without problems. The problem that I consider particularly challenging is the one that questions the instrumentalisation of goods. If the contract is the means for establishing a just distribution of goods, does that imply that primary goods such as freedom can be instrumentalised (Glintić 1998, 143)? Unfortunately, I will have to leave this important and problematic issue open because it is a separate topic. Secondly, the hypotheticity of the contract implies that it does not exist as a fact, or at least as a binding force. In other words, contractual relations do not exist beyond the original position. The only thing that should remain after the original position are the principles of justice reflected in the conception reached by the means of hypothetical contracts and on the basis of the representative individuals' dominant sense of rightness.

Acknowledgement The work on this paper has been granted by the Ministry of Education and Science (Republic of Serbia), through the project "Constitutionalism and the Rule of Law in the Process of Nation-State Building – The Case of Serbia."

References

Gaus, Gerard. 2000. *Political Concepts and Political Theories.* Boulder: Westview Press.

Glintić, Tatjana. 1998. Teorija pravde Džona Rolsa. In *O pravdi i pravičnosti*, edited by Miloš Knežević 132–146. Beograd: Studetski grad.

Hampton, Jean. 1980. Does Rawls Have a Social Contract Theory? *The Journal of Philosophy* 77.6: 315–338.

Hampton, Jean. 1997. *Political Philosophy.* Boulder: Westview Press.

Kymlicka, Will. 2004. The Social Contract Tradition. In *A Companion to Ethics*, edited by Peter Singer, 186–196. Malden, MA: Blackwell.

Kymlicka, Will. 2002. *Contemporary Political Philosophy.* Oxford: Oxford University Press.

Kis, Janoš. 1998. Iza vela neznanja. *Nova srpska politička misao* 2–3: 7–36.

Loux, Michael J. 2006. *Metaphysics: A Contemporary Introduction.* Abingdon: Routledge.

Newey, Glen. 2001. *After Politics.* Hampshire: Palgrave.

O'Neill, Onora. 1993. Kantian Ethics. In *A Companion to Ethics*, edited by Peter Singer, 175–185. Malden, MA: Blackwell.

Pavićević, Đorđe. 2004. *Politička koncepcija liberalizma Džona Rolsa.* PhD thesis, University of Belgrade.

Pavlović, Dušan. 2005. *Autonomija ličnosti u Rolsovoj teoriji pravde.* Beograd: Fabrika knjiga.

Plant, Raymond. 1991. *Modern Political Tought.* Oxford: Blackwell.

Podunavac, Milan. 1998. Politička Pravda u demokratskom društvu. In *O pravdi i pravičnosti*, edited by Miloš Knežević, 118–123. Beograd: Studetski grad.

Podunavac, Milan. 2001. *Princip građanstva i poredak politike.* Beograd: Čigoja štampa.

Rawls, John. 1971. *A Theory of Justice.* Cambridge (Mass): Harvard University Press.

Vincent, Andrew. 2004. *The Nature of Political Theory.* Oxford: Oxford University Press.

Future Generations: An Almost Rawlsian Perspective

Miklós Könczöl

I

In public deliberation concerning possible policies, references to the rights or interests of future generations are sometimes made in order to justify choices that are likely to result in sub-optimal outcomes from the perspective of present people. Quite often, such arguments are received with a great deal of scepticism. I think, at any rate, that the concept of future generations is a useful one, as it helps to formulate a problem on the one hand and an intuition on the other. The problem is that given the present state of technical advancement, present people are capable of making decisive impact on the life circumstances of people they are never going to meet as their life spans do not overlap. The intuition, then, is that no harm should be done to future people.

Now, one can interpret the expression 'future generations', broadly speaking, in two ways, emphasising either 'generations', i.e. the fact that future people will be descendants of present people, or 'future', i.e. that those people do not exist yet. Any plausible discussion has to keep a balance between these two aspects. Still, it has to be borne in mind that the real potential of arguments based on future generations shows only if we exclude any overlapping between the present generation and those considered as future ones.[1] Also, it is only this way that problems related to the notion of future people having rights or to intergenerational justice come to the surface and can be addressed.

In what follows, I shall briefly mention some of these problems before turning to possible ways of dealing with them. Then I am going to have a look at John Rawls's

1 This is not to say that a theoretical approach based on the chain of overlapping generations would be useless: as it will become clear in the final part of this paper, the continuity of generations is essential for my argument as well. Yet if one wants to weigh future interests against present ones in terms of rights or justice, one should not allow present and future to overlap. As Aristotle puts it in his *Nicomachean Ethics*, 'it is another's interest that justice aims at' (1130a 4–5). See also Hubin (1976, 70 and ibid., n 1).

way of extending his theory of justice to future generations. I hope to conclude by showing why some of Rawls's ideas may be fruitful for making plausible arguments with reference to future generations.[2]

II

Arguments based on the rights or interests of future generations are, in general, plausible and implausible at the same time. Their plausibility is due to the fact that imagined this way, the future has got a human face, as it were. In moral and legal thinking, references to rights have to be countered by references to other rights, references to interests with references to interests. And if we think of people who are going to live after us, no matter how far they are remote in time, it seems natural that these people, *qua* human beings, will have rights and interests. Our task is, then, to represent these future interests in present decision-making processes and to strike a balance, as far as possible, between future and present rights and interests.

The implausibility of such arguments results, in turn, from the potential nature, or, to put it in negative terms, the uncertainty of these rights and interests. Indeed, the mere existence of future persons is something we can only assume. Derek Parfit's formulation of the 'non-identity problem' goes one step further by showing that even if future people are going to exist, it is very difficult to conceive of duties or obligations towards them (see Parfit 1979). Moreover, if we put this theoretical problem to one side for the moment, and focus on the question of why we should care at all about the interests of future generations, i.e. the problem of motivation, potentiality and uncertainty appear again. Why should we seek to formulate future rights and interests if we do not see how they are relevant for us?[3]

2 A similar endeavour is that of D. Clayton Hubin (ibid.) and in much what follows I do, in fact, concur with him. Our final conclusions being the same, i.e. that we do not owe any obligation *to* future people but we do have obligations towards our contemporaries *with regard to* future people, there are, as I see, two main differences between Hubin's approach and mine. On the one hand, his argument is based on the assumption that people are going to have children (see ibid. 81–82), while I try to describe obligations with reference to communitarian ideas of identity and membership. On the other hand, as a consequence of focusing on that particular kind of relationship, his 'psychological principle' only motivates the parties to the contract to save for the next generation (see ibid. 82–83).

3 In an article published in some thirty years ago, Norman Care identifies some motivational factors which, however, are in his opinion incapable of establishing any motivational link between present and future people (Care 1982). Love or concern, he argues, fails to do so because of the non-particularity of not yet existing persons. Community bonding, the second candidate, has reciprocation as its condition, which just does not obtain between different generations. Finally, the 'sense of common humanity' is something that is 'somehow beyond us, or too difficult for many of us to develop, at this time'. Non-particularity and the absence of a 'sense of common humanity' are, I think, problems that can be traced back to uncertainty.

III

In his 1971 book, *A Theory of Justice*, John Rawls formulated a contractualist framework for determining principles of justice for a given society. As opposed to contractarian theories,[4] his 'original contract' is not a historical one, but rather a symbol of his claim that rights and duties can be determined through a political consensus of rational and reasonable persons. In a famous thought experiment, Rawls speaks of the parties to the contract as being under 'the veil of ignorance', i.e. when deliberating about principles of justice, one should eliminate any information concerning one's social position.

Rawls was one of the first thinkers to look at inter-generational issues as matters of justice and rights. As we are going to see presently, he was not so much concerned with whether it makes sense to speak of not-yet-existing people having rights as with the question of how future interests can be formulated as obligations for a given generation.

Discussing the principles of justice, Rawls writes that '[e]ach generation must not only preserve the gains of culture and civilization, and maintain intact those just institutions that have been established, but it must also put aside in each period of time a suitable amount of real capital accumulation' (Rawls 1971, 285). The amount of this accumulation, the just savings rate, is one of the questions the members of a given generation have to agree upon. In order to ensure impartiality in this decision, the contracting parties – being under the veil of ignorance – do not know which generation they belong to (although they know that they all belong to the same generation).

It is interesting to note that Rawls does not say explicitly that just savings are a matter of *inter-generational* obligation, only that they are necessary to make the accomplishment of principles of justice possible and render acceptable the situation of the least advantaged. On the other hand, by extending the veil of ignorance to the parties' place in time, he seems to conceive of the just savings rate as something that is 'just' because it promotes inter-generational impartiality.

Moreover, Rawls adds a 'motivational assumption', which he thinks necessary to prevent 'generational egoism', i.e. to ensure that the participants of the contract are not going to determine the principles of justice in a way that excludes any kind of savings. According to this assumption, '[t]he parties are thought of as representing continuing lines of claims, as being so to speak deputies for a kind of everlasting moral agent or institution. They need not take into account its entire life span in perpetuity, but their goodwill stretches over at least two generations' (ibid., 128).

Again, having something like 'goodwill' towards future people does not necessarily mean that a given generation has got obligations to another or that future

4 The distinction of contractarian and contractualist theories follows Gardiner (2009, 79).

generations would have rights. Yet critics and interpreters of Rawls read it that way, and it is also in that sense that Rawls developed his theory further. In his 1993 book, *Political Liberalism*, he describes what is at stake in the original position in the following way: 'The correct principle is that which the members of any generation (and so all generations) would adopt as the one their generation is to follow and as the principle they would want preceding generations to have followed [...]' (Rawls 1993, 274). Finally, in the second edition of *A Theory of Justice*, published in 1999, he summarised his position as follows:

> The question arises [...] whether the persons in the original position have obligations and duties to third parties, for example, to their immediate descendants. To say that they do would be one way of handling justice between generations. However, the aim of justice as fairness is to try to derive all duties and obligations of justice from other reasonable conditions. So, if possible, this way out should be avoided. There are several other courses open to us. We can adopt a motivation assumption and think of the parties as representing a continuing line of claims. For example, we can assume that they are heads of families and therefore have a desire to further the well-being of at least their more immediate descendants. Or we can require the parties to agree to principles subject to the constraint that they wish all preceding generations to have followed the very same principles. By an appropriate combination of such stipulations, I believe that the whole chain of generations can be tied together and principles agreed to that suitably take into account the interests of each [...] If this is right, we will have succeeded in deriving duties to other generations from reasonable conditions. (Rawls 1999, 111)

While several aspects of Rawls's motivational assumption have been challenged since the first publication of *A Theory of Justice*,[5] I think it is exactly this part of his theoretical construct that may serve as the starting point of a different approach. To be sure, the motivational assumption as an element of Rawls's theory of inter-generational justice is open to objections on several points. Yet the approach I am going to outline below is not one that seeks inter-generational justice.

IV

The first point to be taken seriously in Rawls's conception is that according to him, it is not necessary that we conceive of the 'continuing lines of claims' as families. In the original version this was obvious, but also the wording of the second edition makes it clear that family lines are but an example of such going concerns. Fortunately enough for future generations, there are continuing lines of claims that are available

5 See, e.g., Hubin (1976), Barry (1978), Manning (1981), and Singer (1988). See Könczöl (2007) for a selective overview of the main points of criticism.

for those without a family or for people whose life plan does not include having children (cf. Singer 1988, 221 and ibid., n 7). Communitarian theories have since long tried to approach the problem of intergenerational justice from this angle.

There are, however, two problems that quite often appear in such theories. The first one is related to the future existence of the respective line of claims, or, otherwise put, a community. It was pointed out in an 1972 article by Martin P. Golding, who discussed the possibility of grounding present obligations to future generations on the assumption of moral community. According to his reasoning, obligations to future people can be justified only if we assume some kind of a moral identity, i.e. that the present generation's values are accepted as such by future generations. He claims, however, that such assumptions become increasingly uncertain as we look at generations more remote in time. As their life circumstances may differ considerably from ours, we cannot be sure whether our conceptions of the good life hold for them.[6] What follows from this is that arguments in favour of our obligations to prefer the interests of future generations to present ones are unconvincing: either their interests coincide with ours (or with the interests of those less remote in time), or we would be sacrificing more certain interests for less certain ones. Yet Golding makes it clear that as the life circumstances of future generations can be influenced by present actions, so can be their values. In his conclusion which seems to anticipate, albeit in a positive form, Derek Parfit's non-identity problem (cf. Parfit 1984), he says that '[i]t actually appears that whether we have obligations to future generations in part depends on what we do for the present' (Golding 1972, 99).

The second problem arises when communitarians try to establish some kind of a reciprocity between different generations. Some authors argue that here are real harms and benefits posterity can do to us or, more precisely, to projects that are constitutive of our present selves.[7] While this may be true, it is hard to see how this would bring about any kind of obligation on either part. Fortunately, however, it is not necessary to accept the possibility of harming past people to agree with them on the trans-generational nature of communities.

Janna Thompson's brief statement in an essay published in 2009, according to which '[a] political society is intergenerational' (Thompson 2009, 25), adequately summarises why communitarian theories can be helpful where individualist ones fail: having an identity as a member of a certain community (in this case, a polity) implies that one is interested in the past and the future of this community. If we conceive of present persons as bearers of such identities, then we also have to accept that these persons have interests in respect of both past and future generations. And present interests seem to be a much more adequate candidate for counterbalancing other present interests than (assumed) future or (reconstructed) past ones.

6 For a more detailed analysis, with examples of particular communities, see de-Shalit (1995).

7 E.g. O'Neill (1993, 28–36) or, more recently, Thompson (2009).

V

It seems that Rawls's conception of the contract is not entirely incompatible with such an approach, either. In the concluding paragraph of his chapter devoted to justice between generations, he writes:

> We can now see that persons in different generations have duties and obligations to one another just as contemporaries do. The present generation cannot do as it pleases but is bound by the principle that would be chosen in the original position to define justice between persons at different moments of time. In addition, men have a natural duty to uphold and to further just institutions and for this the improvement of civilization up to a certain level is required. (Rawls 1999, 258)

Of these two claims, the first one reflects Rawls's basic approach to future generations, together with the problems it entails. What is more important for us here, however, is the second claim, where he speaks of 'a natural duty to uphold and to further just institutions'. While the notion of 'natural duty' may be open to certain objections, this claim seems to provide the explanation we are looking for. It is for the sake of upholding just institutions that present people should make savings for future people, thereby enabling them to improve or at least to preserve the conditions of a just structure within their own generations.

What we have here, then, is a trans-generational project of achieving just institutions through the cooperation of several generations. While our contribution to the project does not establish any obligation on the part of future generations, we still have a reason to contribute.

We may conceive of various trans-generational projects which are important for individuals who are contemporaries ('important' here meaning constitutive of their selves). In the context of the Rawlsian contract, it may be considered a matter of *intra-generational* justice that these projects be taken into account when choosing between policies that are likely to have an impact on our posterity. This way, we are not going to be able to formulate obligations *to* future generations. It will become possible, however, to speak of rights *with respect to* the posterity of present people, and consequently, to regard the due consideration of future generations' interests as one of the duties present members of political communities owe one another.

Acknowledgements Earlier versions of this paper were read to various audiences in Miskolc (Hungary), Belgrade (Serbia), Frankfurt am Main (Germany) and Durham (UK). I owe a particular debt of gratitude to Péter Cserne, who has read and commented on a longer draft, saving me from some big claims and hazy arguments. For any of these remaining it is me who has to bear responsibility.

References

Barry, Brian. 1978. Circumstances of Justice and Future Generations. In *Obligations to Future Generations*, eds. Brian Barry and R. I. Sikora, 204–248. Philadelphia: Temple University Press.

Care, Norman. 1982. Future Generations, Public Policy, and the Motivation Problem. *Environmental Ethics* 4: 195–213.

de-Shalit, Avner. 1995. *Why Posterity Matters: Environmental policies and future generations.* London & New York: Routledge.

Gardiner, Stephen M. 2009. A Contract on Future Generations? In *Intergenerational Justice*, edited by Axel Gosseries and Lukas H. Meyer, 77–118. Oxford: Oxford University Press.

Golding, Martin P. 1972. Obligations to Future Generations. *The Monist* 56: 85–99.

Hubin, D. Clayton. 1976. Justice and Future Generations. *Philosophy & Public Affairs* 6: 70–83.

Könczöl, Miklós. 2007. Problems of Justice and Community in the Discourse on Future Generations. *Jogelméleti Szemle – Journal for Legal Theory* 2007/1 [http://jesz.ajk.elte.hu/konczol29.mht].

Manning, Russ. 1981. Environmental Ethics and Rawls's Theory of Justice. *Environmental Ethics* 3: 155–165.

O'Neill, John. 1993. *Ecology, Policy and Politics: Human Well-Being and the Natural World.* London: Routledge.

Parfit, Derek. 1984. *Reasons and Persons.* Oxford: Oxford University Press.

Rawls, John. 1971. *A Theory of Justice.* Cambridge, MA: Harvard University Press.

Rawls, John. 1993. *Political Liberalism.* New York: Columbia University Press.

Rawls, John. 1999. *A Theory of Justice.* 2nd rev. ed. Cambridge, MA: The Belknap Press of Harvard University Press.

Singer, Brent A. 1988. An Extension of Rawls's Theory of Justice to Environmental Ethics. *Environmental Ethics* 10: 217–231.

Thompson, Janna. 2009. Identity and Obligation in a Transgenerational Polity. In *Intergenerational Justice*, edited by Axel Gosseries and Lukas H. Meyer, 25–49. Oxford: Oxford University Press.

Electoral quotas and John Rawls's idea of justice and equality

Anna Kalisz & Magdalena Półtorak

> Free people need to agree on some ground rules in order to live together in harmony
> (John Locke)

I

John Rawls's *Theory of Justice* is usually considered as an attempt to reconcile liberty and equality as well as to solve the problem of distributive justice by bringing back the idea of the social contract based on principles of justice.

The idea of social contract implies a basic assumption that since people's nature is neither entirely altruistic nor purely egoistic, the society is a combination of common and conflicting interests. The conflict situations result in the need for the existence of some rules of distribution of various social goods.

Thus, the '*well-ordered society*' (see Rawls 1993, 73–79) shall be effectively regulated by a public conception of justice that derives from common acceptance. According to Rawls (1999, 5), such an acceptance – a '*civil friendship*' – is based on the fundamental agreement, held among other different conceptions of justice within society, that the institutions are just when no arbitrary distinctions are made between persons in assigning basic rights and duties.

Therefore, the primary subject of justice is the basic structure of society, as a factor mutually affecting the ways of distribution of such rights and duties and determining the division of advantages from social cooperation. These established 'ways of distributions' influence every person's life-prospects. In short, 'the basic structure is a primary subject of justice because its effects are so profound and present from the start' (ibid., 7). Since we are born into different positions and have different expectations of life determined partly by the political and social system, certain starting places are favoured over others. These inequalities have an influence on our initial chances in life. And the principles of social justice must be applied to these (ibid., 5–7). Thus, the principles of justice serve the elimination of inequalities.

Rawls's famous idea about the provenience of justice, formulated through the metaphor of a 'veil of ignorance', implies that

> no one knows his place in society, his class position or social status, nor does anyone know his fortune in the distribution of natural assets and abilities, his intelligence, strength, and the like. I shall even assume that the parties do not know their conceptions of the good or their special psychological propensities. The principles of justice are chosen behind a veil of ignorance. (ibid.)

Thus, according to Rawls's understanding of social justice, it is based on extreme equality, which means that the minority must not cede its freedom to the majority. All basic social goods – liberty and opportunity, income and wealth, and the bases of self-respect, etc. (the catalogue of goods as well as the conception of justice itself were, except for philosophical discussion, a subject of political debate since the very beginning[1]) – are to be distributed equally, unless an unequal distribution of any or all of these goods is to the advantage of the least favoured.

The paper is an attempt to interpose one more item to the catalogue above, an item the Author of *A Theory of Justice* probably did not think of – the gender question (see further Magill 1995, 1180–1181) – and to examine Rawls's conception of justice from this very perspective.[2]

II

The *'strict compliance theory'*[3] predicates that, as mentioned, in the hypothetical well-ordered society the rational principles of justice serve the elimination of any inequalities that do not depend on human beings themselves and are accidental – just like gender matters.

Despite the pure fact that women are the majority (in number) in contemporary society, within the structures of power and decisional processes, they still remain in the status of a minority: the less favoured. Through most of its history, law has constrained women and legal regulations have supported their exclusion from socio-political processes based on biological differentiation.

1 See the works of Rawls's opponents such as Nozick (1974), Buchanan (1975), Sandel (1998), Gauthier (1986).

2 The paper refers – taking the risk of generalisation – solely to the chosen elements of Rawls's theory, relevant to the matter of equal participation of males and females in public life. The article has no ambitions to deal with all the – numerous and various – conceptions of justice, equality or different issues deriving out of them.

3 A normative approach to the principles of justice as rational rules that would regulate an ideal and hypothetical well-ordered society.

This fact has created the sources of inequality and leads to a situation of social injustice (understood as the lack of justice) and inadequacy.

Nevertheless, not every case of unequal distribution must lead to social injustice. It is worth deliberating what, then, could justify unequal distribution.

The first justification that Rawls's conception argues with – an *argumentum ad utile* (the principle of utility) – does not seem to be compatible with the conception of social cooperation, since

> it hardly seems likely that persons who view themselves as equals, [...], would agree to principle which may require lesser life prospects for some simply for the sake of a greater sum of advantages enjoyed by the others. Since each desires to protect his interests, [...], no one has a reason to acquiesce in a enduring loss for himself in order to bring about a greater net balance of satisfaction. (Rawls 1999, 14)

And further: 'it may be expedient but it is not just that some should have less in order that others may prosper' (ibid., 23–33).

Also the second argument that usually enters the debate, permitting an unequal distribution (for example of wealth and authority) exceptionally, only if it results in compensating benefits for everyone, and in particular for the least favoured (Rawls 1999, 14–15; 1993, 35) is not to be applied, because the aforementioned situation does not benefit everyone; on the contrary, it deprives the 'less advantaged' of their benefits.

In the light of these considerations on just and unjust distribution of goods within society, the electoral quotas and similar devices can be perceived and interpreted in two ways: either (1) as a guarantee of just distribution of such goods as power (where it is a matter of parity, i.e. equal gender quotas – 50–50%), or (2) as a denial of the just distribution of such goods (with quotas other than 50%, or where these are not gender-neutral – since justice shall be understood as fairness).

This paper seeks to show that the first interpretation is appropriate here.

III

Since the distribution of goods is just if it is fair, i.e., if it is able to provide equal possibilities for each person, it seems appropriate to present here the mechanism of electoral gender quotas as a device of ensuring equal and fair participation of men and women in political life.

Today, women constitute approximately 19.5 per cent of the members of all the world's parliaments.[4] This fact means that women are still underrepresented in political decision-making assemblies. Many initiatives have been started to promote

4 Based on information of the Inter-Parliamentary Union (2011).

an increase in women's representation in politics. One of these is – though a controversial one – electoral gender quotas, which are in use in almost half of the countries in the world today (Dahlerup et al. 2008).

Until recently, Europe has not been in the forefront of this new development. Recently, however, many new measures – such as quotas and parities – have been adopted also in a European context in order to achieve a gender balance in political assemblies.

The difference between the concepts of 'quota' and 'parity' seems to be worth explaining. Quotas in politics may be defined as an affirmative measure that establishes a fixed percentage or number for the nomination or representation of a specific group, in this case women, most often in the form of a minimum percentage, which may be 20, 30 or 40 (see Dahlerup 2006, 19). An equal quota is called a 'parity', in this case a 'gender parity', i.e. its value amounts to 50%.

As mentioned before, justice implies creating a system of certain proportions, which – following democratic theories and political science – is called a principle of descriptive representation. According to this rule: 'women should be present in decision-making in proportion to their membership of the population' (see Lovenduski 2005, 17). A variety of such solutions are electoral gender quotas, which are generally used to increase the participation of under-represented groups in decision-making positions, for example, in parliaments, governments and local councils (see Dahlerup 2006, 19; Squires 2007, 91; Phillips 1995, 62–63).

A closer analysis shows that many types of electoral gender quotas are in use today. The classification takes into account, in the first place, the main dimensions of a given quota system, such as the place where it is provided for: the constitution/the electoral law or party statutes.

Legislated candidate quotas are included in the constitution and/or electoral laws of a country, and they target the gender composition of the electoral lists of all political parties, for instance, requiring a certain minimum of women candidates/candidates of same sex.

Voluntary party quotas are adopted voluntarily by political parties and take the form of internal party requirements to nominate at least a minimum number or percentage of women for electoral lists.

Moreover, quotas can be designed as *gender-specific* or *gender-neutral*. Quotas for women require a minimum number or percentage of women. Gender-neutral quota provisions set a minimum and maximum for both sexes, typically no more than 60 per cent and no less than 40 per cent of positions for either sex. In the case of gender-neutral quota provisions, the quota sets a maximum for both sexes whereas quotas for women do not (see Dahlerup 2005, 142).

As for the international level, the 'quota mechanism' first appeared in the *Convention on the Elimination of All Forms of Discrimination against Women* (CEDAW

1979). This 'international women rights act' – apart from the abolition of discrimination based on sex (gender) – created a possibility of applying temporary 'special legal measures' for accelerating real gender balance in decision-making processes.

In Europe, where some kind of a dualism of legal acts can be found, the regulations of both the Council of Europe and the European Union contain the principle of indiscrimination and the stipulation of equality of rights.

Firstly, following the adoption of *Recommendation Rec(2003)3 of the Committee of Ministers* [of the Council of Europe] *to member states on balanced participation of women and men in political and public decision making*, 'positive action measures' have been taken.

Secondly, the gender balance in decision making is a stated goal of the European Union as well. Recommendations for the introduction of legislated, regulatory and incentive measures to redress the underrepresentation of women in decision making have been adopted by all of the EU's major institutions. For instance, *Commission Decision of 19 June 2000, relating to gender balance within the committees and expert groups established by it*, is based on the *Council Recommendation of 2 December 1996 on the balanced participation of women and men in the decision-making process (96/694/EC)*.

Moreover, the European Commission's 'roadmap' for equality between men and women for 2006–10 included the promotion of their equal representation in decision making as one of the six priority areas for action.

However, the most important regulation seems to be the *Charter of Fundamental Rights of European Union*, especially Article 23:

> Equality between men and women must be ensured in all areas, including employment, work and pay. The principle of equality shall not prevent the maintenance or adoption of measures providing for specific advantages in favour of the under-represented sex.

As for the domestic level, since January 2011, the Republic of Poland has its own Act on Quotas, which has changed electoral law at the local and national levels for councils/parliaments and also the elections for the European Parliament. This Act introduces the rule that every electoral list must comprise a minimum 35% of candidates of each sex. In the event of non-compliance, the authorities in charge of receiving parties' lists of candidates would not accept the list.

Generally, out of 27 EU countries, six – Belgium, France, Portugal, Slovenia, Spain and Poland – have introduced quotas by law that are binding for all political parties. In 13 of the countries, at least one of the three largest parties has written electoral gender quotas into its statutes, which are defined as voluntary party quotas for elections. In 8 of the countries, no gender quotas are in use for national elections (Dahlerup et al. 2008, 11).

Electoral gender quotas are not only used at the national level for parliaments but are also applied in local, regional and autonomous state elections and in elections for the European Parliament.

In order to be effective, a quota system must be compatible with the electoral system, and quota rules – for example, 30 or 40 per cent women on electoral lists – must be supplemented with rules concerning rank order as well as – in the case of legislated quotas – effective legal sanctions.

In general, it seems easier to construct a quota system that is compatible with a proportional electoral system (PR system), since it is possible to introduce a greater number of candidates on party lists and since parties consciously try to balance their lists in order to win seats, and – inversely – it is much more complicated to construct gender quotas that are appropriate for single-member constituency electoral systems. Only one-third of the countries around the world with plurality/majority electoral systems have introduced some sort of gender quota, as compared to four-fifths of the countries with PR systems (see Dahlerup 2007, 80–81).

In most plurality/majority systems the parties only select one candidate per party and electoral district, and, consequently, it is not possible to introduce both men and women at the same time, as in a PR system. Instead, quotas can be introduced at the aspirant stage of the nomination process.

It has been suggested that a movement towards gender-balanced political representation can take an incremental track or a fast track (Dahlerup, Freidenvall 2005, 26–48; Dahlerup 2006, 6–10).

> The incremental track and the fast track not only represent two different accounts of the actual speed of historical development in women's political representation. They can also be viewed as two different types of equality policy, where the first one promotes formal equality based on the principle of gender equality as equal opportunity and the latter promotes substantive equality based on the principle of gender equality as equality of results.
>
> The two tracks can also be seen as involving two models, constructed as an analytical distinction between two ideal types, which are based on different problem identifications with regard to the diagnosis of women's under-representation, different goals in terms of women's political representation and, as a consequence, different political strategies for change. The two models are also based on different perceptions of historical development. (Dahlerup et al. 2008, 22)

By and large, the fast track route has entailed the introduction of legislated gender quotas (Dahlerup and Freidenvall 2005, 26–48).

The incremental track model and the fast track model
(Dahlerup et al. 2008, 22, adapted from Dahlerup and Freidenvall 2005, 29)

	The incremental model	The fast track model
Diagnoses	Women lack resources	Discrimination and mechanisms of exclusion
Goal	More women in politics	Gender-balanced elected bodies
Strategy	Capacity-building Activities	Active measures, such as gender quotas
View on historical development	Gender equality will be reached in due time	Gender equality will not be reached by itself

To sum up the quota issue: gender quotas can lead to remarkably rapid increases in women's representation, but also may result in disappointment. The condition of effectiveness of quota system is their correct structure. If adequately constructed, gender quotas are an effective policy tool for increasing women's representation in political bodies. Both legislated quotas and voluntary party quotas may lead to permanent increases in women's political representation at all levels. But quotas do not automatically result in equal representation of women and men in political decision making. It is also possible that the introduction of quotas may fall short if they are not compatible with the electoral system in use and do not include rules about rank order and sanctions for non-compliance (Dahlerup et al. 2008, 26).

Rank-ordering rules are critical to the successful implementation of legislated quotas and party quotas in list PR electoral systems. If 40 per cent of a party's candidates on the electoral list in a PR system are women but they are placed at the bottom of the list, this may result in no women being elected at all. In plurality/majority electoral systems, rules are needed with regard to the gender distribution of 'winnable' or 'safe' seats (ibid., 32).

Furthermore, gender quotas must be specific and stipulate details of implementation. When there is a lack of clear criteria or when quota provisions are vague, considerable discretion is left to the local political parties to apply quotas as they see fit.

Finally, for quota provisions to be effective, there must be sanctions for non-compliance. On this point, legislated quotas and party quotas differ. In countries with legislated quotas, effective sanctions take the form of strong financial penalties on parties that do not comply with the law or the right of electoral management bodies to declare a party's list of candidates invalid. The successful implementation of legislated quotas therefore requires institutional bodies that administer, supervise and control the application of quotas. In parties that have party quotas, on the other hand, there are no legal sanctions for non-compliance. The sanction available is pressure from central party organisations, women's groups and the electorate (see Dahlerup et al. 2008, 34; Matland 2006, 278–291).

IV

Trying to connect the strictly political issue of quotas not only with democracy, but also with the jurisprudence, it shall be emphasised that law, as a system of binding norms regulating individual and collective maintenance, does not act in a social vacuum. Being a part of culture, law derives from it and at the same time has influence on it. In other words, law is both a product and a source of social axiology. Such liaisons are identified as 'social functions' of law.

Legal regulations of electoral quotas seem to be linked mostly with the creative, distributive, preventive, motivating and – last but not least – educational functions of law, which in this case is a device for changing social consciousness as well as political manners and practice. There are no doubts though, that law may encourage to some social practice and discourage from another. It may also, eventually, change, form or at least affect social attitudes. Thus, such regulations – as one of the possible methods for balancing the underrepresentation of women in legislatures – preserve the principle of equal participation in social consciousness and then turn into established social and political practice.

Moreover, the quotas as such are – in spite of various suggestions of political provenience – neutral and fair. They perform a purely procedural role and constitute one more conventional element of democracy (such as, for example, the number and magnitude of electoral district or threshold).

The conclusions that derive from the paper are, firstly, that equality is one of the most fundamental elements of the democratic state of law. Worth not solely preservation, but also undertaking affirmative actions (see Clark 2007, 36) that help to ensure substantive equality and shape social attitudes and practices.

Secondly, a procedural mechanism of balancing the participation of male and female representatives in authorities corresponds – perhaps surprisingly – with Rawls's idea of the society as a 'fair system of cooperation',[5] and his concept of one of the main components of egalitarianism: an authentic equality of chances (Rawls 1993, 36, 47–56). Fair equality of opportunity implies that not only must the competition be procedurally fair, it must also minimise the impact of differences in the social background of the competitors as a result.

5 The society as a fair system of cooperation is based on rationality, reciprocity, impartiality and mutual advantage.

References

Buchanan, James M. 1975. *The limits of liberty: between anarchy and Leviathan.* Chicago: University of Chicago Press.

Clark, David S. (ed.) 2007, *Encyclopedia of Law and Society.* Washington: Sage Publication.

Dahlerup, Drude. 2005. *Increasing Women's Political Representation: New Trends in Gender Quotas, In International IDEA, Women in Parliament: Beyond Numbers. A Revised Edition.* Stockholm: International IDEA.

Dahlerup, Drude, and Freidenvall, Lenita. 2005. Quotas as a "Fast Track" to Equal Representation of Women: Why Scandinavia is No Longer the Model, *International Feminist Journal of Politics* 7.1: 26–48.

Dahlerup, Drude (ed.). 2006. *Women, Quotas and Politics.* New York, London: Routledge.

Dahlerup Drude. 2007. Electoral Gender Quotas: Between Equality of Opportunity and Equality of Results, *Representation* 43.2: 80–81.

Dahlerup, Drude, Freidenvall, Lenita (and others). 2008. *Electoral Gender Quota Systems and Their Implementation in Europe*, [study requested by the European Parliament's Committee on Women's Rights and Gender Equality], *WIP, Women in Politics Research Centre, Department of Political Science, Stockholm University, in cooperation with International IDEA*, Brussels: Directorate-General for Internal Policies, Policy Department C, Citizens' Rights and Constitutional Affairs. PE 408.309.

Gauthier, David P. 1986. *Morals by Agreement.* Oxford, New York: Clarendon Press.

Inter-Parliamentary Union. 2011. *Women in National Parliaments (Situation as of 31 December 2011)* [http://www.ipu.org/wmn-e/world.htm, retrieved on 31. 03. 2012].

Lovenduski, Joni. 2005. *Feminizing Politics.* Cambridge: Polity.

Magill, Frank M. (ed.). 1995. *International Encyclopedia of Sociology.* London: Fitzroy Dearborn.

R. E. Matland, *Electoral quotas – frequency and effectiveness.* In *Women, Quotas and Politics,* edited by Drude Dahlerup, 278–291. New York, London: Routledge.

Nozick, Robert. 1974. *Anarchy, State and Utopia.* Oxford: Blackwell.

Phillips, Anne. 1995. *The Politics of Presence.* Oxford: Clarendon.

Rawls, John. 1993. *Political Liberalism.* New York: Columbia University Press.

Rawls, John. 1999. *Theory of Justice.* (2nd rev. ed.) Cambridge, MA: Harvard University Press.

Sandel, Michael J. 1998. *Liberalism and the Limits of Justice*, 2nd ed. Cambridge: Cambridge University Press.

Squires, Judith. 2007. *The New Politics of Gender Equality.* New York: Palgrave Macmillan.

From Defending the Minimal State to Examining the Good Life: Continuity and Change in the Work of Robert Nozick

Antonia Geisler

Introduction

Robert Nozick (1938–2002), the US-American philosopher and representative of libertarianism, is known for his defence of a minimal state in his first work *Anarchy, State and Utopia* (1974) which is presumed to be the libertarian answer on John Rawls' *A Theory of Justice* (1971). Libertarianism is a political philosophy which deduces indefeasible rights of individuals from a subordinated right of self-ownership. It means libertarians assume that individuals are complete owners of themselves, and therefore, of their justly acquired property, too (see Cohen 1995, 12). From his libertarian view, Nozick treats the individual rights to life, liberty, and property as fundamental rights which take priority over all other considerations (see Nozick 1974, ix–xi).

The article discusses continuity and change in the work of Robert Nozick and elaborates the contrast between *Anarchy, State and Utopia* and Nozick's later writings. Firstly, Nozick's minimal state, which he develops and defends in *Anarchy, State and Utopia*, is outlined. Secondly, Nozick's conception of justice – the Entitlement Theory – which he introduces as an alternative to John Rawls' principles of justice in part two of *Anarchy, State, and Utopia*, is examined. The antagonism between John Rawls' welfare state and Robert Nozick's minimal state which is based on the authors' antithetical perception of justice is emphasised, too. Nozick especially criticises Rawls' concept of distributive justice, in particular, Rawls' second principle of justice which postulates that social and economic institutions should be arranged in a way that inequalities in wealth occur to the benefit of the least-advantaged members of society (see Rawls 1971, 303). Finally, some of Nozick's later writings are employed exemplarily for the supposed modification within Nozick's works. It is shown that Nozick mitigates some aspects of his libertarian political philosophy, especially his view on the minimal state, in his later works, but basically sticks to his central arguments developed in *Anarchy, State and Utopia*.

The genesis of the minimal state

The theoretical basis of Nozick's libertarian assumptions is formed by *Anarchy, State and Utopia*. Rawls asks how a state should be organised, whereas Nozick argues if there has to be any state at all (see Nozick 1974, 11). In *Anarchy, State and Utopia*, he shows that only a minimal state, which powers are limited to the protection of the named fundamental rights, can be morally justified. Therefore, he proceeds in two main stages: First, he explains how a minimal state would arise from an anarchical state of nature. Second, he develops his own theory of justice in contrast to Rawls' theory and argues that every state beyond a minimal state, in order to constitute a certain vision of distributive justice, cannot be morally justified.

For showing the evolvement of a minimal state out of an anarchistic situation, Nozick employs the idea of an anarchical state of nature similar to Locke's state of nature in the *Second Treatise of Government*. In that state of nature, the individuals already have certain natural rights, in particular, the right to live, the right to freedom, and the right to justly acquired property. Deduced from these rights, the inhabitants of the state of nature are justified to defend themselves against assailants, to demand compensation for an occurred violation of their rights, and they are permitted to transfer these rights to their fellow human beings. For gaining a better and constant protection of their rights, the individuals will soon form a mutual protective organisation (see Nozick 1974, 10–12). They will transfer their right to defend themselves against assailants and their right to demand compensation to the agency and have to pay for protective services. On closer inspection – Nozick continues – the protective agency resembles a minimal state (ibid., 16–17). By installing reasonable and reliable procedures about right violations and compensation and by pursuing the valid claims of its clients, the organisation will exercise a monopoly over rights-enforcement in its territory and has the power to punish people for infringing the rules. What is important for Nozick is that this minimal state develops and receives legitimacy because the individuals voluntarily transferred certain rights to an organisation. Therefore, the competences of that kind of state are limited to these voluntarily transferred rights, namely, the protection of life and property of its citizens, and must not go beyond (ibid., 113–118).

Nozick's Entitlement Theory vs. Rawls' Theory of Justice

In the second part of *Anarchy, State and Utopia*, Nozick starts with the introduction of his Entitlement Theory which contains three principles of distributive justice:

(1) The principle of justice in acquisition, postulating that the original acquisition of holdings has to be just (based on Locke's theory of acquisition).

(2) The principle of justice in transfer, postulating that the transfer of holdings has to be just (justly acquired property has to be transferred voluntarily).

(3) The principle of rectification which determines the compensation of illegitimate acquired or transferred holdings (see Nozick 1974, 151–153).

Thus, according to the Entitlement Theory, a person is legitimately entitled to a holding if it has acquired the holding in accordance with principles one and two. Distributive justice in Nozick's understanding is generated by the voluntary actions and transactions of individuals. The state has to guarantee the compliance with principles one and two and needs to execute principle three if illegitimate acquisitions or transfers occur. Nozick calls these principles of justice, which guide the state's action, historical principles, because whether a distribution is just is determined by the process by which it was achieved. In contrast, the principles of justice presented by Rawls, Nozick calls structural or end-result principles, because they want to realise a certain structure of distribution (ibid., 153–155), precisely a structure where departures from equality benefits the situation of the least-advantaged members of society (in comparison with an equal distribution). For Nozick, end-result principles imply the following – and here Nozick's criticism is rooted: If the state wants to guarantee this certain kind of distributive justice, it gets the competence to interfere with people's life; in particular, it is legitimated to limit property rights in order to realise distributive justice. Thus, the criticism of Robert Nozick on Rawls' theory of (social) justice is founded on the justification of limiting fundamental rights of individuals, namely, the right to justly acquired property. That is why he explicitly criticises Rawls' theory of justice as a system of forced labour (ibid., 169–172). According to Nozick, the welfare state delineated by Rawls is stealing people's lawfully obtained property with the objective of redistribution. A state like the one developed by Rawls, which promotes redistributive measures in the cause of distributive justice, is permanently infringing people's rights, and therefore, is lacking any legitimacy.

It occurs that Nozick's criticism on Rawls' theory of justice derives from different assumptions about justice, especially distributive justice, and from different assumptions about what rights take priority over all other considerations. Indeed, concerning justice in the political sense, Nozick and Rawls are close to each other, because both Nozick's minimal state as well as Rawls' welfare state has to guarantee equal basic liberties. What is important here: They differ about what exactly are these basic liberties. Rawls' list of basic liberties does not include certain kinds of property, for example, means of production, which, therefore, are not protected by the first principle of justice and can be limited in order to realise the second one (see Rawls 1993, 298). The two authors also differ in their economical perspective on justice. Nozick defines distributive justice as a naturally generated process of the voluntary actions and transactions of individuals, while Rawls considers distributive justice as something that has to be established by the state. In this context, the different concepts of liberty also have to be emphasised. Robert Nozick's minimal state implies a concept of negative liberty which stands for the absence of exterior constraints. The functions and the role of the state are limited to the guarantee and enforcement of civil liberties which contain the individuals' fundamental rights to life, freedom, and property. In contrast, John Rawls puts forward a concept of positive liberty corresponding to the intuition that freedom from external coercion does not imply resources and capacities for the realisation of freedom and that this itself might be a restriction on freedom. For Rawls, it is not sufficient to realise the demand for equality only under the law. The state has to take care of an equal distribution of material resources too in order to ensure that individuals are able to exercise their rights and pursue their concepts of life.

Continuity and Change

Robert Nozick is heavily criticised for his libertarian view presented in *Anarchy, State and Utopia.*[1] He, indeed, has noticed this criticism, but refused to make the defence of his minimal state the starting point of his further works. In the introduction of one of his later works, he emphasised that he did not want to spend his life writing the 'Son of Anarchy, State and Utopia', 'The Return of the Son of Anarchy, State and Utopia' etc. because he had other philosophical questions to think about (see Nozick 1997, 2). He dedicated himself to questions of personal identity as well as to free will and ascertaining truth in his second book *Philosophical Explanations* (1981). In *The Examined Life: Philosophical Meditations* (1989), he explores love, happiness, sexuality, death, and the foundations of ethics amongst others.

Nevertheless, or maybe even because of exploring these fundamental questions, a set of phrases can be found in his later works, contesting the minimal state developed in *Anarchy, State, and Utopia*. In one of the essays (The Zigzag of Politics) from *The Examined Life*, Robert Nozick mentions that 'the libertarian position [he] once propounded now seems to [be] seriously inadequate' because the minimal state, in fact, leaves room for 'humane considerations and joint cooperative activities' (Nozick 1989, 286–287), but it does not knit them closely enough into its structure. He

[1] See, for example, the criticism of Murray N. Rothbard (1977) on Nozick's conception of the state and G. A. Cohen's (1985) or Paul Russell's (1987) critique on Nozick's Entitlement Theory.

agrees that there 'are some things we choose to do together through government' (ibid., 287) expressing our human solidarity and that the minimal state defended in *Anarchy, State and Utopia* cannot provide this kind of action directed to common welfare.

However, *The Examined Life* offers more than phrases challenging the minimal state. Here, Nozick introduces a four-layer-structure of ethics, with each of the layers resulting in certain rules and principles (see Nozick 1989, 212–215) which exceed the competences of a minimal state. The first layer is named the Ethic of Respect which 'mandates respecting another [...] person's life and autonomy'. Ethic of Respect means non-interference 'with the person's domain of choice [and] forbids murder or enslavement' (ibid., 212). It postulates an ethic of individual rights, namely, those fundamental rights known from *Anarchy, State and Utopia*. That means that the first layer guides and legitimates the minimal state in executing its power. The Ethic of Responsiveness forms the second layer. Its core principle is the equality of all individuals. It postulates that we have to act 'in a way that is responsive to other people's reality and value' (ibid., 212). Nozick has already presented this kind of ethics in his second book *Philosophical Explanations*, where he emphasised ethical responsiveness as demanding 'principles against murder, coercion, manipulation, and lying' (Nozick 1981, 472). In summary, this kind of layer postulates mutual respect for different concepts of life. The third layer represents the Ethic of Caring which mandates 'nonharm to all people (and perhaps to all living things), and love ("Do unto others as you would do unto those you love")' (Nozick 1989, 213). According to Nozick, on this layer, one can often find religious core values like Christian love or Buddhist compassion, but nonreligious forms of caring are also possible. Out of this layer, a legitimisation for a welfare state can be deduced. The fourth and last layer is the Ethic of Light, the layer of saints and heroes. Nozick links this layer to terms like truth, goodness, beauty, and holiness. On this highest level of ethics, the 'divergence between self and other is overcome' (Nozick 1989, 214), you become a pure vehicle by which something else, for example, certain higher moral goals, can be transmitted. As an example, Nozick mentions the self-sacrifice of Jesus for mankind. According to Nozick, each layer is fundamental to the next one; for example, the Ethic of Responsiveness is higher than the Ethic of Respect and rests on it.

What is interesting now is that Nozick allows constraints of the rules and principles of a lower layer when this constraint is necessary to realise the rules and principles of the next higher layer. This means that the fundamental individual rights mandated by the Ethic of Respect can be restricted 'when in some particular situation responsiveness calls for something different' (Nozick 1989, 212). The Ethic of Respect and the Ethic of Responsiveness can be restricted when they diverge from the Ethic of Caring and so on. This means that the right to property, which, for

Nozick, is a fundamental individual right emerging from the Ethic of Respect, can be constrained if welfare measures, which can be deduced from the third layer, afford it. Here, Nozick really concurs with John Rawls. What seemed impossible to be morally justified in *Anarchy, State and Utopia* now becomes feasible. With the four-layer-structure of ethic, Nozick provides the foundation for legitimising a welfare state.

In fact, Nozick implements a principle of minimum mutilation which requires the minimum deviation from the rules of the former layer. The principle of minimum mutilation approves, for example, deviations from the rules of respect for the sake of responsiveness, 'but only when this is enough greater to outweigh the loss in adhering completely the norms of respect' (Nozick 1989, 213). Divergence from a former layer is only approved under restriction of commensurability. Thus, the principle does not permit achieving maximum responsiveness, no matter what costs to respect. However, Nozick leaves it open if restrictions of certain property rights are commensurable to realise considerations of material welfare. For this reason, it is a legitimate question if Nozick has left libertarianism behind, and even worse for libertarians, become a proponent of the welfare state.[2] As already mentioned in the introduction, this article argues that, in fact, Nozick himself questions the finality of his defence of the minimal state, but he, by no means, is departing from his libertarian position which treats the rights to life, liberty, and property as fundamental. An evidence for this assumption is delivered by Nozick himself in his last work *Invariances: The Structure of the Objective World* (2001). In the chapter 'The Genealogy of Ethics', he goes into detail concerning the relation between the four layers of ethics. Nozick considers the layers as layers in the evolution of mankind in general and in our personal ethical and moral development in particular. For Nozick, 'living and behaving at each layer [...] may make the next step a natural one to take' (Nozick 2001, 281). He furthermore emphasises a point which brings him back on the libertarian path: Only the first layer should be made mandatory for all societies (ibid., 281–282). By emphasising this, Nozick takes up the normative position that further ethical layers 'are matters of personal choice or personal ideal' (ibid., 281). This results in the fact that societies should only coercively demand the Ethics of Respect and no one can be forced to move to higher layers because this has to be an individual decision.

2 After *The Examined Life: Philosophical Meditations* was published in 1989, it was broadly interpreted as Nozick's renunciation of his libertarian view presented in *Anarchy, State, and Utopia*. See the articles of Roderick T. Long (2002) or Jane O'Grady (2002).

Conclusion

What does all this mean for continuity and change in the work of Robert Nozick so far? The change arises from Nozick's conclusion that individuals might need more than a minimal state just promoting their negative liberty. During his creative development, during examining the life philosophically, he realised that the individuals' need for self-expression does not involve only respecting its fundamental rights. The individuals' need for self-expression is also linked to an experience of collective identity, to a feeling of being part of a community with the same values. In *Anarchy, State and Utopia*, Nozick only focused on the non-interference with people's lives as expressing each individual's respect for its fellow human beings, but in his later works, he highlights that marking human solidarity through official action could not just mean to respect their rights, but to express the common values jointly and politically (see Nozick 1989, 287–288). Having this in mind, Nozick had to admit that he had only concentrated on the purpose of the state and not on his potential meaning for its citizen (ibid., 288).

Therefore, Nozick perceived a tension between the primacies of individual rights, in particular, the right to property, and the need of human beings for community – community aimed at a certain kind of common welfare which might involve the redistribution of goods, and thus, the infringement of fundamental rights. But what is important for accentuating the continuity in the work of Robert Nozick: He neither dissolves the tension in favour of a welfare state nor does he dissolve the tension at all. However, by clarifying his position on what kind of ethical layer should be legally institutionalised in a society, Nozick remains a proponent of a minimal state which competences must not exceed the enforcement of the principles and rules settled on the first layer; in other words, the fundamental individual rights to life, freedom, and property. That is why, he is, by no means, a proponent of a welfare state like the one designed by Rawls. Maybe one can say that Nozick underwent a process from a resolute defender of a libertarian vision of a minimal state in *Anarchy, State and Utopia*, to someone who pursues a more flexible libertarianism which is aware of the priority of individual rights, but which does not assume that the minimal state is, in any case, the ideal solution.

References

Cohen, G. A. 1995. *Self-Ownership, Freedom, and Equality*. Cambridge: Cambridge University Press.

Cohen, G. A. 1985. Nozick on Approbation. *New Left Review* 150: 89–105.

Long, Roderick T. 2002. Robert Nozick, Philosopher of Liberty. *The Freeman. Ideas on Liberty* 52.9: 30–33.

Nozick, Robert. 2001: *Invariances. The Structure of the Objective World.* Cambridge, MA: Harvard University Press.

Nozick, Robert. 1997. *Socratic Puzzles.* Cambridge, MA: Harvard University Press.

Nozick, Robert. 1989. *Examined Life: Philosophical Meditations.* New York: Simon & Schuster.

Nozick, Robert. 1981. *Philosophical Explanations.* Oxford: Clarendon Press.

Nozick, Robert. 1974. *Anarchy, State and Utopia.* New York: Basic Books.

O'Grady, Jane. 2002. Robert Nozick. Leftwing political philosopher whose right-ward shift set the tone for the Reagan-Thatcher era. *The Guardian* (26 January).

Rawls, John. 1993. *Political Liberalism.* New York: Columbia University Press.

Rawls, John. 1971. *A Theory of Justice.* Oxford: Oxford University Press.

Rothbard, Murray N. 1977. Robert Nozick and the Immaculate Conception of the State. *Journal of Libertarian Studies* 1.1: 45–57.

Russell, Paul. 1987. Nozick, Need and Charity. *Journal of Applied Philosophy* 4.2: 205–216.

Amartya Sen's Justice: An Idea and a Proposal

Jakov Bojović

Introduction: two points of view

Amartya K. Sen begins his latest book, *The Idea of Justice* (2009), by emphasising a basic paradigmatic distinction which is in close connection with the concept of justice. Social contract theorists, from the Age of Enlightenment as well as modern political theory, constitute the first paradigm. These diverse thinkers, from Hobbes to Rawls and beyond, argued that institutions should be founded on the basis of one unique set of just social principles or norms in order to be righteous. They also assumed that, hypothetically, autonomous individuals would agree to these norms in some sort of a *state of nature*. Sen names this widely-accepted approach *transcendental institutionalism* and assigns it with two distinct features. First, its attention is concentrated on defining perfect justice, rather than on relative comparisons of justice and injustice. Second, in searching for perfection, it is not directly focused on the actual societies that would emerge (Sen 2009, 5–12).

In contrast with *transcendental institutionalism*, a number of other Enlightenment theorists took a variety of comparative approaches that were more concerned with social realisations. These *pragmatists* were interested primarily in the removal of manifest injustice from the world they saw. Different versions of comparative thinking can be found in the works of, among others, Adam Smith, Marquise de Condorcet, and especially John Stuart Mill.[1] Amartya Sen shares a point of departure with these exceptional and extremely influential philosophers, but that does not imply the correspondence of his ideas with their substantive theories. However, his theory does borrow a lot from J. S. Mill's postulates of *practical eclecticism*.

In this essay, we will argue that it is practically impossible to define the principles

1 'He [Mill] has written about the problem of social contract in almost all of his major works. The very idea of basing a political theory and political practice on such mechanism, represented the whole system of thought against which Mill has debated – abstract, ahistorical, quasi-universalistic and an opinion closed for real problems and situations' (Đurković 2006, 187; my translation).

of a perfect, just society, even as an ideal-type. In fact, the vast majority of previous theorists have been asking themselves the wrong questions. It is not about finding perfect justice (what we cannot achieve) – it is about defining what is unjust (what we may be able to agree upon). Therefore, what we need is to identify the injustices in society and eradicate them rather than focusing on perfect ideals that can never exist. Utilitarian thinkers also take such a point of view (Riley 1988, 203–207), but more generally, so does social choice theory, to which Sen has already contributed a lot during his abundant career. Utilitarianism is commonly criticised for relying only on utilities and therefore ignoring everything else that should be important for the notion of justice. Information about the satisfaction of needs and basic interests, opportunities and freedoms, and rights and duties must also be included for many purposes (Morris 2010, 5–6).

Sen explains: 'This departure has the dual effect, first, of taking the comparative rather than the transcendental route, and second, of focusing on actual realizations in the societies involved rather than only on institutions and rules' (Sen 2009, 9).

The first point of departure, in fact, refers to the possible contribution of the economic social choice theory to a broader, comparative theory of justice, while the second mostly refers to his famous *capability approach* which he has commonly used in his works on justice (e.g. Sen 1980, 197–220; 2005, 152–160; 2009, 223–319 etc.), development (e.g. Sen 2000, 87–111), and identity (e.g. Sen 2007, 174–175). Social choice theory as a *comparative* view on justice instead of a *transcedental* social contract, is mainly a methodological shift, while the capability approach is Sen's proposal of a universal measurement of just-ness, and therefore an approach that tells us what should we evaluate and ameliorate in order to expand justice in our societies.

What are the arguments on which Amartya Sen conceivably builds up his anti-contractual theory? After elaborating on this issue, it will be easier for us to understand some possible reasons for crossing to a comparative approach.

Sen (2009, 13–14) illustrates the problems of the aforementioned theories in his style: through very inspiring instances. Imagine that three children, Anna, Bob and Carla, argue over a flute. Anna made the flute, Bob's family is on the verge of poverty, while Carla is the only child that knows how to play the flute, so possessing it will provide her with the most pleasure or happiness. Sen points out that, under these circumstances, even after a long deliberation, there would still be different positions with *equal legitimacy*: a libertarian would think that it is fair to give the flute to Anna, an egalitarian would go for Bob, while a utilitarian thinker would assume that Carla should possess it. This is just one of the many possible examples for a problem named *feasibility*: the fact that 'there may be no reasoned agreement at all, even under strict conditions of impartiality and open-minded scrutiny' (ibid., 9).

This shows an important limitation of previous theories of justice which demand only one ending as justified and it shows a need for a broader theory of justice that will not always make such decisions. Certainly, definitive conclusions are desirable, but when they emerge, there is no necessity to look for a guarantee that a particular choice must emerge in every similar case in the future. This problem tends to show that none of the existing distributive justice theories as such, can have a universal meaning: there will always be situations in which we cannot use a one-dimensional approach.

The second problem, *redundancy*, highlights that 'an exercise of practical reason that involves an actual choice demands a framework for comparison of justice for choosing among the feasible alternatives and not an identification of a possibly unavailable perfect situation that could not be transcended' (ibid.). It is further explained using an interesting analogy with paintings. The fact that a person regards Da Vinci's Mona Lisa as the most perfect picture in the world does not reveal anything about how he would rank a Picasso against a Van Gogh (ibid., 12–20). It is also unnecessary, because when we adjudicate between the various merits of a Picasso and a Van Gogh, we do not have to identify the most perfect picture in the world. Hence, comparison is important because it keeps us in the real world, rather than in an imagined, hypothetical world.

We argue that every attempt to define perfectly and universally fair institutions or principles which should be our guides in real-political modeling of a political society, represented a wrong approach to the problem. First, theorising in such a rigid manner shifts the justice paradigm from the discourses of the societies to an ideological discourse in which, we believe, there can be no reasonable consensus because every such theory claims universality. Second, constituting rigid social arrangements would inevitably lead to acts of unfairness towards someone at some point.

Something that really is definable and that reasonable individuals may be able to agree upon is diagnosing and eradicating particular injustices. For instance, the expansion of political rights in the 20th century represented an advancement of justice in the World, even without a vision of perfect justice. Therefore, what people as citizens can and need to do is to identify the particular injustices in society and eliminate them rather than focusing on perfect ideals that can never exist. This implies the existence of a framework for comparison of justice or injustice, what actually means that we need to establish an efficient, democratic social mechanism for aggregating individuals' considerations and for measuring the *just-ness* of a decision, institution or the society as a whole. That is also the primary concern of Amartya Sen's work on (in)justice.

Defining the framework: public reason and social choice

There are two essential questions. First, what should be the role of reason in a theory of justice? Second, in what way can a diagnosis of injustice be objective and impartial?

What connects the aforementioned theorists from the Enlightenment era, despite the differences, is the indisputable reliance on human reason, which has long been a target of criticism in contemporary political philosophy. Jonathan Glover is just one of the authors who join this line of criticism, arguing that 'now we tend to see the Enlightenment view of human psychology as thin and mechanical, and Enlightenment hopes of social progress through the spread of humanitarianism and the scientific outlook as naive' (Glover 1999, 7).

It is clear in the nature of Sen's theory that it relies on human reason to a significant extent. To pre-empt the expected criticisms, such as Glover's, Sen states that 'the claim that people would agree on a particular proposition if they were to reason in an open and impartial way does not, of course, assume that people are already so engaged, or even that they are eager to be so' (Sen 2009, xix).

Therefore, Sen is aware of the limitations of the reach of human reason, and actually points out to its possibilities if used in a right way. It is simply not realistic to believe that people can act reasonably in every possible situation, but we do not see that fact as an argument for not broadening and ameliorating reasonable thinking to the highest possible extent. This answers our first question.

The second question emphasises the differences between Rawls's and Sen's theory and leads us to social choice theory as a logical answer.

The proper reasoning is the one characterised by objectivity. In this paper, we argue that objectiveness can be achieved through a process of public reasoning, a device that was originally introduced to the theory by John Rawls in his *Political Liberalism*. 'To say that a political conviction is objective is to say that there are reasons, specified by a reasonable and mutually recognizable political conception, sufficient to convince all reasonable persons that it is reasonable' (Rawls 2005, 119).

Sen elaborates against Rawls's use of *reasonable persons* as a category, since he is convinced that 'all of us are capable of being reasonable through being open-minded about welcoming information and through reflecting on arguments coming from different quarters, along with undertaking interactive deliberations and debates on how the underlying issues should be seen' (Sen 2009, 43). The second distinction consists in Sen's claim that the principles which survived public critical scrutiny, need not be a rigid, unique set, what was discussed previously in this paper (ibid., 43–44).

Rawls's and Sen's common demand for objectivity, in characteristics of which they differ, is the demand of impartiality. Sen makes a distinction between *closed* and *open* impartiality. Rawlsian impartiality is named *closed* impartiality, because it invokes only the members of a given society or a sovereign state. Rawls has also thought of the *veil of ignorance* as some kind of a *filter* for ideal impartiality. That is how Rawls narrows the process of reasoning that leads to the principles of justice, both territorially and mentally, to protect them from the influence of these characteristics (Rawls 1999, 118–123). This approach is in contrast with the impartiality that Adam Smith proposed, *open* impartiality. Smith argues that there is clearly a strong case for not leaving out the perspectives and reasoning presented by anyone whose assessments are relevant, either because their interests are involved, or because their way of thinking can enlighten our own investigation (Sen 2009, 44–46). The key concept of Smith's approach to impartiality is the concept of the *impartial spectator*. It assumes that whenever we want to make a decision, individual or collective, we should approach the problem from a point of view a fair and impartial spectator would have (Raphael 2009, 32–43). The Smithian impartial spectator is a device for public discussion and therefore it need not seek unanimity in a way that Rawlsian theory demands. Sen argues that Smith's approach may be able to take note of possibilities that the social contract cannot easily accommodate, including:

(1) Dealing with comparative assessment;

(2) Taking note of social realisations;

(3) Allowing incompleteness in social assessment, but still providing guidance;

(4) Taking note of voices beyond the membership of the contractarian group (Sen 2009, 69–70).

As in social choice theory, such openness to alternative views of approaching social problems can provide a more solid ground for ranking the *just-ness* or, at least, manifest injustice of certain social realisations, even if they are merely partial and ordinal rather than comprehensive, cardinal rankings. From social choice theory we have learned that sometimes we cannot make a complete comparison of choices because of the *impossibility results*.[2] To be useful, a social ranking must have some coverage, but need not be complete. 'A theory of justice has to rely on partial orderings based on the intersection of distinct rankings drawing on different reasons of justice that can all survive the scrutiny of public reasoning' (ibid., 399).

Kenneth Arrow's revolutionary *impossibility theorem* shows that democratic pro-

2 Social choice theory is on the one hand a mathematical discipline and on the other a theoretical framework for aggregating and transferring different individual choices into a collective decision. It combines and connects the subjects of mathematics, economics, politics and philosophy. The pioneers of this theory, French mathematicians from the time of the Revolution, had a motivation to avoid arbitrariness and instability in procedures of social choice. Unfortunately, most of them were rather pessimistic regarding the end results of their researches. For instance, Marquis de Condorcet is the author of the well-known voting paradox that shows the limitation of democratic procedures (Sen 1985a, 1764–1765). The subject was revived by Kenneth Arrow who popularised his impossibility theorem in the book *Social Choice and Individual Values* (1963).

cedures cannot satisfy what members of the society want, even with mild conditions of reasonable sensitivity to social conditions. It presents an empirical proof that there does not exist a social welfare function (SWF) that would satisfy the following four conditions:

(1) Unrestricted domain: All possible individual preferences must be in the domain of the SWF;

(2) Pareto principle: If everyone prefers any X to any Y, then X is socially preferred to Y;

(3) Independence of irrelevant alternatives: Only the individual rankings of any X and Y determine the social ranking on the two states;

(4) Non-dictatorship: The presence of a dictator is prohibited (Arrow 1983, 73–74).

Various theorists have tried to find ways to convert aggregate individuals' preferences into a more efficient social choice. Some of them postulate that the main thrust of analysis must be to create laws and conventions that would lead to a desirable outcome, recognising that virtually all individuals are self-interested. One development considers the possibility of devising ways of using people's self-interest to achieve socially desirable outcomes (Craven 1992, 7–8). Amartya Sen (2000, 67; 2004, 71–82) convincingly argues that such impasses can often be resolved by *informational broadening about interpersonal comparisons of well-being and relative advantages*:

> It is not surprising that the rejection of interpersonal comparison must cause difficulties for reasoned social decision, since the claims of different persons, who make up the society, have to be assessed against each other. We cannot even understand the force of public concerns about poverty, hunger, inequality or tyranny, without bringing in interpersonal comparisons in one form or another. The information on which our informal judgements on these matters rely is precisely the kind of information that has to be – and can be – incorporated in formal analysis of systematic social choice. (Sen 2004, 96–97)

Social choice theory's point of view on justice involves a comparison of outcomes, considering, at the same time, everyone's preferences. The flute problem is merely an example of an *impossibility result* that leads to ordinal rankings, while informational broadening can be understood as being *openly impartial* and taking in consideration more information on the situations that emerge. This is where we have to raise the key question: What are the information that institutions need to seek in order to make social choices more fair? Sen's comparative idea of justice passes this critical issue to public reason, as it *knows best* what is to be considered as important when the issue of justice is invoked. However, Sen does propose us, in our opinion, the most universal, neutral and intercultural metric for the measurement of justice, which we will try to defend in the following chapter.

Materials of justice

Informational broadening is a very widely used conception in Sen's works. It emphasises that by broadening the information about particular situations or individuals, we can avoid injustices that would emerge if we did not take those information in consideration. Particularly, the widening should be done in the direction of findings about what Sen himself named a person's *capabilities to function*. This is actually where we get to the distributional part of Sen's theory, which implies answering to the ever-lasting egalitarian question: *Equality of what?* With that, we deviate from the theoretical discussion about the ways of getting to the just principles and the reliance on human reason in this process (an *idea*), and move on to the practical and essential question of all theories of justice: What do we actually owe to each other (a *metric*), to what extent and how to distribute the same (a *rule*)?

This chapter is divided into three parts. The first part describes the main purpose of the capability approach, the concepts of functioning and capabilities. The second part describes its relation to the resource-based Rawlsian approach. We will try to show that the capability approach is a logical continuation of a comparative idea of justice, since it is broad and neutral to different societies and cultures and is dependable on actual public reason. In the third part, we will compare different versions of the capability approach to prove that Sen's is the *most neutral* one.

Sen defines two distinguishable and equally important aspects of human life, which should be taken into account in our understanding of how individuals and groups are doing: *well-being* and *agency* (Sen 1985b, 169–221; Sen 1992a 39–42). Before going further into explanation of these concepts, we must attend to a cross-cutting distinction, namely achievement and freedom:

> A person's position in a social arrangement can be judged in two different perspectives, viz. (1) the actual achievement, and (2) the freedom to achieve. Achievement is concerned with what we *manage* to accomplish, and freedom with the *real opportunity* that we have to accomplish what we value. (Sen 1992a, 31)

Well-being and Agency (Crocker and Robeyns 2010, 62)

	Well-Being	Agency
Achievements	Well-Being Achievements (Functionings)	Agency Achievements
Freedom	Well-Being Freedoms (Capabilities)	Agency Freedoms

A person's well-being comprises his or her functionings and capabilities. Functionings can be seen as various things a person acomplishes during his or her life: 'Living may be seen as consisting of a set of interrelated functionings, consisting of beings and doings. A person's achievement in this respect can be seen as the vector of his or her functionings' (Sen 1992a, 39). Sen adds that a person's well-being consists not only of the realised functionings but also of the person's abilities to function in various ways, namely *capabilities*.

Agency, like well-being, has two dimensions. 'Agency freedom is freedom to achieve whatever the person, as a responsible agent, decides he or she should achieve' (Sen, 1985, 204). A person's agency achievement, on the other hand, refers to the realisation of goals and values (s)he has reasons to pursue, whether or not they are connected with his or her own well being (Sen 1993, 30–37). Without agency freedom, without 'the liberty of acting as citizens who matter and whose voices counts, people run the risk of living as well-fed, well-clothed and well-entertained vassals' (Drèze and Sen 2002, 288).

The capability approach evaluates policies according to their impact on people's actual functionings and their capabilities to function. Proponents have addressed the question of whether capabilities, functionings, or a combination of the two should be the appropriate measure of justice. There are several considerations that are relevant for this choice. First, by focusing on capabilities, we do not privilege a particular amount of good lives, but instead aim at a range of possible ways of life from which a person can choose. A second consideration stems from the importance given to personal responsibility in modern political philosophy: each person should be given the same capability, but once that is in place, each individual should be held responsible for his or her own choices. Third, as capability sets may include freedoms that are conditional (because they depend on the choices of other people), it might be better to focus both on the individual's capability set and also on what people have been able to realise, i.e., their functionings. The question of choice between functionings and capabilities can also be bridged by a conceptional move. Sen has proposed the concept of *refined functionings* to designate functionings that take note of available alternatives. Sen (1992b, 52–53) notes that *fasting* as a functioning is not just starving, but 'choosing to starve when one does have other options'. There are also concerns related to measurability: for example, it is often easier to observe and measure functionings than capabilities (ibid.).

Sen criticised Rawls's use of primary goods because they are mere *means*, not worthwhile *ends*. Individuals often don't have the same capability to use their primary goods and convert them to what really matters to them, even when they are equally redistributed. That is why Sen elaborates that the concept of primary goods misses the concern of greater equality of capabilities. Sen writes: 'if people were basically very similar, than an index of primary goods might be a good way of judging advantage [...] judging advantage purely in terms of primary goods leads to a partially blind morality' (Sen 1980, 216–217). As a result, if we take the primary goods as the measure of well-being we may treat people unfairly. The conversion factors discussed in Sen's writings can be categorised into three groups. *Personal conversion factors* are internal to a person. The best example for this kind of conversion problems would be a person in a wheelchair (Daniels 1990, 279–280). *Social conversion factors* are factors from the society, such as social norms, power relations or public policies. For example, if there is a stigma towards homosexuals in a society, it would surely narrow their capabilities. *Environmental conversion factors* emerge from the geographic location in which a person lives. Among those aspects are climate, pollution, volcano activity and so on (Crocker 2008, 171–172; Robeyns 2005, 99–100).

The fundamental difference between resource based theories and capability theorists lies in the degree to which their principles are sensitive to these individual differences. Resourcism relies on institutions to provide access to a standardised package of primary goods that individuals need to achieve basic functionings, while the capability approach insists that the basic structure should provide, to each person, access to a package of resources adjusted to that person's individual ability to convert them into relevant functionings, sensitive to above mentioned environmental, social and personal conversion factors. Whether a theory of justice should be sensitive to such variations is what divides these two approaches (Anderson 2010, 87–88).

Thomas Pogge has recently criticised the capability approach, questioning its ability to specify a plausible criterion of distributive justice that avoids stigmatising the naturally less well-endowed:

> Can the capability approach be justified? Can it conceivably deliver at least one candidate public criterion of social justice that would be as clear and as workable and as plausible as the leading resourcist criterion, Rawls's two principles? Would such a capability criterion do better in addressing and highlighting the horrific injustices of the world in which we live? The evidence to date suggests that the answers to these questions are *no*. (Pogge 2002, 228)

Elizabeth Anderson answers the criticism and defends the capability perspective with four basic reasons. First, since both sides agree that resources are means to functionings, there is a presumption in favour of articulating principles of justice in terms of ends rather than means. Second, capability measures are sensitive to structural and psychosocial injustice, for example, *de facto* group segregation, stigma and other unjust social norms. Third, a capability approach can handle better the variations in access to funcitionings needed for equal citizenship. Fourth, democratic institutions are formed in way that enables them to answer the concerns of justice couched in terms of capabilities. Individuals recognise this and express their claims in those terms, not just in terms of primary goods (Anderson 2010, 87–88).

We have presented the reasons for applying the capability approach as a more sensitive approach to actual problems of the societies. Now we will present some different versions of the capability approach which have emerged in the past two decades and try to show how Sen's theory is the most universal one, one that can have a larger grasp on actual societies.

There is a split among capability approach theorists over the question of selecting and weighting capabilities that we owe to each other. Anderson (1999, 287–337) argues that, for purposes of political justice, the only relevant capabilities are those needed for a person to participate as a citizen. Nussbaum presented a full list of various capabilities, which, she argues, should be enshrined in every country's constitution (see Nussbaum 2000, 70–86; 2003, 33–59; 2006, 76–78).

Sen draws on his ideal of *agency* to argue that through the process of public reasoning each group should select, trade off, categorise and prioritise capabilities in relation to other normative considerations (Sen 2005, 158–159).

As opposed to the approach developed by Martha Nussbaum or Elizabeth Anderson, Sen's approach has an *informational focus*. It just tells us what we should be concerned with in the measurement of advantages, it does not tell us what to do with the information once we achieve it. The theory is thus neutral between different approaches to distributive justice: egalitarian, sufficientarian, prioritarian, etc. There is a range of things that we have reason to value, that cannot be reduced to one metric. This is another aspect of neutrality which we have pointed out at the beginning of this chapter.

Concluding remarks

Now that we have defended some general postulates of Amartya Sen's theory of justice, we have come to two conclusions regarding the *reach* of his ideas. First, we believe that Sen's theory of justice can be considered as an *unfinished theory of democracy*. These two concepts are seen as dialectically connected: the more we expand democracy (in the way Sen pictures it), the better are the possibilities for the amelioration of justice. As democracy is a normative ideal, so is perfect justice. We had elaborated that the main task of social choice theorists is to empirically prove the failures of democratic choices. However, it is a general misunderstanding that social choice theory takes a negative attitude towards democracy, in favour of some other kind of social and decision-making organisations. In addition to the above mentioned task, their main objective is to find ways to overcome those failures. Amartya K. Sen is among the social choice theorists having an optimistic attitude towards the possible achievements of democracy. Criticising Schumpeter's minimal model of democracy *in terms of ballots and voting*, he points out to the contributions of Jürgen Habermas and Joshua Cohen in deliberative democracy. Sen also emphasises the role of free media and human rights as indispensable elements of democracy that extends justice (ibid., 319–336). In that picture we can also fit his capability approach and Smithian open impartiality. All this makes the democratic institutions appear as *promoters* of justice and not as *manifestations* of justice themselves. Still, Sen's theory is far from a complete theory of democracy, since he does not define in detail how exactly the institutions should be organised, but only gives us directions: *who to listen to* and *what to value*. The conclusion is that justice can be satisfied if we hear as many voices as we can coming from different quarters and if we collect the most information possible on the situations concerned. This means that democratic institutions need to be defined in correspondence with these challenging demands.

Second, we believe that Sen's theory of justice is a significant attempt to bring this metaphysical conception back to the real lives that people lead. Our general impression is that current theories of justice have not led to a reduction of injustice in the world. Sen's approach is oriented to defining conditions under which the decisions made would be more reasonable and therefore equitable. Hence, it is in conflict with rational choice theory which claims that when people act rationally, they act in a selfish and self-centered way. For Sen (1988, 15–22), rationality is a much broader and more permissive concept, a matter of basing our choices on reasoning that we can *reflectively sustain*. If someone, let us say, decides to pursue an idea of social good, even at a great sacrifice to himself or herself, Sen would hardly see that as an irrational behaviour. However, while rationality can easily allow for non-self interested motivations, it does not in itself demand this. In a social context, it is necessary to go beyond the requirements of rationality in terms of *permissive self-scrutiny* and to consider the demands of *reasonable conducts towards others* (Sen 2009, 181–185). Amartya K. Sen has not set himself high targets of defining a perfectly just society. He tends to define conditions under which citizens would be able to organise their societies, directly and through their democratically elected and effectively controlled representatives, on the principles that reduce injustices and expand justice, constantly adapting them to the time that always changes, and their cultural norms and circumstances in which they find themselves. Whatever someone thinks about his obvious anthropomorphic optimism or his often criticised, but also glorified, capability approach, it is beyond doubt that Sen's theory is a valuable attempt to reduce the gap between theory of justice and social reality.

References

Anderson, Elizabeth. 1999. What is the Point of Equality? *Ethics* 109.2: 287–337.

Anderson, Elizabeth. 2010. Justifying the Capabilities Approach to Justice. In *Measuring Justice: Primary Goods and Capabilities*, 81–101. Cambridge: Cambridge University Press.

Arrow, Kenneth. 1952. Principle of Rationality in Collective Decisions. *Economie Appliquée* 5: 469–484.

Arrow, Kenneth. 1963. *Social Choice and Individual Values.* New Haven: Yale University Press.

Arrow, Kenneth. 1983. *Collected Papers of Kenneth J. Arrow: Social Choice and Justice.* Cambridge, MA: Harvard University Press.

Craven, John. 1992. *Social Choice: A Framework for Collective Decisions and Individual Judgments.* Cambridge: Cambridge University Press.

Crocker, David. 2008. *Ethics of Global Development: Agency, Capability and Deliberative Democracy.* Cambridge: Cambridge University Press.

Crocker, David, and Robeyns, Ingrid. 2010. Capability and Agency. In *Contemporary Philosophy Today: Amartya Sen*, 60–91. Cambridge: Cambridge University Press.

Drèze, Jean, and Sen, Amartya. 2002. *India: Development and Participation.* Oxford: Oxford University Press.

Daniels, Norman. 1990. Equality of What: Welfare, Resources, or Capabilities? *Philosophy and Phenomenological Research* 50 (Supplement): 273–296.

Đurković, Miša. 2006. *Politička misao Džona Stjuarta Mila.* Beograd: JP Službeni glasnik.

Glover, Johnatan. 1999. *Humanity: A Moral History of the Twentieth Century.* London: Jonathan Cape.

Morris, Christopher. 2010. Introduction to *Contemporary philosophy today: Amartya Sen*, 1–13. Cambridge: Cambridge University Press.

Nussbaum, Martha. 2000. *Women and Human Development: The Capabilities Approach.* Cambridge: Cambridge University Press.

Nussbaum, Martha. 2003. Capabilities as Fundamental Entitlements: Sen and Social Justice. In *Feminist Economics* 9.2–3: 33–59.

Nussbaum, Martha. 2006. *Frontiers of Justice: Disability, Nationality, Species Membership.* Cambridge, MA: Harvard Uniersity Press.

Pogge, Thomas. 2002. Can the Capability Approach be Justified? In *Global Inequalities*, 167–228.

Raphael, David. 2007. *The Impartial Spectator: Adam Smith's Moral Philosophy.* Oxford: Oxford University Press.

Rawls, John. 1999. *A Theory of Justice.* Cambridge, MA: Harvard University Press.

Rawls, John. 2005. *Political Liberalism.* New York: Columbia University Press.

Riley, Jonathan. 1988. *Liberal Utilitarianism: Social Choice Theory and J. S. Mill's Philosophy.* CUP Archive.

Robeyns, Ingrid. 2005. The Capability Approach: A Theoretical Survey. *Journal of Human Development* 6.1: 93–117.

Sen, Amartya. 1980. Equality of What? In *Tanner Lectures on Human Values*, 197–220. Cambridge: Cambridge University Press.

Sen, Amartya. 1981. *Poverty and Famines: An Essay on Entitlement and Deprivation.* Oxford: Oxford University Press.

Sen, Amartya. 1985a. Social Choice and Justice: A Review Article. *Journal of Economic Literature* 23: 1764–1776.

Sen, Amartya. 1985b. Well-being, Agency and Freedom: The Dewey Lectures 1984. *Journal of Philosophy* 82.4: 169–221.

Sen, Amartya. 1988. *On Ethics and Economics.* Oxford: Wiley-Blackwell.

Sen, Amartya. 1992a. *Capability and Well-Being: The Quality of Life.* Oxford: Clarendon Press.

Sen, Amartya. 1992b. *Inequality Re-examined.* Oxford: Clarendon Press.

Sen, Amartya. 2000. *Development as Freedom.* New York: Anchor Books.

Sen, Amartya. 2004. *Rationality and Freedom.* Cambridge, MA: Harvard University Press.

Sen, Amartya. 2005. Human Rights and Capabilities. *Journal of Human Development* 6.2: 151–166.

Sen, Amartya. 2007. *Identity and Violence: The Illusion of Destiny.* London: Penguin.

Sen, Amartya. 2009. *The Idea of Justice.* Cambridge, MA: Harvard University Press.

Central and Eastern European Forum for Legal, Political, and Social Theory Yearbook

Edited by Jürgen Busch / Péter Cserne / Michael Hein / Miodrag Jovanović / Marta Soniewicka

Vol. 1 Péter Cserne / Miklós Könczöl (eds.): Legal and Political Theory in the Post-National Age. Selected papers Presented at the Second Central and Eastern European Forum for Legal, Political and Social Theorists (Budapest, 21–22 May 2010). 2011.

Vol. 2 Miodrag A. Jovanović / Bojan Spaić (eds.): Jurisprudence and Political Philosophy in the 21st Century. Reassessing Legacies. 2012.

www.peterlang.de

www.ingramcontent.com/pod-product-compliance
Ingram Content Group UK Ltd.
Pitfield, Milton Keynes, MK11 3LW, UK
UKHW020836290926
15470UKWH00004B/1382

9 783631 622070